WHAT REALLY HAPPENED

JOHN EDWARDS, OUR DAUGHTER, AND ME

Rielle Hunter

BENBELLA BOOKS, INC.

DALLAS, TEXAS

BenBella Books, Inc.
10300 N. Central Expressway
Suite #400
Dallas, TX 75231
www.benbellabooks.com
Send feedback to feedback@benbellabooks.com

Printed in the United States of America
10 9 8 7 6 5 4 3 2 1

Library of Congress Cataloging-in-Publication Data is available for this title.

ISBN 978-1-937856-40-3

Editing by Erin Kelley
Copyediting by Lisa Miller
Proofreading by James Fraleigh
Cover design by Kit Sweeney
Text design and composition by John Reinhardt Book Design
Printed by Berryville Graphics

Distributed by Perseus Distribution
perseusdistribution.com

To place orders through Perseus Distribution:
Tel: 800-343-4499
Fax: 800-351-5073
E-mail: orderentry@perseusbooks.com

Significant discounts for bulk sales are available.
Please contact Glenn Yeffeth at glenn@benbellabooks.com or (214) 750-3628.

For

Frances Quinn

I love you most.

Contents

"The heart has its reasons which reason knows nothing of."

—BLAISE PASCAL

Christmas and New Year's Holiday, 2011. We are on Johnny's basketball court—Quinn's favorite indoor playground.

Introduction

"Fame means millions of people have the wrong idea of who you are."

—ERICA JONG

A LOT HAS BEEN SAID ABOUT ME, about John Edwards, and about our relationship. You may feel like you know the true story. You may even feel like you know me. But the truth is, you don't.

There have been many lies told, many judgments made. Even Erica Jong, who from the quote above would seem to know better, said, "When you think of John Edwards being taken in by someone like Rielle Hunter, you think, what a child he must be, how infantile he must be!"

Apparently everyone is ready to judge me, to judge Johnny, and to judge our relationship. That's okay. This book isn't about changing anyone's mind. It's simply about telling the full truth, which, up until now, no one has heard.

At its heart, this is a love story. It's about two people who fell in love, made terrible sacrifices for that love, and did terrible things in defense of that love. I have regrets about some of the things we did— of course I do. But I don't regret loving Johnny and I certainly don't regret the birth of our amazing daughter, Quinn.

I originally thought that I could get through this whole ordeal without needing to write a book. But in the summer of 2010, I finally grasped the full depth of the story and my role in it and I changed my mind.

I have endured a lot—a great deal of embarrassment, pain, and sadness beyond measure. The disrespect to my life and my privacy are still somewhat astonishing to me. This has not been an easy road to walk, but I'm not writing this book to garner sympathy.

I am writing this book because the truths of this story are not yet in the public domain. In reality, there are facts that even I didn't become aware of until 2011. I'm hoping that by sharing the truth and my experiences, this book will shed some light on the untold side of the story.

Many people invested their hearts, their time, and their energy into the image of John and Elizabeth Edwards. While this image wasn't exactly true, I did play a role in destroying this myth and many supporters ended up feeling hurt, betrayed, and disillusioned. I feel that I owe them the full story.

I also believe that I have a responsibility to Johnny and his entire family to offer the truth.

In addition to all of those reasons, I have a stronger, more personal force driving me to write this book. Her name is Frances Quinn. I want my sweet girl to have one entirely truthful public account of how she came into the world. After all, this is her history too.

I am not writing this book as a defense, but everything in it I would repeat under oath.

It is the truth.

Our daughter deserves it.

ONE

Sixty-First and Park

"We must let go of the life we have planned so as to accept the one that is waiting for us."

—JOSEPH CAMPBELL

DON'T LIKE TO THINK OF MYSELF as a stupid person but I have done a lot of things in my life that were just plain stupid. Snorting cocaine is stupid. Snorting cocaine for just under a decade, desperately attempting to recreate the euphoric high from the first line ever snorted, is so far beyond stupid it may even qualify as criminal. Fortunately, I recognized this in my twenties and stopped. I then began to devote a huge amount of my time and energy to spiritual growth. I know that sounds weird to most people and I'm not one of those gullible New Age–types who believes everything any swami says, but I have always been very attracted to the idea of happiness, self-improvement, and change, which in my youth seemed to be somewhat elusive. For many years I studied astrology, went to spiritual retreats, practiced transcendental meditation and much more. Even as I was drawn to these practices, I also was somewhat skeptical. If there were a joke to be found, I would find it. And yes, while there is a lot of silliness out there, I do sincerely believe there are also a lot of positive things to be learned.

On May 4th, 2004, it suddenly occurred to me that what I had been looking for all those years couldn't come from someone or something else. I realized that I was the source of my own happiness. It was kind of like, if in forty years of life, you had never once seen your own reflection and then one day you just simply looked in the mirror. The realization was so simple yet so weird. I think of that day as the day I woke up and started living, because there was a fundamental shift that happened in my mind and my perspective changed. Overnight, I no longer had any ongoing internal wars. I still had negative emotional reactions, but instead of hanging on to those feelings, I moved to acceptance seamlessly. It took me about two years to adapt to this new way of operating and during that time, I felt extremely high, quite similar to a high from drugs but much better. Actually way better.

Johnny and I took Quinn to school together the day after her fourth birthday. Afterward, we were standing in the kitchen while I made coffee for myself (he doesn't drink coffee). I asked him, "What attracted you to me that first night?" He responded, "Your lightness. When you walked into the room there was a lightness about you."

When this "lightness" happened I (stupidly) assumed that I would do what countless others have done when "waking up" had happened to them—I would teach. I had emerged from more than a decade of intense spiritual study as a person who was committed to being as honest and authentic as I can be with myself and to helping others to the same. I also had a knack for being able to help people see where they were stuck, and what was keeping them from being happy. I'd been an actress, a producer, a filmmaker, and a writer. With my newfound "lightness" (accompanied with a few people asking me for guidance), teaching seemed the most logical thing for me to do next.

So on February 21st, 2006, I was in the process of becoming a spiritual teacher, or to put it in more traditional terms, a life coach.

If I were writing this as a screenplay, here is the part where GOD (played by LENNY KRAVITZ or if Lenny is too busy touring, BONO) would ERUPT into laughter.

I mean, really, what a joke.

I was living in South Orange, New Jersey, with my best friend, Mimi Godfrey Hockman, and her two sons (and my godsons). It was late afternoon and I was getting ready to head into New York City. I remember feeling very happy. Ever since my new outlook on life had happened, my emotional state rarely varied from one of satisfaction. No matter what the circumstances were on the outside, life was just fun.

By early evening I had finished a downtown meeting with a guy from Plum TV about a TV show that never happened, and Mimi had finished getting her hair done, so we met up for dinner. As we approached Park Avenue, Mimi suggested that we stop for a drink at the Loews Regency Hotel.

I liked that idea. I had never been inside the Regency. More importantly, Mimi was in love and wanted to revisit the places that she and her boyfriend had been visiting in the city.

We walked into The Library, the Regency's street-level bar/restaurant. A waiter escorted us to a table. I looked around the room. Diagonally from me on a couch were two men sitting side by side; two more men in chairs flanked the couch. One of the guys on the couch was attractive, wearing all dark Barneys New York type of attire: leather coat, turtleneck, and jeans. He smiled at me; I smiled back. I guessed that he was in the music industry. Directly behind Mimi sat three men who appeared to be having a business meeting. The one closest to Mimi was the most attractive of the three, looking very Southern and conservative but still casual in blue jeans, a blue blazer, and no tie.

After my initial scan of the room, I drank some wine. Then my cell phone rang; it was my friend, Glory Crampton. I asked her to join us, given we were in her neighborhood. She told me she wasn't dressed for the Regency; I told her I wasn't either. (I had on jeans and a black cashmere turtleneck.) She said she would be there soon.

I spotted a guy in a blue blazer sitting directly behind Mimi. I pointed him out to her and said, "He looks like someone who went to University of Virginia or someone that I showed horses with." He was very familiar to me, as if I had known him a long time ago in the South.

She turned briefly to glance at him and said, "You know who that is? John Edwards."

I said, "No, John Edwards is a geek. That guy's got it going on."

"It is. I recognize the accent."

I still didn't believe her.

We spotted an empty table and headed there since Glory would soon be joining us. It also happened to be the precise spot where Mimi and her man sat the previous week.

Seated at our new table, I was now directly facing the alleged John Edwards. He looked directly at me, not smiling. I returned his gaze, also not smiling. He rested his face in his hands and continued to glance at me during the rest of his meeting. This was weird. I knew this man. There was a strong sense of familiarity that I couldn't shake. I was intrigued because there was something so different and so very interesting about this man. This looking back and forth at each other went on for a while, and then he and the younger gentlemen got up and left.

That surprised me. I would have thought that he would have walked directly over to me and asked, "Who are you? And where do I know you from? Because I know you."

Mimi said, "That was definitely John Edwards."

I said, "No way. John Edwards the politician is disconnected and as deep as a puddle. That man has depth and awareness."

The man they had been sitting with remained at their table. Mimi got up, walked over to him, and asked if he had been sitting with John Edwards. The man said he had.

"It *was* him, I told you," she said to me from John Edwards's table.

Mimi sat down with the man and I joined them. We chatted briefly. He introduced himself as a lawyer and campaign donor named Tony; if he told me his last name, it didn't stick.

"I can't believe that was John Edwards. He is so hot." I didn't say this in the voice of an adoring fan, but more like I was surprised to find that it was true.

Tony said, "You should have come over and told him that. He would have loved to hear that."

After some pleasant small talk that included Mimi expressing a strong desire to work for John Edwards, Tony the lawyer raving about what a great guy John Edwards is, and John Edwards's uncanny ability to inspire people to want to help him wherever he goes, there was an exchange of business cards between Mimi and Tony. We went back to our table and Glory arrived. Mimi told her that she had just missed John Edwards and expressed again how much she would like to work for him. Glory seemed a bit disappointed that she had missed out. She sighed, "Oh, I would have loved to meet him."

I replied, "You will." I told Glory about the weird connection I felt between the two of us and that I was confident our paths would cross again one day.

And that was it about John Edwards. The conversation turned to Glory's upcoming wedding, and we were soon discussing details like flowers and venues.

A bit later, I got up to use the ladies' room and on the way I noticed the younger gentleman who had left with John Edwards was back and now sitting with a young woman. I stopped at their table in order to pick up a card for Mimi. His name was Josh Brumberger. He gave me his card and I gave him mine.

I thought about the card exchange for a split second after it happened. I realized that I, the self-described spiritual guide, and my website (which was unfinished and targeted at a much different demographic) could possibly trigger a little ridicule from a young political staffer but I let the thought go. I had picked up his card for Mimi and didn't think that he would ever actually look at the site.

On our way out of the Regency, Glory, a musical theater actress, noticed a poster advertising a friend's upcoming singing engagement. She asked us to wait for her. So while she popped back in to inquire about her friend, Mimi and I waited outside for her.

And then out of nowhere it happened: Johnny Reid Edwards came waltzing around the corner and into my life.

This was *the* moment. Not a "love at first sight" moment but it was the moment when something electric exploded between us. For me it was a little like one of those slow-motion movie moments; it felt like an eternity and yet it all happened very quickly.

As he rounded the corner, he saw me and just lit up. I was very surprised to see him so soon, even though I had felt certain our paths would cross again. I could feel his joy when he saw me and I responded to it. Much to my own astonishment, "You are so hot!" came flying out of my mouth. Not a usual greeting for me. And his friend Tony was right—he did like it. His smile got even brighter. He shook my hand so eagerly it felt as though he might jump into my arms as he said, "Thank you."

And then another little surprise flew out of my mouth: "I can help you."

He replied, "I want your help. I need your help."

"Do you email?" I asked.

He said, "No. I am staying here under the name Matthew Nelson. Call me."

"How long are you staying?" I asked.

He replied, "Until tomorrow morning. Call me. Call me."

And then he was gone.

I had never in my life experienced anything like that meeting. It actually made me feel dizzy. There was a very strong connection between us, I was certain of it.

Mimi was standing next to me, just inches away during the entire exchange. She claims that she saw two people in their own world when Johnny and I shook hands. Mimi held her hand out the whole time attempting to shake hands with John Edwards, the man she wanted to work for. And not only did he not shake her hand, I found out later that he never even noticed her standing there.

Johnny also told me later that he had gone to dinner and could not stop thinking about me. He was mad at himself for not walking over to my table to find out who I was. When he was walking back to the hotel, he looked through the window into the Regency and saw that I was no longer sitting at our table. And much to his surprise he felt very disappointed, even sad. So when her rounded the corner and saw me standing, he felt very happy, with no real understanding as to why.

After the big crazy intro, we girls continued on to dinner and as we sat down, Glory and Mimi kept peppering me with questions and opinions: "What was *that*?" "Are you going to call?" "You have to call." "You could really help him." "You have to call him."

We ordered our food, and I walked outside to call him. No answer. I hung up and figured that I would try again in a while.

A few minutes later, my cell rang. I dug into my coat for it and saw the number.

"What's 212-759-4100?"

Mimi said immediately, "That's the Regency."

"What?" I was floored.

Did the Regency have caller ID?

It was too loud in the restaurant, so I got up and went into the bathroom to call him back.

I asked, "Do you always call women that you don't know, that you meet on the street?"

"Nope, this is the first. I want to hear what you have to say. I am interested in hearing how you can help me. But, uh, my life is, uh, different."

"You can't exactly meet me in a public place."

"Correct."

"Because you can't exactly be seen alone with a woman in the lounge."

"Correct. Would you feel uncomfortable coming to my room?"

"No. I don't feel uncomfortable at all."

And I didn't. There was so much immediate ease between us. He felt very familiar and safe to me, and I really thought I could help him.

"Let me finish my Caesar salad. I'll be there in about fifteen, twenty minutes."

He told me his room number, and we hung up.

I went back to the table to finish eating and informed the ladies that I was headed back to the Regency. They were very excited by this new development, as was I. I remember Glory was adamant about how I could not sleep with him; she had seen the connection and thought he was really attracted to me. More importantly, she thought that I *could* really help him, and that our country needed him. I told her that I had no intention of sleeping with him. I really did just want to help him.

My type of "teaching/life coaching" seems very simple on the outside. I sit with someone and, as they talk to me, I listen and begin seeing where he or she happens to be stuck in his or her head. And then I help them to see it, like holding up a mirror for them.

We all have mental habits that we repeat over and over again, and most people identify the world around them through the lens of these mental habits. They believe they *are* their mental habits. For example, if you have a habit of seeing what's wrong around you, and you don't know you have this habit, everywhere you look you'll see what's wrong, and then you'll get upset about it over and over again. It's all taking place inside of you, and the whole time you think the problem is being caused by someone or something outside of yourself. It's as if you're wearing special eyeglasses, and the lenses have "What's wrong?" written on them. First you have to recognize that you're wearing those glasses and then, at the very least, start reading what's written on your lenses.

When you start seeing that you are not made up of mind patterns but actually the awareness that is *behind* the mind patterns, your whole life starts to change.

This is why I wanted to help John Edwards. I sensed that he was an interesting man who could offer some amazing things to the world, but that was not at all what I saw when I saw him on TV. My thinking was if he could just recognize his mental habits, the man I saw sitting in the Regency would be more likely to shine through on TV.

So I finished my Caesar salad, said goodbye to my friends, and headed back to the Regency to help John Edwards become more aware, to help him to see his mind patterns. That really *was* the plan. At least, it was the part of the plan that I was aware of.

I knocked. He opened the door, a smile lighting up his entire face. I walked in and, after the little hallway and past the bathroom, there was a table with two chairs, where I stopped. He passed me. I looked around the room, which had a king-sized bed with a chair and ottoman next to it. I noticed that he had his opened suitcase on the chair and ottoman. There was something happening between us that I had never felt before. There was a charge, an excitement that filled the room, as much energy as a sold-out rock concert—and it was just the two of us. I didn't understand the force of what was going on between us and it scared me. At the same time, I liked the unknown and the newness of it all. I stayed at the table. He sat on the bed.

"I can't see you way over there," he said. "Come over here—I won't bite." It may sound cheesy now, but to me it felt sweet and charming.

I can see now that what I should have said was, "Sorry, there is more attraction here than I first realized. I need to stop right here or I won't be able to work with you because I won't see clearly."

But, I did not say what I should have said because it did not even occur to me. I was a moth fluttering helplessly toward a flame. Naturally, because he was the most charismatic man I had ever met, he eventually persuaded me to join him on the bed, where we sat and talked. And talked. And talked. We talked about everything—his relationships, his political career, his family. What became clear to me very quickly was that this was a man whose whole self didn't fit in his marriage, which happens a lot. But instead of repressing the parts that didn't fit, he split himself in two and created a double life. A politician who compartmentalizes was not really a shocking development to me because that is one of the abilities that contributes to making a great politician. It had taken him many years to get where he currently was. He told me that he had an entire hidden life that had gone on for decades and that he was currently involved with three different women. One lived in Los Angeles, one in Florida, and one in Chicago. Clearly this behavior of his was not going to change overnight.

I could also easily see the fear—infidelity stems from fear—but I was blinded to the extent of it. I believe that I couldn't see it, partly because I was so blown away by his ability to disclose all the parts of his life to me so openly. The depth of his immediate trust in me was a bit overwhelming.

I remember telling him that the key to being authentic is total honesty with yourself—not hiding anything from yourself. I also told him that if I was going to help him, he couldn't lie to me. He needed to have one person in his life that was safe for him.

He said that wasn't a problem, and when he said that, I felt a wave of total relief roll off of him. He needed this safe space.

Somewhere in the midst of our talk, long after I realized how far off the rails his marriage was, and for how long it had been that way, something happened between us. The connection I felt when I walked in the door had only grown, and the amount of energy between us was huge and unstoppable. And then a moment came while we were talking when something in my heart clicked and I surrendered. I took off my teacher hat, let go of all my resistance to him, and let him lead.

And lead he did. He led me toward the most extraordinary night of my life.

There was a lot of talk, a lot of laughter, and zero sleep.

When I left, I really didn't expect that I would ever hear from him again. From our conversation the night before, I knew that he was a very busy man and because I had forfeited the teacher role, and I am not remotely the type of girl that would ever fit into the role of mistress, let alone occupy the space of girlfriend number four, I just couldn't imagine how our lives would ever intersect again. I honestly thought that I'd just be left with memories. I gave him my phone number but I never asked for his, and he never offered. Walking out of the hotel, I was sleep deprived and walking on air.

On the train back to Jersey that early morning, if my Lenny/Bono GOD sat down next to me and said, "At this exact time, on this exact date six years from now, you will be in North Carolina driving your daughter to school and that man is your daughter's father," I would have ERUPTED with laughter. Because to me, in that moment (especially with all the information that I had acquired in the previous ten hours), that would have sounded just plain stupid. Funny, but stupid.

TWO

Becoming a Mistress

"People say I make strange choices, but they're not strange for me. My sickness is that I'm fascinated by human behavior, by what's underneath the surface, by the worlds inside people."

—JOHNNY DEPP

REALLY HAD NO IDEA whether or not John Edwards would call me. So when he called around 9:30 P.M. later that night, my response was, "I can't believe you are calling me!"

He told me that he had left New York that afternoon and was at his next hotel. He informed me that he had just canceled his previous plans—"the Florida ones I told you about last night." He went on to say, "In fact, I permanently canceled. That one is all done. Which speaks volumes about how I feel about you."

I swooned.

We talked for two hours. He said repeatedly that he couldn't believe how easy it was to talk to me. He asked if he could call me on Saturday night from Davenport, Iowa. It would be around 11:30 my time. Would I wait up for him?

I said yes. I was completely fascinated by him. Where could this possibly be headed? And was he really already changing his behavior, based on our one night together? Love does evolve you and encourage you to behave differently. Was he in love with me?

I was in the kitchen when my cell rang late Saturday night, February 25th. The first thing out of his mouth was, "I miss you! I can't believe how much I miss you. I miss you so bad."

I couldn't believe how vocal he was about his feelings! A man expressing his feelings? I loved that! He came across as open and fearless, though I would learn later that this was not exactly the case.

"You know how bad I missed you?" he continued. "I almost broke all my rules yesterday. I went to my phone; I had it in my hand and just about called you before I stopped myself. I thought, 'What are you doing?'"

I wondered to myself: what are his "rules"?

He paused and sighed. "By the way, I'm in Iowa. What am I doing in Davenport fucking Iowa?" The way he said it cracked me up, like he was completely bewildered to find himself mired in the crazy political landscape of Iowa. It was like he knew he didn't belong there.

I burst out laughing. And just like that, I was head over heels in love. My heart had a reaction to him like no other man, ever. His sense of humor sealed the deal. I couldn't believe it—I had absolutely no control over my heart—not that I wanted any, but oh my God, this was CRAZY!

That night began our frequent extended phone conversations, usually four hours in length.

It felt to me like he was starved for authenticity and he was finally getting fed. He had the freedom to say anything and not get punished for it. He told me that I didn't have the negative reactions that most women had when he said things that were a little off the wall. He said that he found me to be so refreshing and couldn't believe how easy I was to talk to. He also told me that I was the first person in his life that gave him energy instead of taking it.

I loved how much he needed and wanted more awareness, joy, and love. I had a lot to give and I very much wanted to give it to him.

The problem with our relationship is pretty obvious: someone who is living a life devoted to spiritual truth is probably not going to be the best mistress. Mistresses are supposed to be a secret. It's a hidden relationship by nature, but given that I had never been a mistress and because I never set out to be one, I did not attend mistress school, I never read any mistress handbooks, and therefore didn't realize how important it is (outside of your relationship, of course) to *keep your mouth shut!*

I also find it very ironic, given I am actually somewhat knowledgeable and talented in other areas, that I would become world-famous for something that I am *not* very good at.

If you have ever been in love, you know that when it happens, you are bursting with happiness. It is very difficult to contain yourself, so everyone who crosses your path will instantly realize that something is different about you.

Johnny told me that many people he worked with around that time said to him, "What's going on with you?" And he would tell them, "I'm happy. It makes a big difference."

Because I had no experience at this type of thing, when I was asked about my over-the-top happiness, I stupidly said a little too much.

It was during this same time period that I was attempting to fix my website with a woman named Pigeon O'Brien.

I met Pigeon on October 25th, 2005, at an anniversary book party in New York City for Jay McInerney's book *Bright Lights, Big City*. Pigeon approached me and acted as though she was my long-lost friend. I did not know her so I asked Jay, my ex-boyfriend, who she was. He said Pigeon was in love with him and was around him a lot after I dated him in the 1980s and that she built websites. I asked around and, with the exception of Jay, none of my old friends from the 1980s knew her either. Despite her odd insertion into my life as my long-lost friend and disclosing many of her emotional problems in the first few minutes of chatting, she seemed quite harmless and very quickly offered to help me with my website. She spent a month or so in 2005 building the initial site and then disappeared before it was completed.

In 2006 I reached out to Pigeon again and asked if she could fix her original work. And like our original verbal agreement, instead of a money exchange for her work, I was helping Pigeon with her problems, one of which was a situation where she found herself chasing after a guy. In my bursting-with-love state I (stupidly) used my life as an example and mentioned to Pigeon that I had seen a guy in the Regency who seemed interesting, different to me than most men, but I never went after him. And then later I just magically bumped into him on the street. But then (bad mistress) in response to her inquiry, I revealed that the guy from the Regency was from North Carolina, his name was John, I had fallen for him, and the hard part for me was that he was (still) in a bad marriage and he had small kids. I (stupidly) answered questions, offering too many details that would enable her to later put the puzzle together. Yet, at the time, she expressed her joy over my newfound love and over those first few weeks, when I was falling hard, she sent my some examples for the splash page, which, to put it nicely, were not at all what I was going for. I thanked her anyway and stopped talking to her. I never spoke to her again nor did I retain her last name. Unfortunately, Pigeon didn't forget about me and would show up in my life later, in a much more sinister aspect.

Johnny came back to New York for two days at the beginning of March. He phoned me in the late afternoon to confirm our plans to meet later. He was totally in his work mode, which to me felt cold and a bit guarded. He told me if I could just be somewhere near his hotel around 8:30 that night, he would call me when he was done.

I wasn't accustomed to his work mode and asked him if he was nervous. He replied no, not at all, and that he was really looking forward to getting together. I was feeling a little nervous, after so much intimate phone time and not a lot of face time, but because he didn't ask, I kept my feelings to myself.

The "state of affairs" of his life made me very uneasy and scared for him. He seemed to want to clean it all up and not hurt anyone in the process, yet, like a lot of very successful men who compartmentalize, he had not, in his fifty-odd years, acquired the tools needed to handle any kind of deep emotional territory. And from what he told me, his other girlfriends would understandably not be very happy with this new development in his life.

I was really impressed with his strong desire to clean up his life, and at the same time, the mess of it all seemed so dangerous to me. Apparently, though, not too dangerous to stop me from going forward with him, partly because I really thought I could help him and if he didn't change his ways, his life was bound to implode. Secondly, and more importantly, I was already madly in love.

Around 8:15, I went to the Four Seasons and my phone rang just as my glass of wine arrived.

"What are you doing?"

"Having a glass of wine."

"Get your butt over here right now. I can't wait to see you."

I paid my tab and didn't drink my wine.

I walked into the hotel, right through the lobby, and up the elevator. His door was ajar, and when I walked in, he ran over to me as he said, "You are even more gorgeous than I remembered."

I was blown away, not because of him, or that comment, but I just couldn't believe the charge between us. The force of it! I had never experienced anything like it and it was increasing, not diminishing.

If you have ever wondered whether that movie magic, that mysterious love connection, beyond your wildest fantasy, really exists? I can tell you unequivocally: *it exists*.

While I was there, the hotel phone rang a number of times, but he did not pick it up. I assumed it was the LA woman who had his alias but not the room number. There was never a knock on the door, and his attention stayed focused on me the entire night.

I left the hotel in the morning; he left New York later that day. We continued talking frequently on the phone.

We would talk on the phone until we both had zero energy left. But even then it was still difficult to hang up. We really could not get enough of each other. We were like a pair of teenagers, completely attached, and it felt awful to separate.

And at some point during this time, he told me that LA was done. We'd only seen each other a couple of times and hadn't been talking for very long, and already he'd broken off two of his other relationships.

The following week Johnny went out to the beach with his kids and told me that he needed to go out to dinner with an old girlfriend. I was very upset about this. I asked, "Why are you opening that door again?" He gave excuse after excuse: "I can't get out of it now. She has come all this way to meet me for dinner—dinner only." Clearly he wanted to go. Why would he be doing this? How could he be going out to dinner in a public place? I told him that this was a big mistake; none of it made sense to me. He went and called me when he got back to say what a mistake it had been. She wanted to stay, wanted to get back together, she cried, and so on. He was acting so weird—drunk, in fact. That's it. He was drunk.

This was the man I thought was so unique? Not bloody likely. That little pattern connects him to almost every heterosexual man on the planet.

I couldn't understand how this man could be so unaware or how I could be so in love with him. Of course, those thoughts separate me from almost no woman on the planet.

And what's up with that anyway? You get rid of two women, and an old one comes back? What kind nightmare is this?

When he called me the next day, he was himself again. And he was really appreciative of how great I was for him. He seemed to be happy to have dodged an old girlfriend bullet. And I was somewhat satisfied that at the very least we were moving in the right direction.

Being down at the beach seemed to inspire a desire in him to have me join him there. He really wanted me to see his world—to share it with me. On the afternoon of March 25th, I flew to Wilmington, North Carolina, and he picked me up at the airport. As I was waiting to pick up my huge Prada duffel bag, I saw him circling. I had packed way too many clothes; I was also nervous but very excited. Would we be walking on the beach? Would we even be in public?

He had called the night before while he was driving out to the beach. We spoke during most of his entire drive out. He told me he almost had to cancel because Elizabeth, who was busy finishing her book *Saving Graces*, had informed him that she was going to come to the beach. He said she would typically change her mind if he didn't oppose her in any way, and that's exactly what she did. This is the first time I remember any real mention of Elizabeth as a potential factor in our relationship, though we had discussed his marriage in more abstract terms many times before. Because there wasn't any physical or emotional intimacy between Johnny and Elizabeth, I had absolutely no jealous feelings about her or their relationship. It was his other outside relationships that were the problems for me.

Don't get me wrong—the idea that he had a wife and two small children at home really bothered me, but the "wife as innocent victim" did not match the reality of their marriage. They had big, big problems, which were created by both of them. You don't go through two-plus decades of extramarital relationships unless both parties are responsible.

It's a very strange way of thinking (to me, at least), but there are plenty of people in this world who think that marriage is some kind of ownership, and that if they are not having sex with their partner— for years—then their partner is not having sex with anyone else because they belong to them. My thinking is if you aren't having sex with your partner, the chances are high that someone else is.

When he mentioned Elizabeth, and how our beach plans would not be interrupted, I had a thought: your spouse does whatever she wants and you (carefully) maneuver accordingly. At the time, I didn't really give the thought that much attention. When you are in love, you don't want to examine things that would diminish your extra dose of euphoria. And that euphoria was so intoxicating, so magnetic, and so forceful that I didn't stand a chance against it.

He drove me to my hotel, a Holiday Inn in Wrightsville Beach, North Carolina. He parked his car while I checked in, and then I went back down to the garage and gave him a key. He came up by himself later.

Once he was in the room, he went out on the balcony. I said, "What are doing? Get in here and away from the window."

"Oh, I didn't think about that."

What? For a celebrity politician with relationships outside of his marriage, he sure wasn't cautious at all. Did he want to get caught or was he just that unconscious?

As usual, we had the greatest time. We laughed together so much, the kind of laughter that you can't stop and makes your eyes tear up. Our senses of humor matched perfectly. We had room service for dinner; Johnny hid in the bathroom while the guy set up the table. The food was fantastic. I had chicken pasta; he had salmon.

The next day Johnny called to tell me he really wanted me to meet his kids. He asked me to meet them at Mayfair, an outdoor shopping mall, where they could just run into me as a shopper and hang out a little. I used the free shuttle service from the hotel and headed over. Johnny had on a light blue Ralph Lauren cashmere sweater and jeans. He looked so beautiful and he was so happy to see me. I was nervous to be with him in public, but he was completely relaxed. He told me his kids were in the kid section, just to go over there. I did. Jack was playing with the "Thomas the Train" display, and I started to play with it and he immediately engaged me in conversation. Totally charming.

Emma walked over and apologized for Jack. "Sorry if he's bugging you."

I said, "It's okay, he's not bugging me."

Emma then said, "Do you know my dad is John Edwards? He ran for president." She broke my heart. My instinct was to hug her and say, "That doesn't matter, you are important because you are you."

In two seconds it was clear to me that Jack got a lot of attention as a small child and that Emma had a harder road. I could see why everyone loves Jack; he was charming like his father. But I really loved Emma Claire instantly.

We hung out in the store for a little while and as we walked out of the store to say goodbye, both kids asked, "Can't she come too?"

He asked me, "Want to?"

So we all walked over to Cold Stone Creamery. I stopped and got a green tea and then joined them and we sat together as the kids ate ice cream.

Jack did this little thing with both his hands—pretending they were puppets and he was making a joke about Johnny and me, indicating that our talking was more than talking. Kids, they don't miss a thing.

Later Johnny told me that Emma had asked, "Do you think I will ever see my friend from the bookstore today again?"

Johnny said, "Maybe."

And Emma said, "I hope so."

When Johnny came to my hotel for dinner that night, he brought a newly purchased CD and a framed picture of Wade, his son who had passed away in a car accident many years before. This really touched me. It was clear to me that he was now in love with me, almost a month to the day after I had fallen in love with him. He also brought me some cash in the neighborhood of a thousand dollars, to pay for my hotel and airline ticket down there. He told me when he was getting the cash that his money person asked him, "Do you want me to get you an ATM card?" Johnny was all excited about it.

"What? You don't have an ATM card?" I couldn't believe it.

"No."

"How can that be?"

"I don't ever need cash."

"Ever? What if you got stranded somewhere that didn't take Amex or you needed to tip someone?" This was completely baffling to me.

"I always have people around me to take care of things."

Wow. He really did live in a different world.

We had room service again, and again the food was outstanding. We were both blown away by it. How do you know when you are really in love? Holiday Inn room service tastes like Mario Batali cooked your meal himself. Johnny stayed for a few hours but not the whole night. He was at the beach with the nanny and the kids. He called the second he got back to his beach house and we talked until neither of us could keep our eyes open.

The next day he called on his way over to my hotel. Apparently, the woman from Chicago had been calling his cell phone nonstop, and he felt like he needed to return the phone call. He said he needed to "manage the situation." He planned to end his Chicago thing when he was there in person on April 7th. This made me *mad*. I was in love with him and didn't understand why he wouldn't just end that relationship now.

By the time he got to the hotel, he was all messed up.

I put on my teacher hat for a while, sitting and talking with him until he returned back to himself. And once he did, we had the *best* time.

THREE

Falling in Love

*"When one is in love, one always begins by deceiving
one's self, and one always ends by deceiving others.
That is what the world calls a romance."*

—OSCAR WILDE

JOHNNY CAME BACK to New York at the beginning of April
2006, and then I took the train to DC to spend the night at his
Georgetown townhouse. It was my first time in Union Station
and it took my breath away; I wasn't expecting its beauty. I also
absolutely loved all the old townhouses in Georgetown.

He gave me a tour of his big yellow house, which the family no
longer lived in. However, it still had plenty of furniture. I was not
completely comfortable in his house—it did not have a homey wel-
coming feel to me. I believe it was on the market; it felt more like a
house that had been staged to sell. He then gave me his credit card
and I went out and got take-out food at Paolo's. I wondered for a second if the guy behind the bar would have any reaction to me using
John Edwards's credit card. He didn't. We spent the night together in
Johnny's house but we didn't stay in the master bedroom. I thought
that would be way too weird. He agreed.

23

The next day he headed to Chicago and I went back to New Jersey. He had told me sometime back that his Chicago girlfriend was the one who had bought him his extra cell phone.

I was not remotely happy about the night ahead of me. He called after he got to Chicago, saying she had picked him up at the airport and that he was going to have dinner with her in order to end it and that nothing was going to happen between them. Her picking him up and them having dinner together? The thought alone pissed me off. I then heard knocking on the door. He said he needed to go; he couldn't just leave her out there knocking. I knew this needed to happen but I was furious. I wasn't finished talking, and he was hanging up to go have dinner with someone he said was in love with him and didn't want to let him go? He hung up and did what he wanted. I called a few times later and he didn't pick up. I don't think I had ever been that angry in my life. I turned my phone off.

The next morning, when I had turned the phone back on, he called almost immediately. He was so mad at me for turning my phone off! He told me that the Chicago relationship was over but that she said she was going to fight for him. He told me that she cried and slapped him when he told her that I made him happy. I asked how this was all going to work out with the phone. (Remember, he said she paid for it.) He believed she was still going to pay the bill because she was that in love with him.

WHAT? The whole thing seemed so nuts to me! I was very uncomfortable about a third party monitoring how much we spoke on the phone and having phone records of it and I told him so. He seemed to think that this woman was never going to do anything to hurt him. That just seemed ridiculous to me.

My biggest problem was I was unable to hold on to any discomfort about anything. I don't know if it was just from the "waking up" or if it was because we were so in love. Or both. Any and all negativity that was triggered by him diminished completely, especially when we were together, or even just talking on the phone. Our connection was the strangest thing I had ever experienced. And I couldn't turn away from it.

On April 20th I flew to Manchester, New Hampshire, for two days, obviously just to see him. After all, it's not like there is a whole lot anything other than politics going on in Manchester. I arrived at the hotel before he did and had dinner in the restaurant. By closing time, he still hadn't called. I sat in the lobby way off to the side, hidden from view. I was certainly excited to see him but not at all enjoying this sitting in the shadows, waiting. And believe me, the irony did not escape me. He finally called. I made a mental note: waiting is definitely one of the least interesting parts of being a mistress.

When I got up to his room and saw him, the rest of the world faded in the background. All of my annoyance at waiting, and any hesitation I had about being with him just disappeared.

The next morning, I went out to explore Manchester while he went to speak around New Hampshire about how bad off our country was under President George W. Bush, and how great he would be at changing and fixing all the problems.

Johnny had given me his brand-new ATM card to take out money for my plane fare, which had been way too pricey because of the last-minute booking. As I was taking the money out, my heart was racing because I thought some bank teller was going to come over, grab the card, and arrest me for withdrawing funds from my boyfriend's bank account.

Nothing of the sort happened. I withdrew around a thousand dollars and got out of the bank as quickly as I could. Once safely outside, I thought my reaction was somewhat hilarious. Secret agent girl I am not.

I returned to the hotel for a few hours, hung out in the room reading, and then went out for dinner. Johnny had called to give me periodic updates as to whether the coast was clear or not.

He returned to the hotel while I was out to dinner and then called to tell me when it was safe to return.

That night, as usual, he told me about being hit on by a woman. However, what was unusual this time was that while he was telling me everything she had said, I started repeating it to him so he could actually *hear* it. Most people listen to others in order to get confirmation of what they already know or to confirm what they want to believe is true. Rare is the person who listens in order to discover something *new*.

This was the first time Johnny had ever removed his "belief that what they were saying was true" from the equation. He burst out laughing. Laughter is a normal reaction when you begin to free your-self from your thoughts. Most of us don't realize that our minds have taken us prisoner, and as we begin to free ourselves, to *see* our thoughts instead of *being* our thoughts, there is usually a lot of laugh-ter and a big release of energy.

Johnny saw for the first time that what women would say to him was a pattern. Once he stopped getting hooked into what they were saying, he could see why they were saying it, that it actually had nothing to do with him, how good-looking he was, how they be-lieved in him, how they wanted to help him—and everything to do with their agenda and how they wanted to use him.

John Edwards got hurt a great deal because he believed what people were saying to be true, because he wanted it to be true. He blinded himself to what was underneath the words. He couldn't see that people were using him.

Years before he met me, he really believed he was the savior, the golden boy for the Democratic Party. People told him that all day long. His wife. People he paid. People he met on the street who want-ed him to be that.

I left the hotel early in the morning before he did, and once again, it was painful to part. At the airport, as I sat at the gate waiting for my plane I was absolutely astonished by my feelings. I had the most intense longing for him and I had just left him. It was so surprising to me. He apparently was feeling it too. When he called me later, during was his run time (two hours blocked out every day on his schedule in order to run), he told me that he actually went looking for me in the airport. He didn't find me, because my plane left earlier than his, but I was very pleased to hear that he had looked.

The next time I saw him was in May, when I took the train to Boston. I arrived late, and it was raining. The hotel was the Fairmont Copley Plaza, two blocks from the Back Bay train station. I was a tad angry when I arrived because Johnny and I were talking on the phone while I was on the train and his other line beeped and he hung up with me to answer it. We talked only on the "other woman" cell phone, so that meant he was hanging up with me to talk to another "other woman." NOT COOL. He had already told me the coast was clear, so I went right to the room. The other woman was the one he'd had dinner with at the beach, his old girlfriend, and that was the last time he made that mistake. After seeing how much it annoyed me, he never answered the phone again if it beeped while he was talking to me. And this old girlfriend (who he claimed was now just a friend) was an issue between us that he also claimed he was going to do something about.

Johnny was in New York a couple nights that month. And true to his word, one of those nights he had a very long conversation on the "other woman" cell phone with this old girlfriend as I sat next him on the bed. He was attempting to wind down their friendship, and, from what I gathered, this was something she didn't really want to do. The fact he did this with me sitting there did show me he was at least trying to clean up his life, but it also irritated me how difficult it was for him to actually cut the cord. He claimed that he didn't want to hurt her. I kept thinking, as he was on the phone: how do I help you see that's just your projection, that you don't want to hurt yourself? But no natural opening presented itself that night so I kept my thoughts to myself. The next morning, to pay for my New Hampshire travel from April that I had put on my Amex, I took his bank card to an ATM on Madison Avenue on my way to Penn Station and took out fifteen hundred dollars—three five-hundred-dollar withdrawals. I returned his ATM card to him when I came back that night. As usual, I was unable to hold on to "issues" about our relationship and there were no more talks that evening with or about the old girlfriend.

I again took the Acela down to DC to see him. The Acela rocks. It is the greatest way to travel. I loved eating at the Daily Grill in Georgetown while I waited for him. It's just a few blocks from his townhouse. It was a restaurant chain I ate at frequently in LA; they serve a great Cobb salad.

From DC I took the Acela to see him in Philadelphia, the City of Brotherly Love. I arrived before he did, dropped my bag off at the Latham Hotel, and went out to explore the city because it was my first time there. I had a delicious crab cake dinner at a seafood restaurant on Rittenhouse Square. He called when the coast was clear to tell me what room we were in, and I happily joined him. In the morning, he called his assistant Josh Brumberger, presumably "to go over the schedule," but it was just a ruse to keep Josh on the phone so I could get out of the hotel without being seen. Josh would recognize me, of course, from our meeting at the Regency.

One day at the end of May, when Johnny called me at home in New Jersey, he said, "We have a problem."

He was at an event, and Elizabeth had called with an emergency. She said, "Someone has stolen your bank card. There was fifteen hundred dollars taken out in New York."

Johnny said, "No, it's not stolen. I took out that money."

"Why do you need that much money?"

They had a big fight. Her radar was up.

He was angry. He knew from the beginning that getting me money to travel to see him was going to be a problem.

I told him I would figure something out.

I found it strange but I didn't say a word about their money dynamic. Couples have the oddest money issues. I don't know many who are exempt from this. He seemed to have no control or awareness of the money he made. She was in charge of spending; he wasn't supposed to spend.

I flew to West Palm Beach, Florida, at the end of May and had dinner in the hotel while I waited for him and his entourage to arrive. Once they showed up, I watched them from the dining room while they unloaded their cars. I remember watching Johnny get his own bag out and wheel it into the hotel. I was touched watching a "big wig" wheeling his own bag. I remember having the same feeling when I watched Al Gore wheeling his own bag through airports in *An Inconvenient Truth*.

Johnny called me and told me when the coast was clear. Josh was not along on this trip, and no one he was with would recognize me. I remember going down to the lobby in the morning and withdrawing the new limit of four hundred dollars out of the cash machine and bringing his card back to him. I saw his staffers in the lobby and walked right by them as I hopped in a cab and went on my way to the airport.

To solve our problems, both logistical and monetary, I came up with the idea of shooting a documentary, which quickly evolved into doing shorts for the web as well. I had made many shorts in LA while one of my scripts was in development, and documentaries are my favorite. When I pitched it to Johnny, he loved it. He was crazy about the idea of showing the campaign "behind the scenes," showing the real him, and also the idea of me traveling with him and putting me to work. I told him I would write up a treatment for him. We were both excited about this development.

In June, I flew to Moline, Illinois, and drove to the Radisson Hotel in Davenport, Iowa—the very place Johnny was staying when I fell in love with him over the phone. The hotel had an open eating area and indoor atrium in the center, with the rooms opening on to the atrium. I went directly into the bar and ordered a glass of wine while I was waited for my call. Johnny called right on schedule to say that they had brought his dinner, but uh-oh, dinner disaster! They had forgotten the ketchup, so he asked me to sit tight while they brought back some ketchup. Sure enough, I saw the man whom I would later meet as John Davis, an earnest blond who was very clearly a political staffer. He was coming down in the glass elevator. I waited for the big ketchup delivery to be complete before joining Johnny for dinner in his room. The food was great. We celebrated his birthday with the presents I brought him. One was a pair of classic aviator Ray-Bans. He was only fifty-three years old, but not the hippest guy in town. He later got many comments about how those sunglasses were "too cool" for his homey Southern husband image. His operatives didn't really need to worry too much because, like most of his sunglasses, he ended up losing them shortly thereafter anyway.

A big mistake I made that night: I taught Johnny how to text. He told me soon after that night he started receiving texts from other women. I assumed that the woman who bought him the phone had noticed on the phone bill that he was now texting, so she started using it as another method to attempt to reach him. I read some of the texts, if one came in while I was sitting there. (He hid nothing from me.) The ones I always read were from the old girlfriend, the one he went to dinner with at the beach. Irritating? That's an understatement. Clearly this "friendship" was not end-ing soon enough for me.

In the morning, we went running together. I went out in my run-ning clothes; and he joined me five minutes later and we ran together, right out in the open, next to the Mississippi River. I really couldn't believe we were running together side by side in light of day. I still can't believe it. Nobody noticed. Nobody cared.

After he left the hotel, I took a shuttle bus to the airport and rented a car to drive to Des Moines, Iowa.

I took a little tour of booming Des Moines and ended up at the Hotel Fort Des Moines. I parked my little white rental car in the parking lot across the street and went into the restaurant. I ordered a burger and red wine. As I was eating, I saw John Davis, the ketchup guy, walking outside, talking on his cell phone. Johnny called me on the phone and told me I had to wait until they brought him food from Centro. I really didn't realize that being a mistress would involve so much waiting. I ordered another glass of wine.

The next morning, I put a bandana over my wet hair, and my small purple Paul Smith sunglasses. As I walked out of the hotel, a tall guy in his late twenties, with disheveled hair wearing glasses, was walking into the hotel as I was walking out. I knew this was a staffer but I didn't look at him closely. I wanted out fast. I went out to my car and realized I'd forgotten to get a validation from the front desk of the hotel to get out of the parking garage. I walked back, hoping that the staffer would be finished with his checkout, but he was standing there, checking out the room number I had just stayed in.

The lady at the desk asked what room I was in before she validated my ticket. I panicked, said, "Never mind," and hightailed it out of there.

I kept thinking that the staffer must have known something. I just had a feeling that he knew me. I was freaked out. Did I just get Johnny busted over a parking validation?

I paid the parking garage and drove to the airport, my mind racing the entire time. This was all my fault, I was in trouble, and I was going to get punished. What would the punishment be? He would break up with me.

When Johnny called me later, he laughed. He said nobody saw anything, and if they did they didn't tell him.

But who was that guy in the glasses? Johnny didn't know which staffer he was. My description did not ring a bell, but more than that, he didn't seem to care. He was more interested in the contents of my mind. He thought it was hilarious that my little run-in had triggered the notion that he was going to break up with me. But mostly he seemed to be in awe of the fact that I shared the whole experience with him. Nobody else in his life was ever open with him.

FOUR

Working Girl

"Love is a fire. But whether it is going to warm your heart or burn down your house, you can never tell."

—Joan Crawford

WROTE UP A TREATMENT but I knew from my years in LA attempting to get projects off the ground that to get the video project up and running, I needed someone who could bring what I was lacking to the table: big credentials. This was low-budget filmmaking in uncharted waters. And at that time, I happened to know a guy, Cary Woods, who was known for being a groundbreaking indie producer. His movies had much bigger budgets than this, but he was an innovative guy, and I was pretty good at guerrilla filmmaking, given my experience writing and directing many shorts on very small budgets, so I thought it might work.

My first step was to talk to Cary about producing or consulting on this documentary and/or the shorts for the web. He wanted to meet with Johnny to see if he liked him. I set up a dinner meeting at Serafina with Johnny and Cary in NYC and they hit it off, as I suspected they would. I joined them for part of the dinner. It was a go, but because of Cary's schedule, he only wanted to commit to consulting.

The next step was for Cary and me to meet with Nick Baldick, the guy running Johnny's political action committee, or PAC as the people in politics call it. I set up the meeting in DC and took the train down the night before the meeting. I was in Johnny's living room, eating takeout from Paolo's, when Nick called to get my date of birth for a flight. Nick wanted our info because Cary and I were invited after our meeting to travel via private plane to Raleigh with Johnny for a Dave Matthews Band concert. I was excited about this because, thanks to Mimi, I was a new Dave Matthews fan.

After I hung up with Nick, Johnny's "other woman" cell rang. He didn't answer, but boy I was not happy about it ringing. It was his old girlfriend (again), which really bugged me. He insisted (again) that she was his friend, and he wanted to handle it the right way. Because I am friends with most of my exes, and he wasn't hiding this from me at all, what could I say? After I expressed my jealousy, I dropped it.

The next day I met with Cary, who had taken the train down from New York. Cary told me he could not go to the concert because he needed to return to New York right after lunch. I called Johnny from the lobby of the Ritz Carlton where we were meeting Nick for lunch to tell him about this new development.

Cary and I had a good meeting with Nick. Both of us were surprised how much we liked him. Despite his political operative side, Nick had a really soft, nurturing side and a good sense of humor.

After the meeting, Cary and I parted way. I went back to Johnny's house, where I met with Matthew Nelson, one of Johnny's staffers. It was funny to discover Johnny's alias (the name his rooms were listed under) was a real person who worked for him. Matthew and I waited and chatted in the living room while Johnny showered and got dressed so we could drive to the FBO, or fixed-based operator. An FBO is basically the small airport, often next to the large commercial airport, used for private planes. Apparently Matthew had earned himself a seat on the private plane and a concert ticket because Cary couldn't make it. I don't know who decided this (Johnny or Nick or maybe both of them), but someone thought that it probably didn't look good for Johnny to be arriving in North Carolina with just me on a private plane. This was my first experience of the micromanaging that goes in politics. Every move was handled: What will it look like? How will it affect the candidate's image? Will this help us or hurt us? Welcome to politics. Many cooks in the kitchen all armed with their own recipes.

We landed, and Johnny's loyal aide Andrew Young was there to meet him. I was told before we landed about Andrew's love for the senator. There were many jokes within the PAC: Andrew was so in love with Johnny that he would meet him with rose petals to scatter under his feet as he walked.

This was my first meeting with him, and initially, I really liked Andrew. He was working for Johnny, someone he very obviously loved, so he radiated happiness. He was completely joyful and a little flirtatious. But he also displayed signs of a pattern I observed with most of the people around Johnny. Like so many of his aides, Andrew had a false sense of his own importance. Andrew was not the first one (nor would he be the last) who believed Johnny was gifted but couldn't cross the street, let alone get to the White House, without his assistance in every last matter. In fairness, Johnny's behavior played into this pattern completely.

With Andrew, though, it was endearing. He so clearly believed himself to be in charge of everything and he so clearly wasn't. As I chatted with Andrew about the great state of North Carolina, I wondered to myself why Johnny surrounded himself with people who believed that he was a very talented simpleton who couldn't function without them. Because the Johnny I knew was no fool.

We got to the concert and went to the back where all of the Dave Matthews Band tour buses were; the number and the size of those buses were humbling. There was an outdoor tent, drinks, and buffet food. Supporters surrounded Johnny while Boyd Tinsley, who I later learned was the violin player for the band, was holding court. I met Cate Edwards (who later told her dad she thought I was cool), a friend of hers, and many of Johnny's supporters. They were all very friendly; some expressed their excitement that I was going to be making a documentary about their guy.

Boyd was giving some of Johnny's supporters an inside tour of his bus, and I was invited to come along. When I stepped inside, Boyd was talking about his passion for tennis and doing musical things outside of the band, like scoring films. I asked if he would be interested in doing some music for the documentary I was about to start making for Johnny, and he said yes, very much. I exchanged numbers with one of his two assistants, we chatted for a second, and then I went to get dinner from the buffet.

We were all sitting in the audience. During the concert Andrew gathered Johnny and some folks to go up to the side of the stage and watch from there. Johnny, of course, had a seat; everyone else stood. After the show, Andrew drove Johnny, Matthew, and me back to the plane.

The night before I wrote this, Johnny, Quinn, and I were having dinner, and because I was working on this section of the book, we were talking about that particular ride. Johnny remembered that *The New York Times* had a piece about him coming out that we read in advance via BlackBerry on the way back to the plane. I remember a lot of laughter and joking amongst the group. Andrew had gotten us all concert T-shirts, and Andrew and I were talking about the band and the song "Steady As You Go." Andrew and I both agreed that we loved that song. Later Andrew would claim it was going to be Johnny's and my wedding song, which isn't something we ever talked about. I had been married once and did not want to do it again.

Boyd and his assistants flew back to DC with us. I remember Matthew and I dropped Johnny off at his place first, then Matthew dropped me off at the Georgetown Inn. And then I walked back to Johnny's, a few blocks away.

In the morning, as I was getting ready, Johnny went running. I left his place and took a cab to Union Station in order to check my bag and then took a cab to go hear Johnny give a speech on poverty in America. Johnny called as I was in the cab and asked if I saw anyone when I left his place. I said no; apparently I had just missed a staffer.

At the speech, I sat with Boyd and his assistants. Josh Brumberger was there. It was the first time I had seen him since the night at the Regency. He did not do a very good job of either hiding his feelings about my new job or his judgments about me. I believe he was mostly bothered by the fact that I was hired without his knowledge or control.

After the speech, Matthew escorted me up to say goodbye to the senator.

The senator and I said farewell, and I told him that I was looking forward to working with him. It was sort of funny, pretending to be formal and acting like I had no other relationship with Johnny. This was the first time I really felt like I was living a double life. And then I hopped a cab to Union Station and headed back to New Jersey.

I had no illusions or doubts as to why I had joined him in this secret life; my choice was to love and support the man I was in love with as he (I hoped) ended his double life. He wanted truth, he wanted authenticity, he didn't want to hide—this I know for sure, even though he sometimes fought himself tooth and nail.

How do I know this for sure? He never would have fallen in love with me if that hadn't been the case. True or not, I believed it.

FIVE

And Away We Go

*"Being president is like being groundskeeper in a
cemetery: there are a lot of people under you, but none
of them are listening."*

—BILL CLINTON

I N EARLY JULY, as the contract for the documentary was getting
worked out with the lawyers, I grabbed a camera and set off to join
Johnny for two weeks of development, in order to check out his
world and the people in it. My biggest concern was how I was going
to turn this world of political preparation into something interesting.

Once I got to DC, I took a cab to the PAC offices and spent a few
hours chatting up some staffers. I still remember John Davis (the
same one who went for ketchup) as such a likeable, fresh-faced Iowa
guy, sitting at his desk explaining the importance of Iowa to me.

Then I took a cab to Nick Baldick's office, where Johnny was making phone calls and having a meeting with Nick and David "Mudcat"
Saunders, a political strategist known for making very colorful statements. To me, Mudcat was quite a character, a man who couldn't
seem to get enough camera time.

Johnny told me later that he and Nick were meeting about Johnny's
desire to replace Josh Brumberger. Johnny's reasoning was that

traveling with someone all the time was hard, and without getting into all the details of why Josh was wrong for him, he just wanted him replaced. But for some reason it didn't happen.

I would soon see a very disturbing pattern from the PAC leaders who supposedly wanted their candidate to reach the highest office in the land: Johnny would request something, and the request would go unheeded because the folks working for him thought they knew better. I wondered, is this from his marriage too? Or is it just youth and ego? Or is it all of politics? Welcome to Washington, DC, the stagnant capital of "I am right and you are wrong."

I went to the Daily Grill, ate my favorite Cobb salad, and checked into the Georgetown Inn, where I stayed the night. Johnny came to visit me later that night for a few hours, which was easy for him because it was just a few blocks away from his house.

We flew to Iowa the next day. Johnny's first event was at a small coffee shop/cafe. I shot a few "man-on-the-street" interviews along with his stump speech. One was with an older female supporter and her husband. She was hilarious. She thought Johnny was the cat's meow, and she had clearly dragged her husband down there to see him. She showed up in the afternoon, at a different event hours away, having ditched her husband, this time with a girlfriend in tow. I would see her at almost every event in Iowa and was beginning to learn that in some cases, there is a fine line between stalker and supporter.

When we pulled up to the event, Johnny's cell rang. He answered and even from the back of the car, you could hear screaming coming from the phone. Johnny said, "I will call you back," and he hung up the phone. He got out of the car and walked half a block away from us, but anyone could see that he was having a heated phone call. He hung up and as he walked by he mumbled to me, "Elizabeth." As if I hadn't already figured that out.

I wasn't allowed to shoot this event so I wandered outside and ran into Jonathan Darman. Darman was a *Newsweek* reporter who was following the senator for a story and had flown in on the same commercial flight with us. I learned that you are always forewarned when press people are around so everyone who is traveling with the candidate is always aware that they are being watched. Johnny even texted me on the plane from the "other woman" cell phone to tell me exactly where the reporter was sitting. Outside this event, Darman gave me his card and his word that he would not write about me or our conversation, given that I didn't have all the details of the upcoming project hammered out yet. Darman and I would later become close friends, at least from my perspective. I came to think of him as a friend first and a reporter second. This was a mistake—a stupid mistake.

After Iowa, Johnny and I flew to Ohio to meet Josh. We were seated next to each other on a small commercial flight. Five months into our secret relationship and we were traveling together, working together right out in the open. It was surreal.

Josh met us, and the ribbing and teasing me started immediately. Sometimes he was very funny, sometimes just plain mean—adolescent displaced anger. Even so, I realized within minutes of being around Josh that I would need to mic him too, and have a second camera, in order to capture the real relationship between Josh and Johnny. Josh would be a great way to inspire a younger generation's interest in politics.

Johnny and Josh had a lot of father-and-son stuff going on. And like any firstborn son, when a new member was added to the family, Josh turned defensive and unhappy when he was no longer getting all the attention. My existence alone irked him, without even counting all the ways I didn't operate within what Josh thought was appropriate parameters for a political staffer. And Josh was right about that: I didn't operate like a political staffer. I didn't falsely bow to Johnny, or talk bad about him behind his back. I wasn't interested in engaging in the pettiness. I really wasn't one of them, nor did I try or pretend to be. I was in my forties and had been hired as a consultant in order to show a fresh perspective of what goes on behind the scenes. I wasn't a staffer; I was removed from that and was also the boss's (secret) girlfriend. Because of that, Johnny was nicer to me than he was to Josh. He often showed his humanity in his interactions with me. If Johnny was eating or getting something to eat, he would frequently ask me if I was hungry. In the airport, Johnny would often offer to help me with my luggage. This was basic kindness, which didn't exactly extend to Josh, the male twenty-something body guy. I am sure Josh felt rejected—who wouldn't?

But Josh was also sporting an attitude, perhaps driven by his exaggerated sense of self-importance as Johnny's gatekeeper. Even the most important donors mostly had to go through Josh to get to the senator. And yet, somehow, I had managed to get hired without Josh's consent or even input. And try as he might, Josh just couldn't control me. I was the new thorn in Josh's side, and he was doing all he could to remove me.

I often thought that it was going to take a miracle just to get their candidate to the next event, let alone the White House, with these kids at the helm. There were *way* too many unaware, underage, wannabe captains on this ship.

While we were in Ohio, Darman's piece appeared in *Newsweek*, and we read it in the car on the way to some event. As with much of his writing, it was quite snarky. He seemed so much nicer in person. Both Josh and Johnny told me that that was almost always the case: the reporters will act and appear to be favorable to you in person and then nail you to the cross in print, twisting and turning everything to fit the story they and/or their editor want to tell, or at the very least, take a few jabs.

I couldn't believe that could be true of all media. I should have listened to Johnny and Josh on this. Instead, I took it all with a grain of salt, which is to say I ignored it and chose to continue seeing the best in the media people. And look how long it's taken me—it's a lesson I'm still dealing with.

I shot a lot of great footage in Ohio, which I remember as being a very fun place. There was a supporter there named Joyce whom Josh and I really liked. She was a hoot, and she clearly got a big kick out of us. Josh nicknamed her "like white on rice," because she was glued to Johnny's side during our entire Ohio stint. Josh is very quick with a joke, and his sense of humor is one of his strongest attributes.

We went on to Arizona, where it was as hot as a sauna. We stayed one night at some fancy resort. Josh, Johnny, and I had margaritas with dinner. I remember Josh expressing concern about how comfortable I was with Johnny, and that his status didn't intimidate me, which was true and would have been true regardless of our shared intimacy. I don't know how successful I was but I certainly tried to explain to Josh my perspective. I told him I knew who I was, and that someone's worldly status didn't make me react as if they are more than I was, or that I was less than they were; I was at ease around everyone.

On our last stop in Arizona, early in the morning, I beat Josh down to the hotel lobby and was waiting on both of them—a very rare occurrence. Josh was always first, then me, then, of course, Johnny. (Once I came down last—*big mistake!* That didn't happen again.) Anyway, when Josh came down, his hair was disheveled and he was wearing glasses. When I saw him like that, something clicked in my brain and I felt my heart drop. Josh was the staffer I'd been standing next to Iowa the morning I went into the hotel for a parking validation! He looked like a completely different person with his hair messed up and wearing glasses. Anyway, he was tired—he, Johnny, and I had spent the night before drinking those margaritas again. He told me he was worried about receipts. Apparently he'd paid for a lot and if he lost receipts, he would not get reimbursed. I really felt for him in that moment, thinking about how much money was spent on food alone.

From there we flew to Atlanta. There were glass elevators at our hotel that opened on to the atrium. On Johnny's floor, you needed a special key to get off the elevator. I remember having a conversation in the hotel restaurant when Johnny had gone somewhere without Josh. During our chat, Josh told me that he was positive that Johnny was not involved with any women outside of his marriage because Josh said he would know, traveling as closely with him as he did.

I later told Johnny about this, and he smiled and said, "Josh thinks he is a little smarter than he actually is."

The next day we went to the Jimmy Carter Library and Museum to record a podcast with Johnny and President Carter.

The former president surprised me. He had such presence and positively radiated peace. He also had a twinkle in his eye.

One thing I didn't understand about political candidates until I traveled with Johnny: It would be almost impossible to campaign without flying privately. You really waste so much time in airports with delayed flights, missed flights, and rebooked flights, not to mention the fact that commercial flying completely drains you of all your energy.

In mid-July Josh, Johnny, and I flew privately to Seattle for the annual trial lawyers convention, courtesy of Fred Baron. I remember I shot a great monologue during the flight. Johnny was talking about climbing Mount Kilimanjaro with Wade, only to discover that I had major audio problems.

Josh told me not to worry, that I would have many opportunities to get that story on tape again, and again, and again.

While we were in Seattle, Johnny had a suite attached to his room that was used for meetings. That's where I met Fred and his wife, Lisa Blue. Fred and Lisa had made a fortune trying toxic tort and asbestos suits, generally on a contingency basis. They were heavy supporters of the Democratic Party and clearly, their favorite leader-to-be—a certain senator from North Carolina named Johnny Reid Edwards.

Somehow the TV show 24 came up in conversation. Lisa was a huge fan of the show and suggested how great it would be if Johnny did something on 24, as Senator John McCain had done. She became very interested in me when she found out that I knew some of the producers on the show. Lisa was a bit of an eccentric for a successful lawyer; I liked her from the beginning. She told me about her love for learning languages and said that she watched the episodes of 24 in Spanish.

From Seattle we hopped a ride to Santa Monica with Lisa on Fred's plane. I talked with Lisa and Josh a bit about awareness. Lisa said she believed I was a witch, like her. I'm not exactly sure what she meant by this. Awareness is difficult to explain but it has nothing to do with being a witch, which I do not believe I am by any stretch of the imagination. So I was trying to explain to Josh that awareness is the part of him that senses that something is going on in the front of the plane with Johnny, while you are back here on your BlackBerry, sending an email and listening to Lisa and me talk at the same time. Awareness is the space that sees all of it, including yourself.

I don't believe my explanation was very successful.

When we got to Los Angeles, we stayed at the Beverly Hilton, which had just been renovated. For some reason, Josh began including me in the small meetings they were having with supporters. Maybe it was due to Lisa's seal of approval. Although when Josh found out

Lisa had already invited me to her annual Christmas party, a huge event that he had never been invited to, he wasn't pleased.

Both Josh and Johnny repeatedly expressed how much they hated LA. I kept saying how much I loved it, partly because there are some really great people who live here, even some who actually work in the entertainment industry. They didn't believe me. I was determined to prove them wrong. After all, I had lived there for thirteen years. I told them I would introduce them to Jay Stern, a producer whom they would both love. Jay ran director and producer Brett Ratner's company, and I had worked with him for a year trying to get a Jeff Goldblum TV comedy that I had created off the ground. (We weren't successful.) Jay had a very endearing and often hilarious habit of injecting "by the way" into every third or fourth sentence that came out of his mouth. We all met up for drinks at Trader Vic's and Jay brought along his friend, who was some big sports trivia fiend like Johnny. I thought Jay and his friend would help Johnny if they decided they liked him. I was right: both Johnny and Josh loved Jay. We all laughed so hard that tears streamed down our faces.

Sometime in July, as we were in development and I was shooting footage and meeting with potential directors of photography, Johnny was in New York for a few days. I remember watching the footage of Mimi being in the car, on camera, in the backseat with Josh and Johnny going downtown to a brownstone for a small meet-and-greet. Mimi and Josh are both so great on camera—hilarious and not remotely self-conscious. I remember meeting Jonathan Prince (a political strategist in the Clinton administration) at that brownstone. Later, right before Johnny announced his run for the White House, I would rally hard on Prince's behalf to get him his job, a high-level campaign position. Prince has a rare ability in the political world that is run so much by ego: the ability to see many sides to a situation, far beyond just his own agenda.

At the very end of July, Johnny was at the beach in North Carolina. He told me that he really wanted to buy me a present and, even though he never went shopping, he wanted to prove to me how much he loved me. He said the act of going to a store all by himself and picking out a gift for me was proof of his love. (I thought the action of going to a store as "proof" was hilarious.) And he did—he went out by himself to a store and bought me a gift. He was so proud! He told me that he would bring it to me the next time we saw each other. He also told me he bought Emma Claire something similar at the store. Into my mind popped the thought: perhaps Emma's gift helped as a cover in case anyone saw John Edwards buying whatever it was. I didn't share the thought.

Before I saw him again, he went to some party down the street from his beach house, where some new woman decided that she wanted a shot at Johnny. When he told me about this, it was almost like he wanted me to be impressed. Instead, I was extremely irritated and even more so the next day when he told me that this woman called him at his beach house. Of course, the first thing I asked was how she got the number. He claimed he didn't know.

She said, "I am calling to invite you out for a drink."

Johnny politely replied, "Thank you, but today is my anniversary, so I am going to do something with my wife."

"Oh." She paused and then said, "Well, I guess she could come too."

Unbelievable.

And yes, where is Elizabeth? From what I gathered from Johnny, at that point she was devoting most of her time and attention to buying furniture and furnishing their dream house. Occasionally, she would check back into his (or her) career, to scream at people or to talk to them in a demeaning way. I would hear reports on how dysfunctional and incompetent she believed everyone was—including her husband. Apparently she was very vocal about how she was the only one in his life with a brain.

I realize that I'm not an objective source when it comes to Elizabeth, so I'm going to quote from *Game Change*, written by political journalists John Heilemann and Mark Halperin. Even though I believe their book has many inaccuracies, they got this part correct:

> ...the romance between [Elizabeth] and the electorate struck them as ironic nonetheless—because their own relationships with her were so unpleasant, they felt like battered spouses. The nearly universal assessment among them was that there was no one on the national stage for whom the disparity between public image and private reality

was vaster or more disturbing. What the world saw in Elizabeth: a valiant, determined, heroic everywoman. What the Edwards insiders saw: an abusive, intrusive, paranoid, condescending crazy woman.

With her husband, she could be intensely affectionate or brutally dismissive. At times subtly, at times blatantly, she was forever letting John know she regarded him as her intellectual inferior. The daughter of a navy pilot, Elizabeth had lived in Japan when she was a girl and considered herself worldly. She called her spouse a "hick" in front of other people and derided his parents as rednecks. One time, when a friend asked if John had read a particular book, Elizabeth burst out laughing. "Oh, he doesn't read books," she said. "I'm the one who reads books."

From everything I heard, his staff loved him and tolerated her, mostly because of their belief in him and the public's adoration for her. There were reports also from the staff that there were some great people in politics that would not work for him because of her.

Not to oversimplify matters, but it seemed to me that all of their marital problems stemmed from Johnny's fear of Elizabeth's wrath. He would give Elizabeth her way on everything and attempt to stay out of her way. This was mixed with Elizabeth's desire to have *only* her way. She would automatically reject most everything that was not her way.

Johnny would tell me over and over again, "Elizabeth doesn't care about the truth. She will insist that she does, but she doesn't."

I didn't believe him. I thought if he could just overcome enough fear, become brave enough to stand up and tell her the truth, they could get to the bottom of their dynamic, the place where it all went off track. I thought he was just afraid of her, *and* that he didn't want to tell her because he had his cake and was eating it too.

Sadly, and I mean *sadly*, he was right, and I was wrong.

SIX

The Real Deal

"Ever has it been that love knows not its own depth until the hour of separation."

—KAHLIL GIBRAN

THE FIRST WEBISODE that I made, *Plane Truths*, begins with us boarding a private plane and flying to a teacher's event in Iowa. It was August 1st, 2006.

After the teacher's event, we flew to Texas. As usual, we drank wine on the plane at the end of the day. Johnny and I were in the front section; all the rest of the guys were in the back. Johnny and I were having a lovers' spat because he was acting like a lunatic, flipping back and forth between a couple of personalities without any awareness that he was doing so. This was his typical behavior after he had spent any time around Elizabeth. It was maddening to be around, to say the least. Anyway, I was sure our spat was not overlooked by anyone in the back, especially Josh Brumberger.

Later that night he gave me a pearl bracelet, the gift he had gone out and bought all by himself, just like a real person. I loved it and, naturally, I forgave him immediately.

The next day we went to a luncheon in Texas where Sam Cullman, my director of photography, covered the senator, and I covered Josh.

49

Johnny forgot he was wearing a mic and as he was getting out of the car, he said something very flirty to me, which I didn't hear, but Sam definitely did given that Johnny was plugged into Sam's camera. Sam looked over at me, laughing out loud.

I loved the stuff I shot with Josh and Fred at this event. We used it in a webisode called *Where's the Party* that was later nixed by the PAC leadership. I believe it was because it contained many opinions about Senator Joe Lieberman's switch to Independent after he lost the Democratic primary election in Connecticut, given that Lieberman eventually won the general election and remained a senator. (Heaven forbid, you speak your truth if it risks pissing off anyone in power.) What I loved most about the webisode was Fred. He was complaining to Josh about Johnny not wearing a tie (as usual). I loved the humanity of it all.

After this event, I remember Johnny in the car talking about his parents naming him Johnny, not John—footage that also never made it into the webisodes. It seems crazy to me that he ran for president *twice* and most people never knew his legal name is Johnny! I caught a lot of "what a bimbo" flak in the media for calling him Johnny instead of John and yet, shockingly enough, I'm the one who actually had his name correct.

On to Oklahoma, where the big news of the evening was Josh had a little "heart to heart" talk with his boss. He informed Johnny that the staff was talking about his relationship with me and was very concerned about it. Johnny related this exchange to me minutes after Josh told him. Johnny also insisted that he wasn't the least bit interested in what his twenty-seven-year-old body guy thought. He used to say to me, "I have one word to describe Josh Brumberger— history." It seemed to me that sooner or later this situation with Josh would come to a head and it probably wasn't going to be pretty.

After Oklahoma, I remember being in Minnesota, along on Johnny's never-ending quest to try to get every Democrat elected, and then driving to Iowa. It was a long drive that began the moment Johnny got off the stage after a large speaking event. After Johnny spoke he would have a post-performance high, which sometimes triggered his belief that the crowd was in love with him and oh, what a great man I am! Of course, some of the staff didn't have any understanding that this was just a "performance high" reaction and reacted bitterly, resenting his egotistical behavior and the fact that he ignored them. Naturally, all of this went unspoken, but on that occasion it did make for a very uncomfortable, very long car ride.

Somewhere during that ride, Kim Rubey, the very intelligent, extremely dry-witted PAC communications director, noticed my pearl bracelet and said, "I like your bracelet." I believed that she knew the second she saw it that it was from Johnny. She had just been at the Ponderosa (which is what Johnny and I call his house in Chapel Hill) for something, probably for one of the many *People* photo shoots, and I assumed she had seen whatever Johnny had bought for Emma, which he had said was similar to my bracelet. Anyway, it was clear to me—she knew.

Later that night, we were all eating at Centro in Des Moines and Newt Gingrich was in the restaurant, so the subject of infidelity came up. Mudcat Saunders, who was with us, went off on it. He had zero tolerance for infidelity, whereas Kim defended it. Of course Johnny and I didn't say a word but we were both surprised by Kim's response. She spoke as someone with a great deal of understanding of the complexities of marriage. We both wondered, because we knew nothing of her personal life, if she had some sort of personal experience with infidelity.

On our next outing (go Democrats go), Johnny, Josh, Sam, and I flew privately to Montana. We stopped in Salina, Kansas, for fuel, and oh no, our plane broke. Thank God it broke while we were parked on the ground! After we spent many hours waiting inside the FBO, the repair crew finally realized that it couldn't get the part before the next morning. So Josh charmed the FBO personnel and got us a courtesy car. When Josh pulled around the building to pick us up, everyone started laughing. It looked exactly like a car from a junkyard. It was amazing to us that the car actually worked.

We piled into our no-A/C, far-from-luxurious car and sputtered down the road to the Courtyard by Marriott, laughing most of the way. Josh then spent the next few hours trying to locate a way out of there, hoping to make it to the scheduled event in Montana. Josh spent much of his time being a travel agent, trying to locate planes from donors and/or commercial flights. In the second webisode, as he is filling out his job description for his visa application to China, he didn't know what to write, and suggested his title should be Political Mastermind, or just Bitch.

It was during this little layover in Salina that Johnny told me that he informed Josh that he took care of his "issue" with me. I assume what Josh thought happened was that Johnny ended his relationship with me and valued Josh's opinion. But what actually happened was that Johnny ignored everything Josh had to say because he felt it was none of Josh's business.

I also remember watching the Lieberman nomination drama un-folding on TV with Josh and Sam. I stopped by Johnny's room only to get into a fight with him over his "other woman" cell phone, which had a text on it from another woman. I didn't read the text, but I threw his phone across the room and stomped out. (Yeah, that will show him!)

Around August 17th I had to strongly pitch—actually, almost argue with—Nick Baldick about going to Connecticut to follow Johnny when he met with Ned Lamont. Nick didn't want me to go, but I already had a lot of great footage about this Lieberman/Lamont issue. I ended up going, but the webisode *Where's the Party?* (the one with Fred that I loved) never saw the light of day.

While still in Connecticut, I got really pissed off *again* about Johnny's cell phone. I read a text from the same old girlfriend (the one he spoke to on the phone next to me months ago) who clearly wanted to take their relationship back to more than friends. I was fed up with that phone. Without it, the other women would have no way to reach him. I was determined to replace it. This, of course, hap-pened *after* dinner (and lots of wine). We had all gone out to dinner, and I remember the dinner fondly because Matt Giobbi was there, whom I called Advance Matt. He was in the second webisode. Matt was great at his job and took it so seriously. There was something so earnest, honest, and humorous about his mannerisms that just seeing him made me laugh. Johnny was also very fond of Matt. (I think this was in part because the mere sight of Matt cracked me up and Johnny loved it when I laughed.) I think Matt liked having me around because ever since I had joined the team, the senator loved eating with the staff, and the staff all loved eating out with him.

At the end of August, Johnny invited me to fly to North Carolina to shoot footage of his parents, Bobbie and Wallace, at the Ponderosa—his brand-new, ever-so-humble twenty-eight-thou-sand-square-foot house. I wanted to capture footage of his father, Wallace, because there was so much continual hype about Johnny being the son of a mill worker. I thought this could potentially be a comedy gold mine. I stayed at a Marriott; Johnny later came to visit for a few hours. He told me to take a cab to a clinic the next morning; he was going in order to get some of his vaccinations for Africa and suggested I should get my shots too. The next morn-ing Johnny was late, which was not a shocking development. I be-lieve Andrew had gotten lost—also not a shocking development. I had my camera on and was already getting my shots when Johnny walked in. As usual he lit up when he saw me, something I cap-tured on camera. I turned it off, finished getting my shots, and then went outside. Johnny's parents pulled up in their car. They had an appointment in the area and arranged to meet us there afterward. This was where I first met Johnny's parents—in the parking lot of a health clinic. I remember Johnny telling Andrew to go ahead and pay for my shots as well, which I would later hear (as usual) be-came an issue with the PAC.

After arriving at Johnny's house, it turned out that Wallace and Bobbie were less than interested in talking on camera, even though Wallace allowed me to mic him as Johnny gave us a grand tour of his new home.

Of course, the press turned Johnny's large house, and over-all lifestyle, into a campaign issue. It frustrated me that the cam-paign couldn't turn this into "the guy from nothing is now living the American dream, able to afford four-hundred-dollar haircuts and million-dollar houses," as opposed to "the hypocrite who says he is for poor people is living the high life." I think the real reason they couldn't turn it around is Johnny wasn't actually proud of it—he was embarrassed by it. Otherwise he would have be able to get out in front of that story, speaking from the heart and with pride, saying, "Yeah, I built that house, all cash. I can afford it and my family de-serves it and now I want to help all of you be successful as well." In reality, he was judging himself for spending money like that. I know him very well and that house isn't close to who he is, and yet he allowed it to happen. He didn't stop Elizabeth from doing it.

When Jack and Emma came home from school, I interviewed them both on camera in exchange for giving them five dollars cash and promising them I would never show anyone. I kept my word on that, although this was one of the tapes that "magically" disappeared out of my hatbox (more on this later).

I remember Andrew being there the night after Bobbie and Wallace had gone home. Johnny, Andrew, the nanny's husband, Jed, and I sat on the porch drinking wine. It was raining. After dinner with the kids and the nanny, Jed, Andrew, and one of the nanny's girlfriends, Andrew drove me back to my hotel. Johnny didn't visit that night. He fell asleep with Jack, in Jack's room.

The next morning I accompanied Andrew, Johnny, and some poverty woman who was really snotty to me to the University of North Carolina, where I shot some footage of Johnny speaking that ended up with lighting issues. Then I went with Andrew and Johnny to some office where I sat outside the office talking on the phone with my editor.

The three of us then drove back to the Ponderosa. I flew out later that day, before Elizabeth returned to the house. Andrew drove me to the airport and before I left, I remember Johnny ribbing Andrew several times about his never wanting to go home. He clearly wasn't doing any necessary work but he was still hanging around. In response, Andrew got very vocal about how he was not interested in going home. Apparently his wife was very bitchy. The more she bitched, the more he wanted to stay away and the more he stayed away, the more she bitched. It seemed that Johnny and he had a lot in common on the marital front.

Back at home, Sam and I were gearing up for a trip to New Hampshire over Labor Day weekend. When I booked Sam for this trip, he informed me that he needed to get back to New York in order to shoot his documentary that he was codirecting. (The documentary, *If a Tree Falls*, was later nominated for an Academy Award.) But the staff was supposed to stay a day later and take a commercial flight home, while Johnny was to fly privately back that night. I told Johnny that Sam needed to get to New York and I obviously would prefer to stay with Johnny, not the staff, and I asked him to please take care of it. I don't actually remember whether he ever addressed it with the PAC leaders or if I just ended up putting my foot down that Sam and I were flying back with him because Sam could not miss his workday. However the details of this silly drama played out, Sam and I ended up flying back with Johnny and Josh did not. And despite Josh's little tizzy about this all that day, we really did miss Josh on the plane ride back to DC. Josh was a major pain-in-the-ass drama queen and whiner but he was also a really good guy with a great sense of humor.

Andrew picked us up at an FBO near Dulles. He had driven from North Carolina to escort Johnny to Bunny Mellon's the next morning. I believe this was the first time Johnny ever met Bunny, but in any case, this meeting was the first I heard of the two of them meeting. One weird thing I remember about that night: Andrew called me on my cell phone very late to ask me if I wanted to join him for a drink in the bar. I answered my cell (not from my own room) but believe me, the last thing in the world I wanted to do, especially after the workday I had just had, was to join Andrew Young in the bar. I declined and as I hung up, I wondered why he had called. I told Johnny that was Andrew on my cell and asked, "Why would Andrew ask me to join him for a drink so late at night?" Johnny gave me a look that told me he had less-than-zero interest in talking about Andrew Young. I briefly thought about how flirty Andrew was to me when he first met me back in June and that Johnny had warned him in funny way when we got off the plane: hands off. Was he hitting on me now? It felt like he was, but it was late, I was exhausted, and I had already given it too much thought. I shrugged it off.

Johnny spoke at some big union event in California in September, and I remember saying to him right before he went on, "I bet you drinks tonight that you can't get through this speech without bashing Bush." He said, "You're on." Of course, I won the bet. Somewhere in nearly every speech, he habitually slipped into automatic pilot, and he would go for the easy applause, how bad President Bush is and how great we Democrats are, and the crowd would go wild. So predictable. So boring.

From there we went to California and then on to Las Vegas. It was my first trip to Vegas. Ever. Every time I vetoed Vegas as a destination, my friend Angela Janklow would say, "Vegas is the exact opposite of everything you are about." She was right, but it was fun anyway. We stayed at the Paris Las Vegas. It was like an indoor Disneyland. After Johnny spoke that morning, we all stopped by some walk-in restaurant at the Paris, one of the many in the hotel lobby; Johnny was looking at salads. He turned and asked me if I was hungry. Not Josh, not Kim, just me. Josh had a *huge* reaction to this. Anger, sulking, back-handed comments. Poor Josh.

From time to time, when I felt especially bad for him, and because I already knew that his days were numbered, I would offer Josh my unsolicited opinion, telling him that he was very talented, and perhaps better suited for a different job. Because my loyalty was to Johnny, I could never do more than hint at that. I felt sorry for him. From everything I could see, Johnny wasn't ever going to be any nicer to him. That's just life. I was the girlfriend; Josh was just the staffer.

From Vegas, Johnny was going to fly to Chicago to do *Oprah* with Elizabeth, for her book *Saving Graces*. It was the first time they had done *Oprah*, and it was a very big deal. Once that I heard that Johnny was doing the show too, I was very upset about it every time it was mentioned. I really didn't want the both of them to go on *Oprah* and lie to millions of people. I thought that he and Elizabeth should wait until they get to a place of honesty in their relationship, and then decide whether to go on *Oprah* and tell the millions of viewers about the journey. You don't do the public stuff and lie. Don't do it until you can be honest. Of course I shared my thoughts but come on, for a guy and his spouse who may actually run for the highest office in the land, do you know how many people watch *Oprah*?

It still astounds me how naïve I was. Of course he went to Chicago and taped *Oprah*. I watched it and found the whole thing to be extremely sad—and extremely irritating.

Toward the end of September, Johnny called me sounding very odd and detached, informing me that he wanted to talk to me later in person. He sounded strange, so I began mimicking his tone and what he was saying, so he could actually hear it. I believe he had gone to church on Sunday and had gotten some good old-fashioned Southern religion. Whatever the case, I got the feeling from his tone that he intended to end our relationship when we talked later in person.

Johnny was set to come to New York to be on a panel at New York University for *The New York Times*, which Sam was going to shoot. I met everyone downtown in front of the building.

Johnny was very odd that night and not at his best, which was not lost on any of us. Afterward Josh, Johnny, and Kim immediately got in the car and left while I was still upstairs. I thought that was so weird of Johnny to leave without asking me if I needed a lift uptown. Was this the end? How would I ever continue working with him if this were the end?

So I got in a cab alone and headed uptown. I figured I'd just go to Serafina and wait for his call. I sat down at the bar and ordered a glass of wine, and who should pop in to get dinner for the senator? Josh. He was a bit freaked out that I was there. It really wasn't that weird, given how often I ate at Serafina, which was in Glory Crampton's neighborhood, but Josh didn't know that and acted as though he had caught me doing something I shouldn't be doing. Granted, I didn't know that this was the restaurant Johnny would order from, but it was a place that I often went, so I didn't act as though it was odd because it wasn't.

Josh and I chatted about how ineffectual Johnny had been on the panel. Josh said, "Yeah, no more panels for us." He left and Johnny called. I went up to his room and we ate dinner together. He told me he wanted to end his relationship with me because he wanted to work on his marriage. Work on his marriage? Was that a joke? Like he and Elizabeth were finally going to enter therapy all of a sudden, all on his incentive? Despite my doubts, he insisted he really wanted to work on his marriage, so the only thing I could say was okay.

I spent the night as though it was our last, and when I left in the morning, I remember looking at him from the door as I said good-bye, thinking that I'd never see him again.

I went back to New Jersey and got into bed, where I stayed most of the day. My heart was broken. I had no idea how I would ever fulfill my contract nor did I want to think about it. I was experiencing way too much pain.

Around 5 P.M. he called and asked, "How are you?"

"Broken-hearted."

"Yeah, I feel it. I felt it all day. Do you want to come see me?"

"Yes."

"Come on."

And that was it. I went back to the Regency.

I think we both realized then that there was no way out of this. We were madly in love.

Two days before we left for Africa, I bought a new phone for myself—a pink Motorola RAZR with a Johnny Cash ringtone—and a black RAZR for Johnny that looked exactly like his work phone.

I took a train to DC to spend the night with him and gave him his new phone. He finally got rid of the ex-mistress's phone, which solved all our ex-mistress problems. Why it took me so long to do that, I have no idea. Maybe because every minute I wasn't traveling, I was logging footage or editing. Or maybe I thought there was a chance our relationship wouldn't survive long enough for it to matter. Johnny told me that he really wanted to move forward, without the ex-mistresses, without all the extra baggage. And now, without anyone having a way to reach him (minus one or two incoming calls to his home phone), we finally could.

SEVEN

The Leaves Are Changing

"Never forget that the most powerful force on earth is love."

—NELSON ROCKEFELLER

THE END OF SEPTEMBER 2006 I drove with Sam Cullman, my director of photography, out to John F. Kennedy International Airport in New York. During the drive I got a call on my phone from Johnny's work phone, but he hung up before I could answer it. Weird. When I arrived in the lounge to connect with our little traveling "Save Uganda" group, I learned what happened. Johnny couldn't figure out where all his numbers had gone on his cell phone so he had handed the phone to Josh Brumberger. But it was the wrong phone—the cell I had just bought for him. Fortunately he realized what he had done before any damage was done.

After everyone arrived, four folks from the International Rescue Committee (IRC) and five people from Team Edwards—Johnny, Josh, Derek Chollet (Johnny's foreign policy guy), Sam, and I—all headed to our gate.

Once on board, we were told that there was a problem with the plane and they were going to contact maintenance to fix it instead of deplaning us. That's when the drinking began.

59

Josh and Sam were very excited to learn that rapper Flavor Flav was on our flight. (He wasn't hard to miss given that he was wearing his trademark clock around his neck.) They wanted to get pictures but seemed a bit starstruck. I had no reaction to Flav so I went up to him and told him that Senator John Edwards was on the flight. "You know, the guy who ran for vice president?" Suddenly Flavor Flav got excited, and soon cameras were flashing everywhere.

After what felt like several hours sitting on the ground, our pilot finally informed us that we all needed to get off the plane, go through customs again, and get on another plane. We realized we were probably going to miss our connection in Brussels to get to Africa, but because the senator's schedule was booked for months, it was decided that we would just fly to Brussels anyway and figure it out from there.

When we finally landed in Belgium, we were met at the gate by some super nice airline folks who were very eager to help. (Traveling with Senator John Edwards was usually a big plus because airline people treated us like real human beings.) We had definitely missed our connection. The next plane to Uganda was a couple of days later, so our best bet was to claim our bags and recheck them with another airline. We headed to London to pick up a connecting flight to another spot in Africa, where we could catch a bush plane to Uganda. While waiting in the bag check line, Johnny managed to express to me how much it meant to him that I was there, how happy he was being with me, and how I made him feel so happy—no small feat to say all that without all our traveling companions hearing a thing.

We flew to London where we had to go through the most intense security I had ever been through. Senator or not, they did not care— he, too, may be packing bombs—and searched through every single bag. Once we made it through security, we hung out in a VIP room where the IRC men briefed us on the crisis going on in Uganda and the details of the Lord's Resistance Army, the army of children who had been kidnapped and forced to fight.

At one point I left the VIP room to use the bathroom and ran into Johnny in the hallway, just as he was coming out of the men's room. He proceeded to plant a huge kiss on me. We were deliriously tired, out of our element, and full of fire, which I obviously liked. But my response was, "Stop! Are you crazy? Someone will see us!"

We finally got on an African airline and were seated in first class. Team Edwards was outrageously comfy. We were all in the front row—Johnny was at the window, I was next to him on the aisle, and then the guys. As usual, Josh was unable to hide the fact that he was less than thrilled that I was next to Johnny. Everyone except me took a sleeping pill. Big mistake. Johnny and I stayed up way beyond everyone else, and he was out-of-his-mind sleep-deprived funny and adorable.

(It is a trait our daughter has inherited. I call it her "running-for-president" phase. Normally she is very shy but when she gets tired, she gets more energized, becomes hilarious, very open, and will talk to everyone. I recently said to Johnny, "She needs to go to sleep, she is running for president." Without missing a beat, he replied, "I hope she does a better job than I did.")

We finally made it to Africa and again had to wait (probably only a few hours, but I had lost all sense of time) to board a smaller plane to get to Uganda. In that airport, we ran into Anderson Cooper, who was on his way to the Democratic Republic of the Congo. Anderson only had eyes for Johnny. He was clearly starstruck, which really tickled Sam and me.

On our last leg to Uganda, the pilot came on the sound system and told us that he didn't think we could land due to bad weather. I can't remember what the problem was but I do recall that our group was about to turn very religious, having decided that God did not want us to get to Uganda. It was beyond comical, given we were in hour *forty-six* of travel time. Fortunately the weather quickly cleared and we finally landed in Uganda.

We were greeted by a nasty woman who was barking orders at everyone (except Johnny, of course). We had missed staying the night in our first hotel because we were still flying but we stopped at that hotel to take a shower before we boarded a puddle-jumper bound for our camp. The woman barking orders informed Sam and me that we were on a different puddle-jumper than the senator. Yeah, that makes sense: spend thousands of dollars on getting cameras to follow you in Africa and then put the cameras on a different plane. I couldn't believe it. After some rearrangements, at least one camera always ended up with Johnny.

After our little day trip, we drove to the hotel in Kampala, which would be our home base for the remaining two nights in Africa. What struck me the most about our time in Africa was how spoiled we are in America and how much we take for granted every day, like fresh water whenever we want. What also stood out were the kids in the camps and the eye contact they would make with us. I fell in love with the curiosity and the openness of the children. They didn't have any computers or TVs, no Game Boys, no iPhone, iPads, or iPods— just total openness to other humans. They were very different from most American children.

In our hotel, Johnny's room was directly opposite mine, and shockingly enough, I overheard Josh complaining about it. Josh was down the hall near Sam. For some reason, Josh was being really mean to Sam and all buddy-buddy with Derek. Sam was not happy about this and ended up being late for one of our excursions, which was way out of character for him. Josh was very snippy with me, but that was nothing new. Derek was also having his own meltdown. He felt that the IRC people were actually doing something that mattered— making a big difference in the world—while he was in Washington "thinking about things."

Oh, it was just a sleep-deprived, life-altering experience for all involved.

After I was already in his room one night, Johnny thought it would be a good idea for me to go get my camera so we could create our own little "private" video. I did and oh have I paid dearly for that adventurous, sleep-deprived run across the hall. We made a short tape and then I put the camera down. Regardless of how sleep deprived I was during this less-than-brilliant escapade, and despite what was reported to the media by some people, one thing I know for sure: I was not pregnant when this happened nor did I look like it from any angle.

During our last excursion to a camp, a woman who couldn't have been more than twenty years old followed me through the camp with her baby. I gathered, as she kept trying to hand me her baby girl, that she wanted me to take her baby out of the camp and give her a better life. This really upset me. She followed me the entire time we walked through the camp. I guided them to Johnny, who held the baby right before he was getting in the car to leave. I don't know what I thought was going to happen, but nothing extraordinary transpired for this little child. The entire event really broke my heart.

The African music that these kids played in the camp also moved me. There was a young guy I nicknamed "Uganda's Bob Marley." He was very talented yet stuck in the camp; I wanted to help him somehow.

After our weekend visit was over, we were once again on the way to the airport. It was after dinner and dark outside. I was in the backseat with Josh; Johnny sat in the front. I asked Johnny a question about something and he answered by calling me "Baby." In my sleep-deprived state I didn't think I heard him correctly, so I kept asking myself over and over, *"Did he just call me 'Baby?'"* When we got out of the car (and away from Josh), I asked Johnny, "Did you call me 'Baby?'" And he said, "Yes, I sure did."

Fabulous.

There was plenty of room in the plane's cabin, so I moved from my assigned seat that was multiple rows behind Johnny to one directly across the aisle from him. Johnny was pleased about that. You could feel Josh's displeasure emanating from his aisle. Johnny clearly didn't care what Josh thought. We arrived in Brussels without a hitch and with more than a few hours to wait for our connection back to JFK. Because it was the next morning, and we still had a very long flight ahead of us, Johnny showed me a place where I could take a shower, which I did, after he did.

I overheard Josh and Sam making fun of Johnny about this, behind his back of course, and I made the mistake of chiming in and said, "What's so weird about taking a shower? I did." Boy, did that shut them up fast.

This Africa trip pretty much sealed Josh's fate. Forget that Johnny and I were in love, which was probably lost on Josh, but between the staffer (the one the boss is *not* having sex with) and the filmmaker (the one the boss *is* having sex with), did Josh really think that he would be the chosen one?

Josh took matters into his own hands and alerted the powers that be at the PAC about the "Rielle" problem. The kid took matters into his own hands because he thought he knew better. It's so amazing to me that this happens in politics over and over again. These young people who worked for Johnny, who presumably believe he has the judgment to become president of the United States, simultaneously believed they knew better about what he should say, how he should dress, how he should behave, and what stand he should take on a given issue. They advised him on everything; they didn't serve his intentions—they wanted him to serve theirs.

I believe that Johnny wanted to send a message to his PAC. He did not want to be their puppet any longer. He was in charge, which he claimed at the time stemmed from his days as Kerry's running mate, but as you can probably guess by now, I think goes back even further. So Johnny took Josh aside in the airport before they were about to board a plane to China and fired him. Johnny told me that Josh had cried.

I later read in *Game Change* that Johnny and Josh had a screaming match and (according to Josh), Johnny said, "Why didn't you just come to me like a fucking man and tell me to stop fucking her?" This is hilarious to me. I wasn't in the room so I don't know for certain what was said, but I seriously doubt this happened. The truth is that in 2006, for better or for worse, the John Edwards that I knew would have never confessed or confirmed our relationship to anyone, especially a twenty-something kid he was in the process of firing.

So Josh was axed, and it was clear within the PAC that most people knew why and a message was sent and received. I'm not entirely sure, however, that the message that Johnny intended was the one that was, in fact, received.

It was clear but, of course, never stated directly to me that the PAC now wanted to keep me away from Johnny. I remember being in Chapel Hill, North Carolina, for two days visiting Johnny during his downtime, per his invitation. I was staying at the Marriott (he could visit) and checking my email from the lobby. There was an email from Nick Baldick stating something to the effect that everyone agreed that I was to stay home and edit and not go on the next Edwards trip, which I think was in Iowa.

In October, I also flew down to Asheville, North Carolina, by myself. I actually went there not just to see Johnny but to get an interview with him to tie the Uganda webisode together.

Elizabeth was speaking at a luncheon sponsored by *Ladies' Home Journal*. And, ironically enough, in response to a question asked by Lisa DePaulo (who would interview me years later), Elizabeth claimed that her choices in life had made her happier than Hillary Clinton, that she was more joyful.

Elizabeth called Johnny in a tirade about it. She somehow blamed what she said on Kim Rubey and on *Ladies' Home Journal*, insisting that the magazine had misquoted her and it was Kim's fault that it had done so. The phone call to Johnny was about whether or not he thought she should she apologize to Hillary.

Nobody I know who heard about this incident believed it was Kim's or *Ladies' Home Journal's* misstep. The consensus was that the incident was more likely to be the real Elizabeth shining through. Johnny's sister Kathy later told me that for years Elizabeth would often call her to gloat about her wonderful life. The manner in which she did this often left Kathy in tears.

No matter what the intentions behind the comment were, I actually felt badly for Elizabeth. The ego frequently has a way of turning the joke right back on us. And the big problem with denial is that your false joy, your "ignorance is bliss," will not last. The day will come when it will end. It's inevitable. And the more you fight it, the more pain you create for yourself.

And unfortunately for Elizabeth, that day came sooner than she wanted.

EIGHT

The End of the Year

"If you make a choice that goes against what everyone else thinks, the world doesn't fall apart."

—OPRAH WINFREY

N THE MIDDLE OF NOVEMBER I went down to DC to stay with Johnny for two nights. He was doing an event at Borders, which I did not go to but remember noticing afterward that he had worn the first shirt I'd purchased for him to the event; it made me happy. He had gotten (via John Davis) take-out food for us from the Daily Grill for our dinner, which also made me happy. (John Davis was now in Josh Brumberger's job, which made me *super* happy. No more dealing with Josh's snide comments and passive-aggressive actions.)

That night, as we were eating dinner, a campaign disaster call came in. One of Johnny's aides had left a message on a Walmart store's answering machine requesting super-special attention for a PlayStation 3 for Senator Edwards. This was pretty funny (in a horrible way) because Johnny was waging a campaign against Walmart, mostly about how the company was unfair to its workers (my second webisode was about this issue). Johnny spoke to Rob Christensen, a reporter from the *News & Observer*, while we were having dinner.

Johnny told the reporter that the kid had made a mistake; he didn't know Johnny's views on Walmart. It was an honest mistake and in the news for a day.

Elizabeth was not about to let this one go, however. She believed that Andrew Young was behind it all, that he had told the campaign volunteer exactly what to say to Walmart and then convinced the kid to claim he had made the call all on his own. It was added fuel for her fire of hatred for Andrew.

Johnny told me that, before he and I met, Elizabeth repeatedly said that she believed Andrew was a thief and liar. She believed he spent a lot of their money on things they never saw. Money and other things went missing when Andrew was around, and now, no matter how innocent Andrew claimed to be about the Walmart fiasco, Elizabeth no longer believed him.

After the Walmart mess she began to harass Andrew with emails and occasional voicemails at all hours of the night. She wanted him gone. Coming from Elizabeth, though, this was a little like crying wolf. It wasn't unusual behavior for her, so Johnny just chalked it up to more of Elizabeth's craziness. Johnny would tell her to stop the harassment, even mentioning that eventually word would leak about the way she spoke to people and damage her saintly image. Elizabeth would then turn her wrath on Johnny. He was now defending a thief and a liar and taking Andrew's side over hers.

Whatever Johnny said to her didn't do any good. The harassment would just continue. According to Johnny, there was no talking to Elizabeth about something when she had made up her mind, and now she was out for Andrew.

From Johnny's perspective, Andrew loved him and would move mountains for him, and Johnny is a very loyal person. He wasn't going to fire Andrew just because Elizabeth had decided he was a liar and thief. Apparently this vitriol toward a staff person was a behavior pattern she had with anyone who got close to Johnny. So he ignored her.

What's so sad about this was that Elizabeth's instincts about Andrew were actually not far-fetched. If she had handled it properly, a lot of misery could have been avoided.

Johnny came to New York City in November to do *The Daily Show* and an event in support of his book *Home*. Sam Cullman and I rode in the car with him to *The Daily Show.* I used that footage to make the final webisode. We then went to a bookstore on the Upper West Side for a signing. Johnny was exhausted afterward; book signings drained him like no campaign event ever did.

Later, after our Serafina take-out dinner, watching the footage Sam and I shot in Uganda air on *Hannity and Colmes,* Johnny signed a bunch of books for me: one for Mimi, her sons Jack and Cole, my younger sister, Melissa, and one for me. By the time we got to my copy, were in a too-tired, too-much-wine lovers' spat. Inside he wrote, "My love—will you marry me?—I love you—your baby."

He wrote that so I wouldn't be mad at him any longer. I did not believe it was an actual marriage proposal, nor do I now. He was attempting to make me happy in the moment.

However, because I was madly in love with Johnny, that book became an important memento to me. Sometime over the next few weeks, I shipped that to a dear friend for safekeeping. Years later he shipped it back to me, which, in hindsight, was stupid. I should have had him keep it for the next fifty years because, sure enough, Johnny's book with that inscription later vanished from my home.

In December, I had a meeting in DC with Johnny and David Ginsburg. This was the first time I had met David, who was the head of public relations for Johnny's campaign. I was getting a ton of push back about putting the webisodes on the Internet. So we watched the webisodes with David, and then I left. I remember asking John Davis on the way out what train they were taking to New York. Johnny had told me to wait for him (something I did not to reveal to John Davis) and get on his train. John Davis gave me some wrong information about their travel plans that didn't involve a train, so I just hopped on the next train. Later, John Davis called me asking what train I was on. They were an hour behind me on the next Acela and he apologized for giving me wrong info. No worries—I was able to get home and shower before meeting Johnny later at the Regency.

Around this time I also had lunch at Serafina on Sixty-First Street with Lisa Blue, who had taken a real fancy to me, sending me her favorite book to read, offering to fly me to their Christmas party, etc. Fred dropped by for a few minutes and said hello. It was clear to me that Lisa had no idea about the extent of my relationship with

Johnny but she did like how Johnny behaved around me. She said more than once that she believed I brought out the best in him. I remember Lisa also saying at this lunch how much she thought I could help Elizabeth who, in her eyes, really, really needed a lot of help. We also talked about Johnny running for president. I was unsure that he would ever announce and said so. Lisa was positive he was going to announce because his ego would not let him sit this one out. I got the sense that his running for president was something she wanted and needed Johnny to do. She would have a strong negative reaction every time I suggested that he might not actually do it.

Another big question going around then was whether the webisodes would ever see the light of day. Andrew had seen a copy of the webisodes and was over the moon about them. He called to tell me how great a job he thought we had done. He later started calling me to get me to one of Johnny's supporters the footage because he wanted to edit a version of his own.

"Andrew, I can't do that. I have a contract. I can't just randomly give you or some guy I don't know footage that the PAC has not approved for this guy to edit his own versions."

I then heard about a meeting at which Elizabeth barked about how everyone was so dysfunctional and afraid of everything. She thought they should put the webisodes on the Internet *now*, even though she had never even seen them.

So thanks to Elizabeth, the webisodes finally got a green light, then I called Jonathan Darman from *Newsweek* (as per prior discussions with Kim Rubey) to publicize them. I had lunch with Darman at a restaurant that he picked.

Wow, did I get my ass handed to me for doing this. Apparently David, the guy I had just met, had a rule that I was not to talk to anyone in the media without his approval. Everything was to go through him. I apologized for my mistake but given I had only met him a few days ago, I didn't really feel that bad.

I also flew to Texas in December and joined Johnny on part of his book tour. What a difference John Davis made as a travel arranger/companion—such a joy. The night after the book event, we all went out to eat with Fred and Lisa. Once again, she commented a few times how great Johnny was with me, how relaxed he was with me, and how well I understood him, which brought out the best in him. Lisa also called her nanny to bring their newborn daughter to dinner so we could meet her. I held her—she was so sweet. Johnny watched all this with rapt fascination, almost as if he couldn't even imagine me with a kid. I love kids but I really had no idea how deep my love for children actually was, because I had never heard my own biological clock ticking.

We also talked about Africa during dinner. I mentioned that I had received an email from the IRC guys about one of the kids from Africa, the one I called, "Uganda's Bob Marley," and was looking for fifteen hundred dollars to make a record. Fred immediately said, "I'll give it to him. Just tell me who to write the check to and where to send it." Done.

That's the kind of man Fred was. He was a fixer and a helper. He had so much money and such a big heart that when he heard about someone having some kind of trouble that he could fix with his checkbook, he didn't think twice. Some kid he didn't know halfway around the world needed help to make a record? He was happy to help, no questions asked.

Andrew called me a couple of times while I was in Texas. Josh was now gone and he didn't trust John Davis so I take it I was the only one to call about his big problem—Elizabeth. She was harassing him nonstop and he wanted me to talk to Johnny about this. I did, and Johnny told Elizabeth to stop, but she clearly ignored him. Much to Andrew's anguish, she steadily continued her harassment campaign to get Andrew out of their lives.

I remember we flew Southwest a lot for the California leg of the book tour. On one of the flights Johnny had headphones on and was jamming out as John Davis and I chatted and laughed a lot. What I admired about John, which was refreshing for someone so young in politics, was that instead of making me feel wrong or bad because I was different from him, he actually liked people who were unique.

We had a glass of wine before the event in Pasadena, which had a good influence on Johnny's performance. He was great. He was a much better speaker after one glass of wine. Another one of my dear friends came to this event with her stepdaughter to meet Johnny and was blown away by his charisma.

Later, after the affair story broke, she said to me, "Honey, you didn't stand a chance. Whatever woman that man wanted, he would get."

We took the signed poster from the event, the book cover of *Home*, and went to dinner at one of my favorite restaurants in Pasadena for spaghetti and meatballs. Then we stayed at the Beverly Hilton, again. Believe me, by 2008 I knew the lay of the land at the Beverly Hilton.

Johnny said something very sweet to me that night, something any woman would appreciate. Most of the time, men don't really understand or acknowledge how much women give emotionally in a relationship. It's different for men than it is for women, and the way our culture sets it up, men can take a lot for granted.

Johnny said, "I've been thinking about you and Kip a lot tonight, given you lived so close to this area when you were married. And I feel bad for Kip. He really lost when he lost you."

Okay, that melted me.

I was married to Alexander "Kip" Munro Hunter III for nine years; we were together for twelve. Kip is a lawyer, shockingly enough, just like my father and the father of my child. He is also the funniest, most quick-witted man I have ever met in my life. We parted as friends and remain friends to this day.

Somewhere around this time, when I was back in New Jersey, Johnny and I decided that we needed to get rid of the intimate tape we'd made in Africa. I think Johnny was seriously considering running for president at that point, and wanted to get rid of any physical evidence of us that could be used against him. He warned me how dirty and awful people in politics are. I thought he was exaggerating a bit, that maybe he thought he was a little more important than he actually was. I mean, really, who would come after me or my stuff? I just couldn't even fathom any of that.

Even though I thought he was being a bit melodramatic, I destroyed the tape, I pulled it out of its casing and cut it. Somewhere in the back of my head, I must have remembered the possibility of someone going through my garbage, so I buried it in the bottom of my hatbox, where I stored my other small, personal mementos.

After I discovered that the tape had been stolen and put back together, I obviously wished that I'd just burned it. I just didn't take it seriously enough. I mean really, who would ever rifle through all my stuff (to find this you really would have to dig), find a random tape, and actually put it back together? I did understand at that time that there are very deeply disturbed people in the world; I just didn't understand that some of their numbers were, in fact, actually stored in my own cell phone. Thankfully I got my tape back (and most of my other belongings that were wrongfully taken), and it is now completely destroyed.

Sometime soon after I thought I had destroyed the tape, Johnny went out to the beach by himself to make a decision about running for president. He was really struggling with it. So many people's livelihoods were dependent upon him; there was a lot of pressure being applied to him from all sides. Elizabeth also really wanted him to run. From what he told me, she was not at all patient about his decision-making process. She even went so far as to guilt trip him.

I should have known right then that he was going to do what Elizabeth wanted him to do. I just didn't understand yet the extent of her "it's my way or no way" attitude.

He really believed his life was a life of service but he was still in deep conflict about how he was supposed to go about doing that. He wasn't comfortable being a politician. It just never suited him the way being a trial lawyer did, but then again, the opportunity to become president is hard to resist. He'd made all the right moves and positioned himself perfectly. Why would he go through all that if he weren't going to run for president?

He asked me what I thought. I thought it was a bad idea. Obviously, he had his "personal" issues to think about. When I brought it up, he would say, "Yes, but I have also already been vetted for VP."

"Yes," I said, "but that was 2004. What about since then?" I thought there were many ticking time bombs on the girlfriend front that could explode at any given time.

In my last attempt at keeping him safe, I told him if he really thought it was something he wanted to do, he should at least wait until April.

After all his contemplation, Elizabeth got her way; John Edwards decided to go for it.

I flew to New Orleans the day after Christmas. I was checking in at the hotel's front desk, talking to the Internet guy, when Johnny (in his brown leather jacket) and his entourage were coming into the building. I said, "Hey there!" He turned when he heard my voice and, as usual, he lit up when he saw me. Every time he does this, my heart just melts.

During a later *20/20* Bob Woodruff interview with Andrew and Cheri Young, it was claimed that I was waiting for Johnny in the Presidential Suite of the Loews New Orleans and allegedly said, "I felt just like his First Lady." Interestingly enough, I also discovered later that this little tidbit was lifted right out of the *National Enquirer's* September 1st, 2008, issue. Was Andrew the original source for the *National Enquirer* story or did he plagiarize it for filler in his book? I really wonder, but, whatever the case may be, my point is: of all the cheesy lines I'm supposed to have said, that one really makes me laugh. There was no Presidential Suite for Johnny, or me; we both had standard regular rooms. To me, waking up before dawn to dress in jeans, a down vest, and a ski hat, and then lug around my camera and all my gear, trying to get a shot of Johnny in the car in the dark on the phone with Matt Lauer—doesn't really conjure up feelings of any First Lady, let alone his.

While we were in New Orleans, Elizabeth finally watched the webisodes. They had been up for a while, and I was getting great feedback on the ground from people in New Orleans. A new employee told me that Johnny's people had sought her out to hire her. She went online to check out Johnny and his politics and when she watched the webisodes, she thought, "Okay, I could work for this guy."

Of course, that wasn't Elizabeth's reaction at all. She made comments to Johnny like, "You'd better not be in that filmmaker's room." Johnny told me his reaction to her comments was to defend me.

A long, grueling trip ensued: four states in three days with very little sleep. New Orleans to Iowa, then back to New Hampshire, where we stayed for the night. New Hampshire to Reno, then our plane broke. Fred came to the rescue with a private plane to North Carolina.

When we landed in North Carolina, Andrew was there to greet his senator. I remember him making a comment to me because I had on a Carolina sweatshirt (that Johnny had given me). Andrew is a *huge* Carolina fan. One of the things about Andrew that was so deceptive, something that blinded me to the real shadow behavior, was how thoroughly he doted on Johnny. Johnny didn't ever have to ask for anything because Andrew had it waiting for him, from having the cooler filled with all his favorite snacks or drinks to having any positive media report on hand for him to read. It's actually quite nice to be treated that way.

A staffer drove me to my hotel while Andrew drove his senator home. Johnny and Elizabeth were going to do ABC's *This Week*, anchored by George Stephanopoulos, before we flew to South Carolina and then back to North Carolina for his hometown ending!

While they was doing *This Week*, and before we got on the plane to South Carolina, I received a new rental wireless microphone package (Johnny was constantly pulling on the wire, frequently breaking it) and I was dealing with audio problems, on top of being exhausted.

It was late afternoon when we returned, and I think we may all have had a glass of wine and a sandwich on the plane. We were in the home stretch of the announcement tour and when we landed, there was a lot of laughter inside the plane upon sighting Johnny's chariot: as usual, there was Andrew waiting for his senator. Truly, the only thing missing were the rose petals.

I rode in Andrew's SUV with Johnny and John Davis. This is when I discovered Andrew's brilliant idea of putting Sauvignon Blanc in water bottles. I couldn't believe I had never seen that before. Andrew seemed very pleased by my approval of his "thinking of everything" in order to keep his senator happy.

As usual, we were late. This may be fine if you're the candidate, but not so good if you are filming the candidate and are supposed to be capturing the behind-the-scenes action, as well as the speech. I was a bit frazzled. I needed to mic Johnny and then get out to the event immediately in order to set up a tripod somewhere in the sea of media. And I had no idea where I was going. I followed everyone into the campaign offices and went into a room in order to get my camera out of its bag. I noticed on the way in that Elizabeth was standing in an adjacent room talking to people. Emma Claire and Jay, Elizabeth's brother, came into the room where I was just to say hello. I wondered for a second, "Do I introduce myself?" Elizabeth was outside talking to people. Awkward situation, yes, but there wasn't a lot of time to fret about it. I needed to mic Johnny and get outside, and in order to do that, I had to find Johnny, who had disappeared. In order to find him, I would have to go through the room Elizabeth was in. So I did. I walked over and introduced myself. Elizabeth did not look me in the eye. In fact, she appeared to be frightened. I have seen this reaction before and I knew in that moment that most of the bullying behavior I had heard about her was true. I really felt bad for her.

I said that I needed to mic Johnny. Elizabeth volunteered to locate him, so Emma Claire and I followed Elizabeth down the hall. He was in the bathroom, so we all walked back to where the offices were. I was finally able to mic Johnny, and thankfully, a guy from New Hampshire helped me navigate where I could stand to shoot the entrance of Johnny and his family coming onto the stage.

When I was shooting at the rope line, while Elizabeth and Johnny were shaking everyone's hands, Johnny turned to me and said, "Isn't this fun?" I looked at him as if to say, are you out of your mind? But all I said was "Fun?"

He smiled and said, "Well, minus a few issues."

And I said "A few *big* issues."

And he was right: the work was fun. I was doing what I loved to do, with the man I loved.

He and Elizabeth and the kids finally got into the car with Andrew and they all drove off. After they left, I felt free—and satisfied. It had been a long tough job, but I had done it well and it was finished. My contract was up.

What wasn't finished was my loving and supporting him because no matter who pushed him into it or how bad a move I thought it was, the man that I loved had just embarked on what I would call, The Path of Hell: John Edwards's second bid for the White House.

NINE

One Night Only

"Life doesn't imitate art, it imitates bad television."

—WOODY ALLEN

N DECEMBER 31ST, 2006 at 9:33 A.M., my cell rang, I looked at the caller ID, saw Johnny's number, and answered as I often did when he called, saying, "Hey, baby."

Instead of a response, the line went dead. I knew immediately that it wasn't Johnny calling me. It was Elizabeth.

Sure enough, at 9:51 A.M., my cell rang again. I answered the phone with, "Hello?" this time, but it was Johnny on the other end. Hoping I was wrong about Elizabeth calling before, I asked if he had just called and hung up. He replied in a very odd voice, "We are done. And I need to get all the tapes from you."

Oh. It had been Elizabeth.

When I didn't respond, he repeated himself. "We are done. And I need to get all the tapes from you."

"What? What are you talking about?"

"You and me, we are done."

"Oh, she's standing right there."

"We are done."

In my head, I was thinking: "We are done? What do you mean? We're just getting started." But what I said was, "Okay."

Then he said, "I need to get all the tapes from you."

"Okay."

"Goodbye."

"Bye."

The entire conversation lasted less than a minute.

I sat there on the bed in my room at the Marriott for a while. I felt very emotional yet, deep inside, I felt a peaceful stillness. And then I pondered the bond between Johnny and me, and yes, there it was again. I was convinced that my previous thought was accurate—this relationship wasn't over yet.

I called Mimi as I was packing, then Andrew called about my departure. He was unable to take me to the airport. I told him my contract was up and this was it, I wouldn't be working for the campaign. "What are you talking about?" Andrew said. "He loves you like a sister. He's not going get rid of you."

That was one of Andrew's tics, that brother/sister love thing. He would constantly say things like, "We were like brothers," or, "I love you like a sister." Clearly, the campaign staff talk of our affair had not hit Andrew yet, or he was flat-out lying.

Andrew continued, "There is no way you won't be working for him."

"Oh no, Andrew, I will not be working for him. Guaranteed."

We hung up and I took a cab to the airport. My cell rang, I looked at the number and it was Johnny's home phone. I answered, but no one spoke. Clearly it wasn't Johnny.

At the airport, Andrew surprised me by arranging to have two drink passes waiting for me in the Admirals Club. I took advantage of that and ordered a glass of wine, attempting to numb my pain.

While I was waiting for my flight, I got another hang-up call. Elizabeth proceeded to do this for the next two days at all hours of the day and night from various numbers, all Johnny-related. Of course I had them all, and I would answer because I never knew if it was Johnny calling until I answered. I didn't understand why she was calling, given she obviously had nothing to say to me, and I didn't really have anything to say to her. I felt miserable for her and for what she must be experiencing upon awakening from denial. But my loyalties were with Johnny.

I think I may have felt differently about this if I had been Johnny's first mistress instead of his last. When I met Johnny, he was leading a life that was completely separate from his married life. He was making his own decisions; I just happened to be a part of that other life. Because he told me when we first met that he was involved with other women and had been for the last twenty years, I felt that Elizabeth's anger had nothing to do with me. But as the third party, I would be the obvious target of her misplaced anger. I did feel like my relationship with Johnny, and our love for each other, did help move him forward, and thus helped bring his problems with Elizabeth out of the dark. And yes, that is a painful experience for anyone to go through.

Suffice it to say, it was the worst New Year's Eve of my life. I stayed in bed and faced my pain head-on, tortured by the hang-up calls from Elizabeth. I answered every single one, always hoping that Johnny would be on the other end.

On the evening of New Year's Day, Johnny finally called. He had gone out to get food. Obviously, he had been going through hell. He told me that Elizabeth was physically attacking him in between all the screaming. He just kept saying to me, "You have no idea. You have no idea."

He was right—I didn't. I had never heard him like this. It sounded like he was drowning. He said he had to go and didn't know how or when he could call because she had taken his phone. But he would be in New York on Thursday as planned, so I should call him at the hotel.

The next day I went to the AT&T store. I changed my number to end my hang-ups from Elizabeth and bought Johnny a new phone to give him on Thursday. There was no way I was leaving this relationship right now. He needed me more than ever—I was sure of it.

But when I called his room on Thursday, I did not recognize the person on the other end of the line. His voice was weird and distant. He said he couldn't see me.

I began to cry, but he was not moved by my tears. In fact, he had a new, strange reaction to my sadness. As I was crying into the phone, I could hear him turning to stone. I realized that he was in survival mode and shielding himself from any possible emotional manipulation.

I told him I had bought a new phone for him. And suddenly his entire demeanor changed. "I want that phone. I want to keep talking to you. But what am I going to do with it? Elizabeth will go through all my bags. I can't take a phone to my house."

The whole situation sucked, but I was in love with this man and I was going to make it work. I thought for a moment. "Why don't you give it to Andrew? Let him keep it and then give it back to you when you leave the house. That may work. He knows you like talking to me. He's already said he loves how happy you are around me. If he asks, tell him you want to keep talking to me. I'll talk to him."

As we continued talking, Johnny started becoming more recognizable.

"I think Elizabeth may have someone following me. I'm afraid to have you come see me tonight. But I really want that phone. It's been bad. You have no idea what I've been through the past few days."

I went to the Regency that night and called from the lobby. I was sitting on the couch in the lobby and I saw Josh walking into the lounge. I assumed he was going to meet his old work buddies, John Davis and Brian Mixer. Josh didn't see me. Johnny told me what room he was in and I went up. He was in a corner room, a suite.

He was a mess. Strangely detached, he reminded me of an abused animal. He was skittish, wary, and withdrawn. I started crying again but like before, my tears had no effect on him. The man I had known and loved had disappeared. He was a shell of himself. I think back on this now and it breaks my heart to know that he was like that, and still had a long road of abuse in front of him.

He told me Elizabeth was going to call and he needed to take the call. I said okay.

When she did, he went into the bedroom. I went in the bathroom to give him some privacy. I sat down on the floor and started thinking. I hadn't given him the phone yet and I thought to myself, "If I leave now, he will never be able to reach me." I thought about just getting up and walking out. But I didn't want abandon him as he was drowning. I decided I didn't care, that it wasn't my problem. "Oh fuck it, I'm going to leave," I thought to myself. I tried to move and I couldn't. What was holding me here? I wanted to go, but I couldn't move. As I was doing an internal scan of my new paralysis, Johnny opened the bathroom door. He looked terrible.

Years later, I would revisit that moment in the bathroom many times over. It was one of those turning points. Would my daughter even exist today had I been able to move my body and get the hell out of that bathroom and out of his suite? What kept me there? Why couldn't I move my body? And what was I doing involved in this mess? The latter was a question I would ask myself repeatedly over the next two years; the only answer I received back was, "learning." Learning about relationships. And now looking back, that is the understatement of the century.

And wow. He wasn't kidding about Elizabeth screaming at him. About two hours later the phone rang again and she went off. I have never heard anyone scream like that in my entire life. I could hear every word and was wondering if the people in the room next door could.

Johnny immediately warped into some person I had never seen before, attempting to calm her down, playing right into her drama. She would hang up and call back. This went on for hours in between me helping translate what was actually happening and showing him what patterns they were in. In Elizabeth's defense, she was bonkers because she had been in denial for years and was now attempting to put the pieces of her life back together. I really get that. She was torturing herself by asking for details of every night we'd spent together—what we did, where we did it, and how we did it. Johnny, in an attempt to be honest, was giving her way too much information. He was revealing way more than the "one-night stand" claims that I would later hear throughout the media. His details were feeding her frenzy, and the phone calls got worse.

What was clear to me was that I needed to get out of there, and that they needed professional help. What was not completely clear to me at the time was that their disagreement wasn't a one-time issue triggered by an outside event. What I was witnessing was their actual dynamic, the way they had always related to each other. Of course, the intensity of her rage varied depending on what she was thinking about. Her own random thoughts about anything and everything varied wildly at any given time, and his reaction varied depending on the intensity of the venom she directed at him. He had lived every day for the last thirty years tiptoeing around land mines. No wonder he liked being away from home so much!

I left well before dawn. He was paranoid that she had a detective following him. I doubted it because, from what I could tell, she did not sound like someone who wanted truth. From everything I had just heard, it sounded like she was stuck in a pattern of avoidance, and he was just playing right into it. That pattern is a deflection, an ego-control game, and it keeps you from discovering the truth. It keeps you in denial of what's really going on inside of you. But there was no way for me to foresee the depth of her attachment, the strength of her will to fight viciously to get her way. I underestimated her desire *not* to know (and her desire not to have anyone else know), as well as her attachment to her life in denial. And even more importantly, I underestimated Johnny's fear of her wrath.

I called a car service and left the suite. The first call came on my way home. Elizabeth was apparently threatening him with all kinds of things. I didn't buy any of it. The problem was, he did. She would beat him into submission with her emotionally charged words, repeating over and over, "How could you do this to me?"

He began calling me often from the new phone. Between being in his bubble, the alternate universe of campaigning, and Elizabeth's hysteria, that new cell phone turned out to be his lifeline to reality. Over the next few days, as he processed everything he had been through, he told me what had been going on the night Elizabeth had discovered the phone.

The night of December 30th, when he called me, Elizabeth was in full accusation and attack mode and had gone looking for him. She found him in the "barn"—a huge four-bedroom guesthouse with an indoor swimming pool that is attached to the basketball court, which is attached to the main house by what feels like a mile-long corridor. Upon hearing her approaching, he hung up quickly, and went to meet her, leaving both his cell phones next to each other.

They went back to main house and, after more fighting, finally went to sleep. Elizabeth had awakened early to take Cate to the airport.

Johnny, lying in bed alone in the early morning, had the thought, "Go move the phone." But he ignored this thought because he was exhausted and didn't want to get out of bed. He went back to sleep.

Elizabeth returned and rang his cell phone in an attempt to find it, suspecting he had been in the barn last night talking to me. She finally found it, and next to his phone was the phone that I had bought for him. She picked it up, and rang the only number in it, the last call the phone had made. I answered and said, "Hey, baby."

She confronted him again, just as she had been doing the night before, and he denied some more, and then finally caved. Yes, he was having an affair.

And that's when he called me, saying it was over and he needed the tapes.

She then stayed glued to his side—screaming, yelling, and attacking—so he would not be able to call me again until the next night, when he went out for food. I guess she thought if she left his side for one minute, he would call me. She was right.

When he got back to the house, Elizabeth was waiting for him at the gate and took his phone away from him. She was now going to attempt to control his every move.

After listening to Johnny's side of the story, I had a fuller understanding that this marriage was a sad and very sick relationship filled with issues that clearly neither Johnny nor Elizabeth wanted to address. They did not want to disclose the truth to themselves, much less to the public. I have learned that such behavior is not only generational but also geographical. It's very Southern to talk around things and to avoid directness at all costs.

What was important to Elizabeth was how she was perceived, what people thought about her, and anything—including the factual truth—that didn't fit into how Elizabeth wanted to be perceived would cause an extreme reaction. She would go on a venomous attack with complete disregard to the people she was hurting. And then she would work very hard at fixing that image by blogging and talking to reporters and her friends at *People*.

The last thing Johnny wanted was to get in the way of Elizabeth controlling her image, because that would cause her a great deal of pain, which, of course, would be directed at him.

TEN

On and On

"Anger is an acid that can do more harm to the vessel in which it is stored than to anything on which it is poured."

—MARK TWAIN

ELIZABETH WAS NOW OBSESSED with getting the tapes back and wanted all the footage I had shot. Johnny told me to go through it all and pull whatever I wanted—anything I might think that would be a bad idea for Elizabeth see, which meant anything that might trigger the venom. I did and stored them with my personal stuff in my hatbox.

During one of my many phone calls with Andrew, I told him that his boss wanted me to have his schedule, so that I would always know where he was, what hotel he was staying in or speaking at, and when his run time was, so I could call the landline if needed. Andrew started sending me all the schedules.

I also informed Andrew about his new duties as master of the cell phone, which he liked because he loved having something on Elizabeth—or Ursula, as he called her, after the sea witch from *The Little Mermaid*.

I knew the one tape that would drive her over the edge more than any of them was the one that I couldn't pull because she knew about it—the day I shot footage of Johnny and was given a tour of her dream house with Johnny's parents. I had no idea at that point how much she disliked his parents or the degree to which she ostracized his entire family, but to see them giving a tour of her house would have been a trigger.

And just as Johnny suspected, Elizabeth took the footage and locked herself in a room to watch it all. Hour after hour. She found the footage of Johnny walking into the room before he got his shots for Africa and she saw his reaction to seeing me, the way he lit up. She apparently told Johnny that he never once looked at her the way he looked at me. So she took that little bit and put it on her computer as a screen saver in order to watch it over and over again.

He wanted to take those tapes away from her, but she hid them from him. It became a battle: whenever he was home, he would search for the tapes, but she would hide them or lock them away in drawer that he couldn't open.

Hiding Elizabeth's craziness from the world was something Johnny had a lot of practice in doing. Apparently, late at night she would often go into what he would describe as the dark place; her voice would change and she would begin saying extremely vile things or emailing such things or calling people and harassing them. According to Johnny, Elizabeth had a very long history of very bad nights.

Johnny and Elizabeth come from the school of "just stay busy," and they both stayed very busy indeed. His campaign schedule was a primary part of his survival tactic. She continued on her path of relentless self-torture, watching footage and calling Johnny to scream at him or disguising her voice and making odd calls to people in search of my number. She went into full damage control, blogging happy stories on the campaign website about their wonderful marriage and romantic time together after the announcement tour.

I found all of this to be beyond heartbreaking and beyond disturbing.

But, of course, I was not about to leave him alone with his mess. I had warned him it was going to be bad, and he had announced his run at the worst possible time. I wasn't about to abandon him at that crucial point. I did continually suggest therapy but I also really did understand the resistance to that. How bad does it sound for a presidential candidate and his wife to be in therapy?

Shortly thereafter, he told me that Elizabeth wanted to renew their wedding vows in July. When he told me, my first thought was, "Yeah right, there is no way that's going to happen."

I flew down to Palm Beach, Florida, to see Johnny on January 17th or 18th. I went to The Breakers for the first time ever and had dinner in the bar until he called around 8:30. I then took a cab to the Four Seasons Resort Palm Beach, where he was staying.

My traveling to see him had become more complicated because I had worked for him and now most of his staff knew me. But now Johnny was actually running for president. I had to stay completely away from John Davis, and now Elizabeth knew about us. Johnny had no idea where John Davis was after they had parted but he guessed the bar. Johnny gave me the instructions on how to get to the elevators and how to stay clear of the bar (in case John Davis was in there and not in his room), so when I arrived at the Four Seasons, I knew where I was going and made it to the room without being spotted.

As usual, when he saw me he lit up, and, as usual, my heart melted. I realize that it's a really lame way to describe what we have, what happens when we are together. But when we looked into each other's eyes, as we did in the hallway when I walked into the room of the Four Seasons that night, it took my breath away, made my heart pound, and my head spin. I loved this man like no other and there was just no way that I was going to leave him alone in his hell.

This visit was far better than the one in New York because we had been talking regularly and because his schedule had kept him away from Elizabeth; he was still beat up but he wasn't as beat up as he was the last time I saw him.

John Davis was set to come to Johnny's room in the morning, so we figured the best idea would be for me to just go wait in the stairwell until John got into the room, and then I would go downstairs and grab a cab.

So there I was, standing in the stairwell of the Four Seasons. I waited and waited and waited. Johnny did not call. I finally gave up, exited the hotel, and sat on a bench outside. The concierge had called a car for me. My phone rang. Johnny said that Davis had still not shown up in Johnny's room. "Where are you? Did you see him?"

"No," I replied, "I'm outside and I did not see him."

As I was checking in at the airport, the computer asked me if I wanted to take another flight, one that was already boarding, or wait another hour? Now please! I hopped on that flight, turned off my cell, thereby missing Johnny's call to change my ticket and fly to Louisiana or Arkansas or Timbuktu, wherever he was headed next, I can't remember. I remember it was a remote location and difficult to get to. But had I not missed his call, I would have tried. Instead, I went home to Jersey.

Somewhere around this time Johnny and Elizabeth finally started seeing a therapist. Praise the Lord.

I flew to Detroit in February for two nights. Johnny and John Davis were staying at a Westin some twenty minutes from the airport. In the elevator at this Westin, you needed a key to get up to your room, so Johnny had to come down and get me. This would always tickle me. There was never anyone on the elevator with him, nor did the elevator stop to pick up anyone. What are the odds?

The next day I left early (with my own key so I could return later) and walked to a hotel next door for coffee and my morning CNN. I then took a cab to a multiplex movie theater and spent the day at the movies. I have always loved going to the movies by myself during the day for as long as I can remember. It's also something I did a lot during my stint as a mistress.

I had dinner at some Detroit basketball sports bar attached to the multiplex, and Johnny called about some "campaign disaster" media crisis that was happening. I think it may have been about the "cutting-edge" bloggers they had hired; one turned out to be a little too cutting edge. Anyway, this delayed my return to the hotel, and when I finally got a cab back, I ran smack dab into John at the elevators. While it was really great to see him, I was a tad freaked.

I went up to Johnny's room and told him, "I just ran into John Davis. Should I go talk to him?" So that's what I did. John Davis opened the door wearing a white bathrobe and opening a bottle of wine. I was very uncomfortable so I wasn't very direct. I never came out and really said anything to John explicitly about my relationship with Johnny;

I just said something like, "Anything you see going on on the road is best kept to yourself." But it was my understanding that he understood exactly what I was saying. I went back to Johnny's room and had yet another unbelievably crazy night with Elizabeth calling to rage at him and Johnny continuing to play into it, attempting to help her. He got very little sleep and was in the bathroom on the phone most of the night. From what I could tell, she believed he was responsible for taking on her pain, taking her punishment, and for making her so miserable.

Don't get me wrong: I am no advocate for cheating, I believe that if a third party pops up, you need to go to your partner and say, "Hey, we have problems" *before* you jump into bed with the third party. But I also know that is not the norm.

And, silly me, I *thought* that running into John Davis was going to make my life a little easier. However, Johnny (as usual), especially coming off a sleepless crazy Elizabeth rage night, didn't trust anyone. Johnny later told me that he told Davis that I had come to see him because I was upset about losing my job and wanted to talk to him.

The week following Detroit, I flew to Fort Lauderdale, Florida, on February 12th and had dinner. For some reason, by the time I had finished, Johnny hadn't called yet. Naturally, I was getting impatient. I tried his cell and it was off, so I called the hotel he was supposed to have checked into and they said there was no reservation under that name. I called Andrew and asked him if he could locate Johnny. Andrew was less than thrilled that I was interrupting Jack Bauer on 24. Of course, he had no idea I was actually in Fort Lauderdale; he thought that I just was trying to reach the senator for another phone call.

Andrew found John Davis and Johnny called shortly thereafter. It turned out they had changed hotels and were now staying at the Sheraton Yankee Clipper Hotel (now the Sheraton Fort Lauderdale Beach Hotel), which was in dire need of an update. On my way there in a cab, I passed by my grandfather's old apartment building on Galt Ocean Mile, where I had learned to play backgammon as a kid. It was one of those weird high-rise buildings directly on the beach. Seeing his building flooded me with memories of my early childhood in Fort Lauderdale.

I remember on my way out in the morning, as I was waiting for a cab, I saw one of Johnny's staffers downstairs. Maybe he was a local guy? He was young and I had never seen him before, so there was no need to worry that he would recognize me.

At the end of February, I remember driving into the city early to beat the snowstorm that was coming. Johnny was somewhere in Westchester, New York, at a fundraiser. I went to my usual haunt Serafina and had wine while I waited for him to call. I walked over to the Regency after he rang. We watched Al Gore win an Oscar on TV together, and Johnny told me about a woman who had been (unsuccessfully) hitting on him that night.

I called or emailed Jonathan Darman for lunch sometime at the beginning of winter. In hindsight, it was sheer stupidity to call him. But the truth is I really liked him, regardless of the fact that I did not like the snarky spin in his writing and hated the piece he had done in December on the webisodes.

I had lunch with Darman and liked him even more than the first time. I'm not sure why he would later take some of the things I said over that particular lunch and claim I had said them much earlier. Was it malicious, convenient for his storytelling purposes, or did he just have a bad memory?

I had lunch at Nobu with Lisa Blue one afternoon when she was in town. Even though I was no longer working for Johnny our friendship continued, and I believe that she still did not have any idea Johnny and I were in love or even intimately involved.

At the beginning of March I went to LA for a little less than a week. As usual, I loved being in LA. I stayed with a friend for a few nights and stayed with Johnny a couple of nights. I remember staying in two different hotels in LA with Johnny. The first night it was the old Hotel Nikko on La Cienega (now the SLS Hotel at Beverly Hills), where you needed a key to use the elevator, so Johnny had to come down and get me.

In the morning, I had to hide in the bathroom when John Davis came in to get Johnny's bags. (The amount of hiding that goes along with being a mistress is downright comical.) I took a leisurely shower before I left. The hotel in Santa Monica had a hot tub on the terrace, which we did not use, but we did avail ourselves of the hotel's great room service breakfast. I remember Johnny calling me in the middle of the night from the plane. He was attempting to hold on to the "goodness in life" because he was about to descend back into the hell of his marriage. As you can probably guess, he and Elizabeth weren't exactly making great headway in therapy. Johnny was taking little baby steps in his attempts to be honest with her, and yet any honesty he expressed would be met with rejection and abuse from her. She continually questioned how in the world he could be attracted to someone like me? The honest reply, "She makes me happy," was not received without punishment. Unfortunately, they could never get past what an awful person Johnny was for cheating on her, because she really believed that she was the victim of his awfulness.

In mid-March I went to DC for a few nights and spent my days in Georgetown going to the movies and shopping. I remember having to hide in an adjoining kitchen in Johnny's hotel room when John Davis again came in to get his bags. I then took a train to Philadelphia and went to the Westin to wait for his call. I had to walk much farther in the cold rain to the Sheraton than I thought I would, and he was late because he was watching a basketball game with his staffers. Neither exactly made me happy. That night turned out to be another crazy Elizabeth night, with her calling to scream all night. As usual, Johnny didn't get much sleep, attempting to calm her from the other room. After she finally wore through his patience, it would turn into a full-blown fight that was beyond belief. And then they'd repeat the whole process. The whole thing was misery beyond belief. I asked him how long this had been going on. He replied, "As long as I have known her."

I asked, "Before she found out about me?"

He said, "Oh yes. It has gotten worse but it has always been there."

Elizabeth took it upon herself to replace Andrew as Johnny's driver by hiring a woman named Kat Lee. When Andrew saw that he was no longer on the schedule he called me, very upset, focusing primarily on how he would never be able to get the phone to Johnny if he wasn't driving. I assured Andrew that Johnny wasn't going to let that happen.

Once again, I was wrong. Andrew was out as the driver, never again to be reinstated.

I sometimes wondered what Elizabeth had on Johnny, what gave her the power to make him fold? It was like no other marriage I had ever seen. It isn't uncommon to be afraid of your spouse, shutting down when he or she walks into the room, which comes from projecting all your childhood stuff into your marriage. But again, I had never seen anything like this marriage. He was so strong, fearless, and honest in every other area of his life, but when it came to her, he was incredibly weak. Did it have to do with losing a child together?

Andrew getting replaced by Elizabeth really helped motivate him to do whatever he could to get Johnny the new phone. No matter how early Andrew would have to rise to put it on the plane, or retrieve it from the oddest of places, he was more than willing. He would even stop Kat en route for Johnny to sign some pictures or some books, but what was really happening was a hand off of the cell phone. In short, I was becoming Andrew's only connection to Johnny.

My birthday was March 20th, and after a birthday lunch at Pastis with Mimi, I was sitting in her car on University Place in Greenwich Village. She had left me in the car while she went to run an errand. My cell rang. It was Johnny, and he was in crisis mode: He told me that the doctors believed that Elizabeth's cancer might be back, that they didn't know for sure, but he was canceling everything and going back to Chapel Hill. "And if it is back," he continued, "I am definitely getting out of the race."

I told him I was there for him, whatever he needed.

He said he would call as soon as he could.

I didn't ask any questions about our future plans to see each other Thursday night in New York and whether we were still on. Those thoughts did not enter my head. All I could think about was the cancer.

My heart really went out to them both, I lost my father to cancer, I know all too well what a bitch cancer actually is.

ELEVEN

The Circle of Life

"I have found the paradox, that if you love until it
hurts, there can be no more hurt, only more love."

—Mother Teresa

O N MY BIRTHDAY, Andrew claimed that Johnny had gotten me something that was going to arrive at my house. Sure enough, red roses came. They were beautiful, and yet it was a gesture that grossed me out because I knew they weren't actually from Johnny. Andrew sent them and claimed they were from Johnny. I knew Johnny would not send me red roses and that he didn't ask Andrew to do that. I already knew Johnny well enough to know that the only birthdays he really acknowledges are his kids'. I didn't stop to wonder who paid for those roses. But where was Andrew getting the money to send me a gift? How many other gifts does he send claiming they're from Johnny?

I did not hear from Johnny the next day, and now that Andrew was no longer driving Johnny, he hadn't either. Andrew saw him the following night at a fundraiser at Tim Toben's house (Tim is a friend of Andrew's) attended by both Johnny and Elizabeth. Because Johnny didn't talk to Andrew about what was going on, I had no way of knowing what had happened at the hospital that morning.

On the morning of the press conference, when the news started breaking that they had had a powwow at Johnny's house with the campaign insiders, and all speculation was that her cancer was back, I still did not know anything because my only connection to what was happening was Andrew, and he wasn't an "insider."

So I watched the press conference along with the rest of the world and was blown away by the hypocrisy of both Johnny and Elizabeth. Johnny stood there claiming that Elizabeth was the most unselfish person he had ever known, which was just a flat-out lie. Whenever he confronted a crisis with Elizabeth, he automatically jumped to her aid and gave her whatever she wanted in an attempt to take away her pain. I had seen him do precisely that over and over again. And now, he was staying in the race.

There was no way that staying in the race was his choice. I was furious at myself. I was flabbergasted because he told me that he was definitely getting out of the race if the cancer was back. Yet there was Elizageth, going on and on about how tough he was and what a great president he would be, and he chimed in with, "See how unselfish she is?"

Life had just offered them a graceful exit and they declined.

I remember talking on the phone with Andrew off and on all day long. By this point, I was talking to Andrew all the time. I always imagined him sitting at a desk "fundraising," which meant calling and chatting on the phone with people about his great love John Edwards, and now I had become one of many that he talked with multiple times a day. He was also always sending me press links. Andrew was elated by the news that they were staying in the race. He couldn't understand why I would be so upset about this news. I said to Andrew, "You just don't understand what our relationship really is."

And he said to me, "Of course I understand."

"No, you don't," I insisted.

"*Yes I do!* Why would I be sending schedules to you? Of course I know."

This was the first time we ever talked about that fact that Johnny and I were intimate. It never got any more detailed than that. But now I knew that he knew. And that bonded us together even more.

I also talked off and on that morning with my friend Jonathan Darman about what a wild decision it was for them to stay in the race. Darman had a fascination with Johnny and the campaign, which may have been our initial bond. (I know it is what bonded me to Andrew—we were both in love with the same guy.) But unlike Andrew, Darman was also fascinated with human behavior, ego, and what makes people tick. He was interested in uncovering real behavior, as opposed to public claims of behavior, like how can a man decide that he is the one guy best qualified to run the entire country?

I really liked Jonathan Darman. He was smart, curious, and actually interesting for someone so interested in politics. I was never fully honest with Darman, meaning I never revealed my relationship with Johnny. I should have steered clear of Darman but I liked him too much, and I was curious to learn more about the media. Live and learn.

Later that night, Andrew called and told me to call Johnny at the Regency. He was there alone and wanted to talk. I called. He sounded odd and tired. He had been through a whirlwind.

"I thought you were getting out."

"She wanted to stay in. It's what she wants."

"Of course." There was nothing else for me to say. The decision had been made.

And even worse, I now believed the sickness of their dynamic was forever sealed by the cancer. How could he possibly defy Elizabeth's wishes now that she was a dying woman? I assumed that her bullying and guilt tripping into getting her way on everything, and his folding to her every wish, was now not only never going to change but it was only going to get worse, and that, sadly, she was going to use this against him as well. Turns out I was right.

And as usual, because their dynamic had nothing do with me, nothing changed between us. Other than the fact that my anger at myself for being in love with him increased, and he was now more concerned that, because the press was all over him, it was much harder for us to see each other.

Sometime after this I remember having dinner with Mimi in New York. A friend of hers joined us. This friend, like a lot of the country, was appalled by the press conference, going on and on about Edwards trotting out old Lizzie and hanging her on the tree, using her cancer to get votes, as if it were all his ambition and she was the poor victim.

I was thinking yeah, not likely, as if he had ever stood up to her once in his life!

I had two very strong thoughts about their campaign (it was always hers as much as his). Even without the cancer, he shouldn't have been in the race. But add the cancer on top of that? Forget the marriage, forget the race, the only question to me is: What about your kids? You know your time is limited, why wouldn't you be spending *every possible second* with your children? That just broke my heart.

I watched their "cancer has returned" campaign tour, including Katie Couric's interview, all from New Jersey. And I found the whole thing disgusting. Every time I saw the two of them on TV, my reaction was the same: I was disgusted with myself for being in love with him. I was also disgusted with myself for being patient with him and his inability to stand up to her and her "This is what we have been working for, we cannot stop" attitude. The real clincher for me was her saying, "I don't want it to be my legacy to take out this good man. The country needs him."

It was beyond irritating to me. And as usual, I could not hold on to any of my upset, disgusted feelings, especially because every time I had them, I immediately saw that they were being created by my own thoughts and judgments.

I went to DC to see him the following Thursday night. There was no press anywhere. One great thing about the media: they usually move on quickly. I remember this was the night Mimi had met a great guy in New York whom she thought should be working for Johnny. Mimi knew (from me and our days with the PAC) that Johnny was (still) not happy with the way his campaign was functioning. She called me just as I was getting to the hotel and said, "Johnny has to meet this guy Steve." I also remember it was unseasonably warm. I had on Robert Clergerie sandals and my brown short jacket from Barneys. And the next morning, walking to Union Station, I was freezing. Johnny was staying at some odd hotel close to Union Station. It was the one and only night I was ever there. I also remember he was different to me that night, he was more comfortable with me than ever before, as if I were a wife as opposed to a girlfriend, and quite frankly I prefer the girlfriend. Why is it that when men marry, they get so comfortable with their wives? They have a tendency to take their wives for granted, killing the excitement of not knowing what could happen—that unknowingness that keeps fuel in the chemistry and the entire relationship. He was comfortable with me this night, like I was his wife, and I was not happy about this new development. Fortunately, that dynamic didn't last long between us.

At the end of April, I flew to Seattle, one of my favorite cities. I stayed at the Westin again, the same hotel Johnny and I had stayed at in 2006 when I worked for him. I remember Mimi's friend Steve calling me as I was out eating breakfast and enjoying the city. He met with Johnny in New York earlier in the month, and was now down in North Carolina assessing what was going on within the campaign. Steve asked me, "Have you met Andrew's wife?"

I said "No. Why?"

He simply said, "Wait until you meet the wife."

Steve went on to tell me that he really liked Andrew but he was also very disturbed about his behavior, specifically the way Andrew was speaking to the young female staffers. Steve told me he was blown away that nobody had already reported Andrew for sexual harassment.

Suffice it to say that after spending a few days around the campaign, Steve decided he didn't want to have anything to do with it, claiming that he was too old for the shenanigans that were going on. After an up-close look, he believed John Edwards had gotten as far as he had on sheer talent alone, because he was surrounded by buffoons and all the talk from staffers was that his wife was a big problem, one that Steve wanted no part of. Naturally this was not new news to Johnny. He knew he had big problems but how was he ever going to fix them if he couldn't get anyone in there to run his campaign properly?

I returned early that evening to find, once again, a Johnny-and-Elizabeth fight that had been very bad. During this one, Johnny threw his phone against the wall and broke it, which he was happy about given she now had no way to contact him.

The last morning in Seattle, Johnny had already left to go to a meeting somewhere else in the hotel, and as I was blow-drying my hair, a room service guy with food kept knocking on the door. My heart was beating fast. The phone started ringing. I didn't answer.

The guy started banging on the door again. I told him through the door he had the wrong room. He left. I was freaked out and wanted out of there fast.

The next week I went to DC and stayed at the Westin again, then the following week I went to the Westin Diplomat Resort & Spa in Hollywood, Florida. (Did they have a deal with Starwood Hotels, or what?) I didn't mind all the travel. I had made plenty of money while working for the campaign, and despite the huge tax bill I had just paid, I had no other real expenses except to go see him. I had no problems spending my money to go see him. After all, I wanted to be with him as much as possible because I was completely in love. The hotel in Florida had a couple of restaurants across the street, so I sat outside and waited for Johnny to call me.

He was always calling me from the plane, from his cell before take-off and in the air from the air phone if he was alone. Then typically he would ring again from his cell upon landing, and then as soon as he got to his room. He would also call during his run time—before and after he ran. I was his lifeline to happiness and I loved it.

This night they were delayed due to bad weather. He said he would keep me posted, and as I suspected, it turned out to be a long wait with too much wine and lots of reading. If you need to learn patience, falling in love with a campaigning married politician is an excellent way to do it.

The following week I remember being in the car in Manhattan, about to go into Soho House New York for dinner with Mimi, when Johnny called to tell me that he had a surprise for me. He believed he had successfully changed his schedule so he was actually going to be staying in New York Wednesday night as well, giving us three nights together that week instead of two.

I remember I wore jeans that Wednesday night. We had Serafina takeout for dinner and, as usual, we laughed a lot. When we were alone together everything else in the world faded away and it was nothing but love and happiness. That night was no different. We really were so madly in love.

On July 3rd, 2007, I would see the ultrasound that, unbeknownst to either of us, resulted from that night. In the wee morning hours of May 24th, 2007, at the very same hotel where our relationship began, was the beginning of an event that changed our lives forever. At the time, we had no idea what had actually occurred and we were certainly clueless about what was to come.

TWELVE

Odd Timing

"Making the decision to have a child is momentous. It is to decide forever to have your heart go walking around outside your body."

—ELIZABETH STONE

OUT THE BLUE ONE DAY at the end of May—neither Johnny nor I had any idea yet that I was pregnant—Andrew said to me something like, "You need to stop paying to go see him out of your own money. This is an expense that you should not be paying. And I am going to take care of it. How much do you think you spend a month on these trips? Like five thousand dollars?"

"Yeah," I replied, "something like that. But Andrew, where is this money going to come from?"

"Don't worry about it. I'm going to take care of it."

"Who is going to pay the taxes on it?" (I had just paid the largest tax bill in my life, so it was a concern.)

He said, "It's a gift from me, so I will have to worry about that."

"So you're going to give me a gift of five thousand dollars a month? But where are you getting that money?"

"Don't worry about it; I am taking care of it. It's a gift."

101

"Are you for real? Is this a joke?"

"I am serious."

"Is this on the up-and-up?"

"Of course. It's a gift. Just send me your banking info and I will put it directly into your account."

"Okay. Thanks. Cool."

I thought this was a little odd but I knew that Andrew had connections to very wealthy people through Johnny. I trusted him and I honestly thought this money was coming from someone who wanted to do what he could to help out the people who were helping out Johnny. In fact, much later on in Santa Barbara, standing in the kitchen, during one of Andrew's many meltdowns about Johnny not calling him, Andrew told me that this money had come from a male lawyer that he knew. He told me the man's name, but I had never heard it before, and unfortunately, I did not retain it.

To this day I am positive that Johnny had no idea about this arrangement of Andrew "taking care of my travel" until I told him about it, which was way after this. Because I have never actually seen all of Andrew's bank statements from all of his bank accounts with my own eyes, I honestly have no idea where the money that he put into my account came from, and I am still skeptical that it actually came from Bunny Mellon as Andrew has publicly claimed over and over again, or if any of Bunny's money was actually used on me (more on that later).

I flew to Vegas at the beginning of June and had dinner at the Four Seasons Hotel Las Vegas while I waited for Johnny to call from his adjoining hotel, the Mandalay Bay Resort and Casino. The next morning, over room service, Elizabeth called to scream at Johnny, and he left the room and paced the hallway while she screamed on and on. He knew how badly his reaction to her irritated me. He would placate her, allowing her to continue on and on with the same behavior, so nothing changed. It drove me nuts.

Speaking of being driven nuts, in the airport I saw a copy of *People* that was filled with Elizabeth's glorious talk of her beautiful marriage to Johnny and upcoming vow renewal. Reading all of this was difficult because it was so disconnected from reality.

The pictures accompanying the "so excited to get married again" article were also not great. Elizabeth and the kids were much more photogenic than what was presented, and I mentioned that to Johnny when he called shortly after I'd read the piece. His response was: "It's so weird—Elizabeth knew you would say that. She was very upset about the pictures because she knew *you* would think they were bad."

Fabulous. It appeared that her spin on the happy couple was also very much directed at me. Nothing spells "happy couple" like the vendetta you have against the other woman.

On June 3rd Johnny had a debate in New Hampshire, which was broadcast on TV, so, of course, Elizabeth (adored by all) attended. It is hard not to become jaded and/or really angry with yourself for being so stupid and actually buying into the illusion—buying into "the media persona"—when you begin to see how far off public images are from the actual person. All of that was very difficult for me. Politics also just goes against the way I naturally operate, which is to let life unfold naturally and speak only if and when it felt right, which usually is not in the midst of some frenzy. I don't want to speak unless I have come to some sort of understanding and I feel that there is a need. In politics you are speaking all the time, getting your story and your agenda out there. And the one who gets their message out first has the best chance of having their message stick, the best chance of driving the storyline they want. Unfortunately, factual truth doesn't have a lot to do with it.

On June 7th, I took the Acela to Boston and went to the first hotel I ever stayed at with Johnny near Back Bay Station. I went straight to the bar and ordered crab cakes and wine. He was staying at the Westin across the street. As I was on my way across the street, I remembered him calling and telling me to wait a few minutes, that they had forgotten something with his food and needed to come back. I popped into the Palm Restaurant to use the bathroom. Suddenly I felt weird, as if I were having an allergic reaction to the crab cakes. I went up to his room. I remember munching on Tums, which made me feel better.

We talked the next morning about me coming to New Hampshire that evening but decided against it. Iowa and New Hampshire were not places for a candidate's mistress to show up. Both are crawling with nosy press and manipulative people. It was just too dangerous. I was going to see him on Monday night anyway in Florida.

After a little shopping for his upcoming birthday, I took the train back to Jersey. When I got home, I felt weird again, a little sick but not like any sick I could identify. Then the thought crossed my mind: Could I be pregnant? I couldn't imagine I was, given I was 43 and had never been pregnant. Johnny and I never used birth control, but I was always mindful of my cycle and I was certain that I had never been ovulating during any of my visits with Johnny. I went to the drugstore and bought a home pregnancy test anyway, just to be sure. I did the test and it was negative. I never told anyone because there was nothing to tell.

I flew off to Miami on Monday, June 11th, the day after Johnny's birthday. Johnny was staying at the Fontainebleau. I went to the Delano South Beach, where I had never stayed, and sat outside for dinner, waiting yet again for his call. Then I took a cab to the Fontainebleau. The problem there was that John Davis's and Johnny's rooms had a shared hallway entrance. There was a door and then a little foyer, and when you went into the foyer, there were two doors side by side, one for each of their rooms. Dangerous. I got in without John Davis knowing.

The next morning Johnny left, and I bolted the door and took a shower. As I was drying my hair, I heard pounding on the door. I called out, "Yes?"

"Hotel security. Open the door."

I did not. Apparently the advance guy (someone I did not know named Jeff Harris) had tried to get into the room when I was in the shower to get the leftover sodas and such and to make sure no papers had been left behind. He couldn't get in (because I had bolted the door) and went to get hotel security.

Through the door I told them I would be done in a few minutes and would then leave.

"Open the door! You are not authorized to be in there."

"Yes, I am. I am the guest of Matthew Nelson."

I let them keep banging away while I went back into the bedroom and called Johnny. He didn't pick up. I then called Andrew and told him I was in a bit of a pickle. I was in Miami and hotel security was banging on the door. He hung up and called hotel security. But the banging continued. Andrew called me back and told me to go to the door and tell the staffer to call him. I did. He didn't know Andrew. I wrote down Andrew's number, opened the door without unbolting it, and gave him the piece of paper. "Call Andrew," I said. He did, and hotel security left.

Johnny called. I told him what had happened and that I was leaving soon. Andrew had gotten them to go away. Surprisingly, Johnny sounded fine about it all. I take it he was focused on whatever campaigning event he was doing.

I was not fine. I was very upset and too old for this shit.

I went back to the Delano for breakfast. Andrew called and told me I should just stay in Miami, relax, enjoy myself, and get a massage. He would take care of it.

"Andrew, you don't have any money. How are you going to take care of it?"

"Don't worry about it. Just let me take care of it."

This went on for a long time. We spoke through my entire breakfast. I finally caved. I told Andrew, "I'm going to the gift shop. If I can find a bathing suit I like, I will stay. If not, I'm going back to Jersey." (I hadn't packed to stay in Miami.) He told me to put the waiter on the phone. I did. He had my breakfast billed to him.

I went to the gift shop and found a bathing suit I liked. Johnny called while I was in there to see if I was okay. He knew how upset I was about "being caught."

"Yeah, I'm a little better. I may stay the night."

"Okay. Just wanted to make you sure you were all right. I'll call you later."

Andrew then called the Shore Club a few doors down from the Delano and faxed his credit card so that it was already taken care of when I went to check in. He insisted that I get a massage and eat at Nobu. After resisting for a long time, almost to the point of fighting, I finally caved.

Looking back now, it makes perfect sense why Andrew was so relentless about letting him take care of it. I suspect that, for him, it justified his soliciting and accepting funds (that nobody knew about) using Johnny's name. And yet four years later, I would see with my own eyes the checks and the dates in the indictment, *United States of America v. Johnny Reid Edwards*, that Andrew had already received two checks from Bunny Mellon, one for ten thousand dollars and one for twenty-five thousand dollars. Of course, beyond the amounts that went to my expenses (if they even went to my expenses) which at that time did not add up to even half of thirty-five thousand dollars, I have no idea how these funds were spent, but it wasn't on me.

I flew home from Florida on Wednesday, and on Thursday I remember feeling weird again. Not well. What was wrong with me? Was it my period? I checked when my period was, and the first day of my last period was May 11th. For obvious reasons, I was always paying attention to my cycle.

I went to the drugstore and bought another home pregnancy test. This one was positive. One was negative, one was positive. I told Mimi about the tests and decided to go see a doctor to get a definitive answer.

Around this time Johnny called me from Detroit; he was very upset and tired. He told me that Elizabeth had begun her full-on harassment campaign of the old girlfriends (the ones before 2004). Apparently when Elizabeth was done raging at Johnny for the night (or if she could not reach him), she would focus her anger elsewhere. Johnny clearly felt powerless against Elizabeth's venom and, on top of his campaign schedule, it simply exhausted him to no end.

Johnny was scheduled to stay the night in New York on June 21st, but something happened that resulted in him and his people opting out of staying at the Regency. Instead, they ended up staying at a hotel next to the Meadowlands so they could get out of Teterboro Airport early the next morning. When he called late that night, I threw on one of my favorite dresses and jumped into the car. It took me only ten minutes to get to his hotel, door to door.

He was so tired and very sweet. My heart broke for him. I loved him so much; I really wanted to give him all of my energy. I remember him saying he really thought I felt different, like I was pregnant. I told him I was going to go to the doctor. I told him I did feel odd, and I really wasn't sure.

I called the doctor on June 25th. The soonest I could get in was July 3rd. I had already stopped drinking just in case it turned out I was pregnant.

The following week I stayed at the Westin Embassy (now The Fairfax at Embassy Row) in DC. I remember Johnny being in a really good mood following a debate that was held at Howard University. He had even ordered chocolate cake with his room service meal to celebrate.

The next morning, I put on a beige summer dress, one that Johnny really liked on me. (I think women remember when men notice clothing because it's so rare!) He called me after I left. I was in a cab on the way to Union Station. He asked if I had seen Sam Myers Sr., Johnny's trip director, on the way out. I had not because I had gone down the side elevators and not the main ones. Apparently Sam had come to his door just minutes after I had left. We must have missed each other by mere seconds. I had met Sam on the announcement tour and even though (like Johnny) I love Sam, I was happy in that moment not to have run into him.

I went to the doctor on July 3rd. I had no plans to speak to Johnny for a while because he had told me during our last conversation that July 3rd was Elizabeth's birthday. They were going to the beach and then on a family vacation to New Hampshire (only in politics do you plan a family vacation in New Hampshire), so he had no way to call because Elizabeth still frequently searched through every one of his bags for surreptitious cell phones.

To say that my entire world shifted when I saw the image on the ultrasound screen would be an understatement. In one second my entire life became about something else.

A protective nurturing power was awakened from the deepest part of my being. It is a part of me that I always had a vague sense was there but did not remotely understand its vastness until that moment. Yet within seconds, this joyful new feminine power streamed through me with the utmost gratitude and I fully embraced all responsibility for this life that had now been entrusted to me. I did not know until that moment that being a mother is a role that means more to me than any other role in the entire world.

I also never uttered one word about the identity of the father of this little child. And I was happy to discover that, besides the necessary generic health questions, the doctors involved really do respect your privacy. I suspect that, with the multiple ways to conceive and all the different family configurations these days, they have seen a lot.

So when my doctor told me, "With your last period beginning May 11th, and the size of the baby, I am going to give you a due date of February 15th and I am going to call this baby a Presidents Day weekend baby!" All I could think was, "Of course you are, because my life, well, it just couldn't get any weirder."

Or could it?

THIRTEEN

Yes, I Am

"Having a child is surely the most beautifully irrational act that two people in love can commit."

—BILL COSBY

THE ONLY PERSON I told about the pregnancy was Mimi. From the parking lot of the OB/GYN office in West Orange, New Jersey, I called Mimi and told her, "I am holding a picture of my baby in my hand." It was completely surreal to me.

Johnny's New Hampshire family vacation came to end; he flew to Vegas on July 10th. Andrew told me he had delivered the phone to him, so when I did not hear from him that night, I tried to call him a few times. His room phone was off the hook—not unusual given that he often did this to avoid Elizabeth. The phone I bought him was switched off, which *was* unusual.

He didn't call in the morning either, so by the time the evening of July 11th rolled around, I was really upset. I obviously needed to talk to him. I had been holding the news too long—since July 3rd, in fact.

Johnny was going to rest overnight in Detroit. After a few calls went straight to voicemail, I called Andrew and asked him to please locate Johnny because I needed to talk to him.

I believe that Andrew heard some urgency in my voice, because he said, "Well, someone has either died or you're pregnant."

I was caught off-guard by hearing the word *pregnant* come out of Andrew's mouth. All I could say back was, "Nobody died. Please get him on the phone for me." It was around 10 P.M. and Andrew and I talked at length while he tried to locate Johnny. I was very unhappy that Andrew knew I was pregnant before I could tell Johnny.

Andrew tried to console me, telling me not to worry and that he wasn't going to say a word to anyone. He said that he was very happy for me, and that I would not be overstating matters if I described his state as over-the-moon with joy. He was a father of three, so I didn't think anything about his happiness. He obviously liked kids and thought they were great. (I had no way of knowing at the time that he probably felt like he had just struck gold with his ability to use me.)

When Johnny finally called me that night, the first thing he said to me was, "Why does Andrew Young want me to call him?" There was in irritated disdain in his voice, as though he thought Andrew was being a gnat. I always defended Andrew because of the bond we shared. We both loved Johnny, and I knew how badly Andrew felt now that Elizabeth had pushed him out of Johnny's life.

"That's me. He was trying to locate you for me."

"Oh." Johnny immediately softened. I could tell that he was tired.

"Why didn't you call me last night?" I asked in a very curious and concerned manner, given it was so out of character. "Or this morning?"

"I don't know."

He sounded really tired and because he had just been with Elizabeth for a long stretch of time, he also sounded as though he was back to his old disconnected self.

"I had a doctor appointment, remember?"

"I do."

"I am pregnant."

He paused and then said, "I'm not surprised." He paused again, softening even more. "I want to be clear that whatever you decide, this is your decision, and I will support you in whatever decision you make." His tone was kind, gracious, and not remotely upset. "This is your body, your life, and it's a big change. I don't think you really understand how big, but there is no way I could tell you what to do with your own body."

I was surprised that his tone was so gentle. I had really thought he was going to be upset. But I think somehow he had already sensed that this was going to be the outcome.

So on July 11th, 2007, both Johnny Edwards, the father of my child, and Andrew Young, the man who would later claim to be the father of my child, became aware that I was pregnant. To me this is an important fact (which my phone records and medical records support) because the criminal prosecution alleges that Bunny Mellon's money was solicited in or around the month of May to support hiding me and my pregnancy.

Johnny also never wavered from what he said to me initially. He never asked me to get an abortion. He always stuck to what he originally said: it was my choice and he would support whatever choice I made. Since the moment I knew that I was with child, I never had a single doubt about what I was going to do: bring this child into the world.

When I found out that I was pregnant, the focus and priorities of my life completely changed. I spent most of the next month reading and educating myself about pregnancy. I discovered (to my shock and surprise) that most women were at their most fertile not during ovulation, but a few days before. IMPORTANT INFORMATION that I did not know! (Commence blond jokes now.)

I remember lunching at Soho House twice with Mimi and Jonathan Darman, and being a little concerned that Darman would notice that I wasn't drinking and would guess the reason. Darman didn't seem to notice or at least never publicly claimed to after the fact. I remember talking about going to Martha's Vineyard with him for Labor Day but I realized at the time that it wouldn't happen because I would probably be showing by then.

Actually, I didn't travel at all until the very end of July and wasn't remotely interested in doing so. The intense need to see Johnny that I had felt before I was pregnant had now diminished.

Lisa Blue flew me to LA at the end of July. I believe it was the same day that Johnny and Elizabeth renewed their vows and *People* got their exclusive article (and photos) of the big event. I had completely let go of my negative feelings about that, which was no mean feat because it went against everything I believe in. But I had to. From everything I could see, their relationship was not going to change, and it was never going to be a real relationship. She wasn't going to stop abusing him, and he wasn't going to stop hiding. I knew Johnny loved her and she wanted this, and now that she was dying, he really wanted to give her anything she wanted. And what she wanted was for the whole world to think she had overcome their little "glitch" in their marriage, and that they were the now a happy couple once again. My feeling was, if what people thought about her was really important to her, so be it.

But the reality of the situation was that Johnny was no longer just my boyfriend; he was now the father of my child. So regardless of what would happen between us, I would be involved with him for the rest of my life.

I also realized the dynamic, good and bad, that would exist between her father and me would be in my daughter's head. So when I discovered I was pregnant, I decided that I would continue doing everything in my power not to complain or be nasty to him in any way, but to love him unconditionally as he grew in awareness and became the man that I knew he was underneath that mask of fear.

So I let any and all anger go. My utmost priority was my child. Also, even though my relationship with Johnny was highly passionate, I decided that I did not want to have any emotional highs and lows. I wanted my child immersed and growing in love, peace, and calmness. I began to monitor all my reactions with a vigilance I had never used before.

I began talking to my unborn baby. I really believed I was carrying a boy. The baby felt so strong to me, so willful. (I sure got that part right.)

While I was in LA visiting Lisa, I saw Johnny for two nights and he had never been sweeter to me. I remember thinking, "Wow, he should renew his vows more often!"

I went to the doctor on August 6th. All was well with my baby, and I got another ultrasound picture. The moment I saw it, I thought, "That's a girl." The forehead and profile looked exactly like a profile picture of me as a little girl that hung in our hallway in Florida. But

I dismissed the thought because my baby felt so strong-willed that I still didn't believe that she could actually be a girl.

I flew back to LA again. Flying across the country is expensive, and I remember Johnny was concerned that I was going to run out of money because I hadn't worked since December and was clearly spending money to come and see him. I told him not to worry about it. I had plenty of airline miles. Lisa had paid for my last trip, and Andrew had been taking care of my travel since June.

He said okay and moved on to the next thing.

I would discover that the problem with this was a communication problem. Most people would assume that taking care of travel meant picking up the bill, that taking care of something automatically meant financially. Johnny doesn't think that way. To Johnny, taking care of something or someone is helping them fix or solve a problem. If Johnny says, "I am going to take care of it," it does not mean he is going to pay for you or support you, so you never have to work again. It would mean he would help you solve or fix whatever challenge you had before you. Johnny later told me that when I told him that Andrew had taken care of my travel, it didn't register with him that Andrew was actually giving me money.

When I read the indictment in 2011, I was shocked to see that Andrew had already received one hundred thousand dollars from Bunny Mellon by the second week of August 2007. One hundred thousand dollars! That is a lot of money for plane tickets! If Johnny really knew that Andrew was receiving that kind of money, why would he be concerned that I was going to run out of money? What I believe is this: Had Johnny known about the money that he had supposedly solicited for me, he would have said something to me about it. He would have wanted to make sure that I, his girlfriend and mother of his child, was getting the money—all of it.

I mean, really? Andrew the employee, who was already making a substantial salary from Johnny, gets eighty-four thousand dollars, and the unemployed girlfriend and mother of his child gets sixteen thousand dollars? Are you kidding me?

I flew to Las Vegas on August 21st for the night. We had room service, and I was so nauseated I couldn't eat. I read in the indictment, almost four years later, that Andrew received another check the next day in the amount of one hundred thousand dollars, bringing the grand total to two hundred thousand dollars! I also remember Andrew offered to give me an additional one thousand dollars that month, which I thought was very nice of him. I was very grateful for his gift of six thousand dollars that month instead of five thousand dollars.

Believing Andrew was a very stupid, stupid thing to do. I shouldn't be too hard on myself, though, because I'm in very good company. Johnny, Bunny, Fred, the media, the US government, and most of America have also taken a little boat ride on this same ship of stupidity. The only one person (that I know of) who actually saw this correctly was Elizabeth.

So let's see: the grand totals we have are staffer, $178,000; girlfriend and mother of his child, twenty-two thousand dollars!

In late August I flew to Orlando, Florida, for one night and then to the Westin Diplomat in Hollywood. In Orlando, Johnny stayed at some weird place that had front and back sections with fifteen or more buildings in each section. It took me a comically long time to find him, and when we found each other, our mutual reaction upon sight was *explosive*. I still remember being surprised about that.

As usual, we had a great night. At one point he said to me very playfully and lovingly, "You are going to keep this baby, aren't you?"

"Yes, I am."

"Well," he said, "I am just going to accept it then."

I smiled. "Yes, you are."

I left long after he did and flew to Miami. This was the first and only time that Andrew reserved a room in his own name for me, in the same hotel that Johnny was going to stay in, which enabled me to have my own room. I put on my bathing suit and went out to the beach café for lunch.

There was a full moon that night, August 28th. Johnny and I sat out on his balcony looking at the moon over the ocean for a long time. He had just been with President Carter, his wife, Rosalynn, and Elizabeth.

Johnny came to New York the first week of September, and, of course, we stayed at the Regency.

I began feeling that I needed to move out of New Jersey. I needed to find a remote place to live and have my baby in peace. But I also wanted to be somewhat close to Johnny. I wanted my baby to grow up near his or her father. I began searching the Internet for places to rent in North Carolina and began talking to Andrew about what it was like to live there. Andrew had sold his house and was moving into a huge rental house while he and his wife built their dream home. He said repeatedly how huge and nice their rental house was and that I should just come down and stay with them. I replied, "I may take you up on that."

When I mentioned to Johnny that I was thinking of moving to North Carolina, he had one response, which he never deviated from: "That is a *bad idea*."

Darman called to tell me that Sam Stein from *The Huffington Post* contacted him, claiming he was looking into my webisodes and asked for my contact information. Darman said he refused and immediately called me to tell me. Darman was naturally skeptical about Stein's claims given that it was September 2007 and the webisodes were long gone. I thanked Darman for not giving out my information and requested that he please continue to refuse to give it to anyone.

I had a doctor's appointment on September 17th, the one where I finally got to find out whether my baby was a girl or a boy. Even though the last ultrasound looked like a girl to me, I really thought the baby was a boy, given how strong-willed the baby seemed. I was blown away when the doctor told me, "It's a girl."

I would never have guessed what my reaction would be.

I went to my car and cried. The reality of it, the shock of it being different than I originally thought and now knowing was just overwhelming. When you're pregnant, emotions really come out of nowhere and wash over you like a tidal wave. It's an odd experience. I can't even begin to express how grateful I am that I was blessed with a little girl—or how surprised I was at Johnny's reaction when I told him later that night in Washington.

I had taken the train down. I did not know it then, but it was to be the last night we would spend together in its entirety for a long time.

He was in a great mood. If I remember correctly, he had just come from Teddy and Vicky Kennedy's house. He was in a great mood anytime he was with them. Johnny would light up whenever he talked about Teddy.

"Guess what the baby is."

"A boy."

"Nope, a girl."

"That is so *cool!*" He kissed me as he rubbed my belly. He was clearly very excited.

We had such a great night. I remember him kissing me goodbye in the morning and the passion involved. To think about it now, even after all these years, still makes me smile.

There was a big debate at Dartmouth College in New Hampshire on September 26th. Johnny told me that he and Elizabeth had had yet another huge fight before the debate and many people on the campaign were concerned their screaming would be heard because they were in a small hotel.

Also before the debate, Andrew sent me a link to a house, near the one he was renting in the Governors Club in Chapel Hill, North Carolina. He thought I might like it, and I did. It certainly looked nice, but I wasn't really focused it because the debate was about to happen.

I watched the debate on TV from Jersey, and then, unbeknownst to me, at 11:34 P.M. on September 26th, 2007, Stein posted his blog, and my entire life was about to change. Again.

FOURTEEN

Knock, Knock

"Today is your day! Your mountain is waiting. So...get on your way!"

—Dr. Seuss

THE NEXT MORNING, September 27th, I was on my way into New York City to have lunch with Glory. Mimi was driving when Andrew called to tell me that the Sam Stein piece about the missing webisodes was up. He read it to me over the phone.

I was wearing a dress that was the last piece of clothing I owned that successfully hid my pregnancy. I had been thinking about sharing the news of my pregnancy with Glory, but now, with the new issues that arose on the drive in, I didn't mention it, nor could she tell.

At lunch, we talked a lot about the Stein piece.

Later that afternoon, after I was back in Jersey, Johnny called. I don't know whether he was in between events or on his run time, but not surprisingly, Elizabeth had flipped out about *The Huffington Post* piece and was screaming at everyone. Apparently what she was most freaked out about was that people would be able to see me in the webisode.

"What are you talking about?" I asked.

"Aren't you in the piece? Isn't there a version with you in them?"

"In the first version, seventeen billion cuts ago, but not the final cut that was online before Elizabeth had them removed."

"Are you sure?"

"Yes."

"Will you look at them and make sure?"

"Yes, I will look at them *again*, and tell you."

"Okay, I gotta go. I'll call you back."

At around 4:30 P.M., I was sitting on the couch in front of the fireplace, about to view the webisodes on my computer again. It was after school, and Mimi's boys were in and out. The outer door at Mimi's house was wide open. Out of the corner of my eye, I saw a guy in khaki pants and a light blue shirt walk past the window, heading for the front door. Mimi saw him from the other window in the family room and told me she immediately thought it was Sam Stein. He had recently emailed her a few times attempting to get information and copies of the webisodes. It never occurred to her that it had gone beyond *The Huffington Post*.

She went to the door and the man with an English accent asked for me. Mimi told him I wasn't there, although I was sitting about six feet from the front door. He gave her his card. She saw the *National Enquirer* logo on his card, and she promptly told him to get the fuck off her property and slammed the door in his face.

She turned to me as she walked into the kitchen and said, "Pack a bag. It's time for you to go. *That* was the fucking *National Enquirer*!"

I walked upstairs and my phone rang again. It was Johnny calling me back about the webisodes. I told him that the *National Enquirer* had just been at the front door.

"Are they still there?"

"I don't know. I am in Cole's room right now and the windows face the rear of the house. I am going to pack a bag and get out of here."

"Okay."

"Okay, I gotta go."

"Okay. I'll call you."

I called Andrew immediately. "The *National Enquirer* just knocked on the door. I gotta get out of here. I'm going to buy a ticket. I'll call you back."

I went upstairs and bought a roundtrip ticket to Raleigh-Durham International Airport, 8:30 P.M. flight, returning in a couple of weeks

As I was on my computer, I saw an email from Pigeon O'Brien, the woman who had designed my website, and to whom I hadn't spoken or been in any contact with since early Spring 2006. I read the message, which was very weird; she was writing as though we'd been in close contact for the last year, as if I had spoken to her the day before. To make things even weirder, it was sent at 4:18 in the afternoon, right around the time the *Enquirer* was knocking on my door.

Her email read: "Okay, so my nerves are on edge and I can only imagine yours. But I am sending good thoughts to you. I am a little baffled.... Call if you can." (She gave her phone number.) "I hope you are well. I know that you are. Big smooches from here. Cats and dogs and fishes are all sending love. As do I."

I knew instantly that Pigeon had something to do with the *National Enquirer*, but I couldn't focus on that because I needed to get the hell out of Dodge. I packed one bag—my red suitcase with wheels that I used when I worked for Johnny. It was easy to pack given my clothing options were limited to the few new pregnancy clothes I had purchased. I packed them and my toiletries.

I did not pack my computer or any personal contents from my room, including my hatbox where I kept my prized possessions. I was the target, and my mission was now to keep my daughter hidden.

I called Andrew and told him what flight I was on. He told me he would pick me up. I changed my clothes, put on my new pregnancy jeans and a black T-shirt, and threw on a black three-quarter-length cotton coat. I kissed and hugged my godsons, Jack and Cole, goodbye. After fully scouting the area for any lurking *Enquirer* reporters, Mimi pulled the car around the back and put my suitcase in the car. I went down the back stairs, got in the car, and crouched down to remain out of view until we were well away from the house.

Andrew picked me up from the airport in his brand-new, souped-up silver Jeep—the tires were the size of tractor wheels. I guess because he wasn't driving for the senator anymore he traded in his Suburban for something a little flashier. Apparently shock absorbers don't come with these mammoth-wheeled machines, either. To make matters worse, Andrew had yet to master how to keep the top securely fastened, and it threatened to blow off while we were driving. I would have found the whole thing really funny had I not been five months pregnant, able to feel every bump in the road, and close to vomiting the entire ride. Johnny called during our ride and asked, "Are you okay?"

"Yes."

"Where are you?"

"With Andrew."

"Yes, but where are you?"

"North Carolina."

"Oh."

And that "oh" was not a happy "oh," or a, "Thank God you're here oh." That "oh" was a deflated "oh," a "that sucks 'oh.'" Johnny never thought it was a good idea for me to be anywhere near North Carolina, yet here I was *in* North Carolina. The *National Enquirer* was after me, and I was going to hide out for a few days twenty minutes away from Elizabeth? He was clearly less than thrilled with this development. I really believe that if Johnny had anything to do with this decision, I would have been on a plane to France or some other country halfway around the world from Elizabeth.

After I hung up with Johnny, Andrew said, "You need to come up with another name for my kids to call you, given that they may run into Jack and Emma. We don't want them saying 'Rielle is at our house.'"

I said, "How about Jaya? Jaya James, James was my dad's name." Jaya was the name of a character in a screenplay I had written and rewritten for about three years. I had to repeat Jaya a few times for Andrew so he could pronounce it.

And that's how my alias was born. That alias ended up on my daughter's birth certificate because the hospital needed to tie my medical records to her birth records.

I got to Andrew's deluxe rental house in the Governors Club and met Cheri Young for the first time. Andrew had told me that she was shy about meeting me because she was wearing a head monitor because she was getting migraine headaches and the doctors were trying to determine what was going on. Andrew had told me over and over that she was just a "sweetie" and that I would love her. Let's just say sweet is not a word I would ever use to describe Cheri.

What appeared to be going on at first glance was not too different from many marriages I had seen before: angry wife is unaware that she is really pissed at herself for staying with this sorry excuse for a human being and projects it all on to him, as if it were his fault for her being in this mess.

Cheri was not someone who would ever be my friend under any circumstances. No friendly vibes, no "same wavelength." In fact, if she were someone I met at a party, I wouldn't spend a moment talking to her. She was clearly the exact opposite of Andrew. He was like a Golden Retriever puppy—sweet, devoted, harmless, and needing a lot of attention. Cheri was more like an abused miniature Doberman Pinscher. But all I could think of at the time was: God bless her. She had some contraption on her head, three kids under the age of six (two with health problems), an absent husband who was avoiding her at all costs, and now he has invited his great love's pregnant lover to stay in their house. Oh, this was going to be interesting.

During the next few days, it became clear that the *National Enquirer* was probably going to publish something about me because its reporters had attempted to contact everyone who remotely knew me. I could see that it was just going to be a matter of time before something was published. I believe it was Lisa who first recommended that I get a lawyer because I needed someone to protect me.

Andrew took me to the AT&T store where I got a new phone and phone number, under a different name and account that he paid for. We also looked at houses to rent. The one from the link he had sent me was also in the Governors Club, a gated community, and it was the one that seemed the best. It was available starting October 11th; the rent was around twenty-seven hundred dollars a month.

According to Johnny, he met with Lisa, Fred, and Elizabeth in Iowa, where Elizabeth screamed at Fred and Lisa for being my friend. I was told that Elizabeth went on to harass Lisa about this long after Fred had passed away. When I heard that, I felt really sad—hadn't Lisa been through enough?

During the meeting in Iowa, as Elizabeth screamed at everyone, Fred and Lisa were talking about a lawyer for me, mentioning two that they thought would be good. One was described as very good-looking, and Elizabeth screamed, "That's what the whore needs, the good-looking one! Give her the good-looking one." I have no idea what her thinking was on that, but thanks to Elizabeth, Lisa called and gave me the number of the good-looking lawyer, who I called immediately.

Oddly enough, given that he came through Elizabeth's request, he turned out not only to be a great lawyer but one of the greatest people on the planet. And even though he is no longer my lawyer, he is someone I will always call a dear friend.

This lawyer, Rob Gordon, made it clear to Fred and Lisa right away that if he became my lawyer, he could no longer talk to them about me unless I gave him permission to do so. He was my lawyer, and my interests were the ones he was protecting, not theirs. I cannot even begin to convey the level of Rob's integrity and selflessness. He worked his ass off in order to protect my privacy (and later my daughter's) and refused any and all payment from Fred for representing me.

I spoke to Rob for the first time while I was sitting on the stairs in Andrew's rental house. I felt immediately emotionally supported and extremely grateful for having him in my corner.

Using one of Andrew's borrowed laptops, I responded to Pigeon's email on September 30th. In my email I wrote, "I have no idea what you're thinking about all this, and I can't talk about anything to anyone to set anything straight...and it's not at all what it seems...." I signed it "with love," which is how I used to sign everything back then. I had no idea what she would do, but given she wasn't actually my friend and had many emotional problems, I thought anything was possible.

Cheri's parents were coming to stay with the Youngs. Andrew was not at all happy about this because he believed they hated him. Clearly I needed to leave their house but I needed a car. Andrew told me I should pick out whatever I wanted. Well, that's fine and dandy, but who is going to pay for it? Andrew told me that he and Cheri had just sold their house in Raleigh and made a lot of money so they had plenty of cash and would just need to get reimbursed at a later date. Andrew mentioned over and over how lucky I was timing-wise given that they had so much extra cash flow. They could afford to float me for a while and Andrew was adamant about I should buy whatever car I wanted.

I picked out a used BMW X3. I thought it would be the perfect mommy car. Johnny had a different reaction. He flipped out! "A BMW? What? How are you going to pay for that? What is Andrew doing buying you a BMW?" (In retrospect, that does not at all sound like someone who had Andrew solicit a bunch of money—three hundred and fifty thousand dollars by this point—to keep me happy.) I told Johnny that Andrew had said over and over that it wasn't a problem because they had sold their house in Raleigh, had plenty of cash, and would only need to be reimbursed later. Apparently that was the same story that Andrew had also told Johnny. (And shockingly enough that actually turned out to be true. They did have plenty of cash from the sale of their house to pay for my expenses.)

As we talked further, it became clear to me that Johnny also thought—or was terrified—that I had some fancy ideas in my head about moving down to North Carolina, just moving myself right in to become the next Mrs. John Edwards. I set him straight about that right then and there. I did not and still do not want to get married. That's just not who I am. I was married once before and it didn't work out. Life is too unpredictable to commit to someone for the rest of your life.

I felt him calming down a bit. I meant what I had said and knew that he believed me.

Because I needed to vacate the Youngs' fancy rental house while Cheri's parents were visiting, I settled on going up to Blowing Rock, North Carolina, for a few days, where I had shown horses and vacationed as a child. I was actually very excited about it because I had not been there in a very long time.

Johnny came over to the Youngs' rental house before I left and brought me one of his black cashmere sweaters for my trip to Blowing Rock. I didn't own a sweater that would fit me because it hadn't got cold yet and I hadn't gotten around to purchasing any cold-weather pregnancy clothes.

Johnny and I were the only ones in the house for a few hours. We sat out on the deck talking for a while and spent some time in the room I was staying in. Johnny was surprised by how much he loved me in North Carolina. I was very calm, peaceful, and relaxed. He claimed that I wasn't like that in New York.

I would later revisit this time with Johnny many times when I heard rumors in 2009 that Andrew claimed he had an intimate video of me when I was pregnant. I wondered whether Andrew had taped us without our knowledge because the only private video we had ever made was in 2006. I had destroyed it (or at least thought I had) and more importantly, I wasn't pregnant in 2006. Did Andrew tape us? Did he steal footage and reassemble a new tape, then lie about the pregnant part? Or was he bluffing? I didn't know.

When I left Andrew's house to go to Blowing Rock, I packed all the belongings I had. I left nothing behind. I made sure there was no trace of me in my room because Cheri's parents were going to be staying in that room. It was easy to do given I had only a few clothes and toiletries. All of my personal belongings were still with Mimi, in my attic room in New Jersey.

I stayed at the Graylyn International Conference Center in Winston-Salem, North Carolina. I headed to Blowing Rock in the morning, where I stayed at the Chetola Resort. I went to some outlet stores and bought a bunch of Ralph Lauren towels for my new rental house. I went shopping on Main Street and found the most amazing Bella Notte pink quilt that I bought for my baby. All of this would eventually disappear from my house, along with many of my personal items that further benefited Andrew's book sales.

(Strangely enough, the statue of St. Francis, which I had also bought for my daughter in Blowing Rock, remained in my rental house untouched—no doubt a weird deity to the Youngs.)

I was in an upstairs store on Main Street looking at bed skirts when my cell rang. I looked at the caller ID. It was Jonathan Prince, with whom I hadn't spoken since I gave him all the video footage in January 2007. I picked up, skipping any salutation, and immediately asked, "How did you get my number?"

"Lisa Blue." Then, without missing a beat, he said, "The *National Enquirer* claims they have emails from you telling someone about an affair with John Edwards. Have you ever emailed anyone about anything that names John Edwards?"

I replied that I had never sent an email identifying John Edwards to anyone, to the best of my recollection. But I could search through my email and see for sure if that's correct. The only email I could recall was one I sent in the spring of 2006, which mentioned a John from North Carolina with small kids. Yeah, so what? There are a million Johns in North Carolina with small kids.

He asked again, "Did you ever identify John Edwards in an email?"

"No, I don't believe so, but let me check and make sure."

"Okay, get back to me."

"Okay."

I hung up and my first thought was: Pigeon. I almost called Jay to say, "WTF?" But I didn't; I saved it for when we had lunch in New York in 2009. Jay's reply was, "Pigeon said to me she had nothing to do with it."

"Jay, please. She sold the *Enquirer* emails. They printed them. It was her."

After Blowing Rock I returned to Andrew's house and parked the car in the second garage underneath the house, adjacent to the basement, because Cheri's parents were still there. I was in the basement talking to Prince. The *Enquirer* was going forward with the story, and he thought I should comment. I disagreed. If the *Enquirer* got a comment from me, it could use my name. Because I was a private citizen, the story couldn't name me until I commented; if they printed it without me commenting it would be libel. From my end, I was attempting to hold on to my privacy and I didn't want to lie.

Prince thought I should comment so that it would dissuade the mainstream media from chasing the story. I just had no idea what the frenzy would be like. He really understood the media; I did not.

The problem was that what Prince wanted was something I couldn't deliver, which he had no way of knowing. I couldn't lie. And not only did he want a denial of an affair, he wanted me to say something about how much I respected John and Elizabeth's marriage.

Yeah, right. Why didn't I just say I was abducted by aliens?

Clearly, I did not respect a marriage filled with lies and abuse nor could I bring myself to say that I did.

I left the basement of the Youngs' rental house and went to a pricey bed-and-breakfast that Andrew had picked out and arranged. I stayed there for a few days before I moved into my rental house.

I was at that bed and breakfast when the *Enquirer* piece came out. I remember going for a walk on a trail near the B&B and feeling paranoid that people would recognize me.

The *Enquirer* did not name me, but the story was filled with BS, like how the affair started and ended. As Prince predicted, the mainstream media went into a feeding frenzy—the first of hundreds that I would experience—in which I was the target and information about my life was under siege. The amount of energy that goes into pursuing a scandal is still baffling to me.

My lawyer, Rob, had to have security escort members of the press out of his waiting room and building in New York City. Mimi and her family were hounded and seriously harassed.

I called Jonathan Darman and asked him what would happen if I responded to ABC, as opposed to issuing a statement online, which is what Prince wanted me to do. He told me that if I responded to mainstream, everyone would report on it, but if I kept it online, chances are it wouldn't jump. But if I were to give it to anyone, I should give it to him. I don't remember if he pitched himself first but I remember feeling angry. I was asking him as my friend to tell me how the media works, and he pitched himself. (He showed me how the media works, all right.) We hung up and soon after, he sent me an email. It's one of the few I saved. It said:

> Hey, Left you a message a little while ago. I wanted to talk with you because our last conversation left me with a weird feeling. I know this is the last thing you're thinking about right now but I think for the sake of our friendship, which has always been based on mutual trust and demands openness and honesty to survive, we need to set up some ground rules for going forward. From here on out, as long as this stupid story is alive, I can't talk to you "between you and me." We can talk off the record from now until the end of time if you wish and I can give you MY WORD—as a friend, as a journalist, as a human being—that nothing you tell me will ever appear in Newsweek unless you want it to. But the fact remains that I cover John Edwards and I have to be able to talk openly with my bosses about a story that involves him. Even if I'm not involved in our coverage, I can't conceal information from them, nor do I want to, especially when you're telling me this whole story is bullshit. I can tell my bosses that anything you say to me is off the record and it can't show up in our coverage, if we ever choose to pursue this story. But I am required to be

open with them about this, and everything else. It's not that I don't value our friendship. This is the way I'd have to operate with a story concerning anyone, even a member of my own family. In fact, it IS the way I operate with a member of my own family, my dad. SO considering all that, I understand if you choose not to talk to me in the same way you would another friend. And I understand if you choose not to talk to me at all. That would suck, of course, because I don't want to lose touch with you, now or ever. And I also think it is in your interest to keep talking to me, because I think this story is total bullshit, while every other journalist in the world starts with the assumption that it's true. Even if I can't be completely helpful to you as a friend right now, I can be helpful to you as a journalist, much more helpful than anyone else around. Anyway, I hope you've read this far without getting really pissed off or feeling dirty. Please understand that I'm saying all of this not to put distance between us, simply to make sure we preserve total honesty. You've got a million other things to think about right now, you don't need weirdness from me. So I hope I hear from you soon. I'll be thinking about you, as always. XO J

I read this and thought, "I will address this tomorrow. Right now I need to write a statement." It was difficult for me but I did the best I could. The *National Enquirer* had inadvertently helped because (thanks to Pigeon's assumptions) it had gotten so many facts wrong. Rob sent my statement to MyDD, a political blog. It read:

The innuendoes and lies that have appeared on the internet and in the *National Enquirer* concerning John Edwards are not true, completely unfounded and ridiculous.

My video production company was hired by the Edwards camp on a 6 month contract, which we completed December 31st, 2006.

When working for the Edwards camp, my conduct as well as the conduct of my entire team was completely professional.

This concocted story is just dirty politics and I want no part of it.

I said my piece. It was a total nondenial, and boy, did I want no part of what was going on. From what I could see online, it looked like it seemed to work. Mostly everyone accepted what I said.

I responded the next day to Darman:

> thanks for your email. what i meant by "between you and me" was in fact "OFF THE RECORD" the mistake in language was my mistake, given the swirl i was in. so let me be perfectly clear, EVERYTHING that i have EVER said to you was said OFF THE RECORD. with the exception of course when you did that piece on the webisodes in nov 06. thanks. i'll be in touch. until then, lots of love to you, rielle

He responded:

> Cool. FYI, Charlotte Observer called me today looking for a number for you, New York mag and NY Post yesterday. Obv didn't return any of the calls. And from what I'm hearing, Sam Stein says he was personally given the original assignment by Arianna. Mickey Kaus, her buddy, had a weird item today on "knowing how this whole thing got started." You holding up?

I did not respond.

I really loved Darman; in fact, I still do. I valued our friendship greatly but there was no way I could talk to him. As any mother knows, my baby was my number-one priority, and I was going to do everything in my power to protect her safety, privacy, and peace. *Everything else* paled in comparison.

I was done. No more media for me.

Or so I thought.

FIFTEEN

"She Even Denied She Was Rielle Hunter!"

"Life is hard. It's even harder when you're stupid."
—JOHN WAYNE

MOVED INTO MY RENTAL HOUSE with no furniture. I slept on an air mattress provided by the Youngs for the few nights before the beds were delivered. Andrew had taken me to a mattress store to buy a queen, full, and two twin mattresses for the small three-bedroom house.

Mimi packed up all my stuff in New Jersey, including my hatbox and all its contents, and drove it all down to me. She helped me unpack it all and stayed for the weekend.

Mimi later brought the boys back down for Thanksgiving, and we had a great time together. In early November I got an email from Jonathan Darman telling me he'd had a dream about me and he woke up thinking about how much he missed me. He hoped I was well and asked me to call when I could. I thought of him lovingly while I read the email but I did not respond.

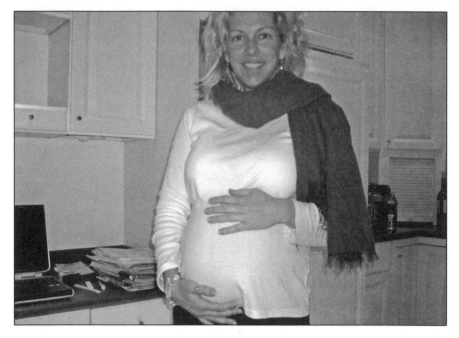

In the kitchen of my North Carolina rental house, November 2007.

I saw Johnny twice while I was living in my rental house. Once, Andrew met him at the gate, and once I did. I later wondered many times whether Andrew somehow taped us without our knowledge on these occasions, but I just didn't know.

Frequently I would go to the Youngs' rental house to walk on the treadmill. I never took anything with me other than a bottle of water and my cell phone. I would drive over, walk on the treadmill (usually during *The Chris Matthews Show*), and then drive home.

After exercising one day, I was standing in the kitchen talking to Cheri about Andrew and how he had such an easy time lying. He could just lie about anything and everything at the drop of a hat. Cheri claimed that she had a difficult time lying, that she couldn't even lie when she was returning something to a store about why she was returning it. Either she was lying then or she learned well by studying at the feet of a master—her husband.

Cheri was always very generous about sharing food. They had a big pantry that was always filled with food, and she would constantly tell me to help myself. I did think the way they shopped was odd. They shopped as though they were made of money, not like a family living on a political staffer's salary. I shrugged it off and figured that having three kids, you'd always want to be fully supplied. I also thought it was odd that Andrew purchased a TV for my rental house. It was too large for the armoire I had ordered from a Pottery Barn catalogue. I thought Andrew would return the super-large TV, but it instead ended up in his house. They weren't using it but it was out of the box, saved. I shrugged that off and decided he just hadn't gotten around to returning it yet.

I never extended the same liberties with my rental house. I value my privacy and have many boundaries about my personal space. The only time they came to my house was to drop off groceries or to help me assemble a piece of furniture. They never came to my house just to hang out. Cheri and I were friendly to each other. We tried hard to bond. We even went out to dinner once, but it was just not easy between us. There was no easy flow of communication. Andrew, on the other hand, was my friend. I loved him. He was easygoing, fun to talk to and joke with, and handy around the house. He would often go to the grocery store for me, put up curtains, or assemble furniture. He was always available and always offering to help.

My house was sparse, but I was trying to make it homey. I was nesting, after all. During the two months in my rental house in North Carolina, even though we saw each other only twice, Johnny and I spoke on the phone constantly.

Once, Johnny told me he was walking into the NPR debate, and Hillary Clinton stopped him and asked if she could talk to him for a minute privately. This was his first real interaction with her, before he began to get to know her and before he began to see her as a real human being and not just an opponent. When he was relating this story to me, I could feel his defensiveness, his posturing at her request. He retorted with, "Anything you need to say to me you can say right here."

She replied, "I didn't have anything to do with the *National Enquirer*."

He said, "What do you mean?"

"The Rielle Hunter story. I had nothing to do with it." Looking him straight in the eye, she went on, "Given my life, it is not something I would do."

He said, "Yeah, you might not have, but that doesn't mean your campaign didn't."

After he told me this story, I was silent. I paused for a long time. It had just hit me for the first time that two different realities had collided. All I could think was: Hillary Clinton knows my name?

While I was busy nesting and making a baby—going for walks, doing yoga, napping, etc.—Andrew told me he was going to ask David Kirby, Johnny's best friend, for money for reimbursement. He told me that he told David that he needed to borrow money for his new house (to pay his builder or something), and David was hesitant. So Andrew told me that he asked Johnny to call David and tell David that he was good for it, and that Johnny would pay him back if Andrew couldn't. Johnny did.

From what I gathered, I was never mentioned as the reason for the reimbursement; it was a loan for Andrew. But there was a problem: Andrew was annoyed that David couldn't lend him more than twenty-five thousand dollars at the time. Andrew wanted more so Andrew said no. Of course, now I am thinking, why would Johnny tell David, his best friend, that he was good for the money if he knew Andrew had already received three hundred and fifty thousand dollars from Bunny Mellon?

What I find even more astonishing is that, after saying no to David, Andrew then told me he was going to ask Bunny for money *and* he told me that she gave him two checks, each for twenty-five thousand dollars. He said that he never deposited those two checks because of what happened on December 12th.

Yes, December 12th, 2007, was a big day.

That was the day that the *National Enquirer* showed up in Cary, North Carolina, and took a picture of me pregnant in the Whole Foods Market parking lot. This is, hands down, the worst picture of me ever taken in my life.

So there I was on December 12th in North Carolina, living a happy, secluded, making-a-baby, don't-even-go-to-the-grocery-store life (unless it's a store that's far, far away from Elizabeth's neck of the woods), and this was my big "I am in so much pain I can barely move" outing of the week, which was to go to the OB/GYN office in Cary, and to the Whole Foods store, which was across the street. It was my first visit to a grocery store in a very long time (Andrew or Cheri would usually shop for me to prevent the possibility of me running into anyone), and, despite my pain, I was very excited about that.

At that point in my pregnancy, I was in a lot of pain. I could barely walk. I was sitting on a "special" pillow in the car, which also didn't help. During the drive to the doctor, I was talking to Andrew on the phone. He claimed he had just returned from Bunny's house in Virginia, and that she had given him twenty-five thousand dollars, which he claimed he never deposited. (According to public records, he actually received $175,000 on that day!) I remember this call vividly, given that later, in my head, I went over and over my drive to the doctor's office, and I am positive I was not being followed. These were long country roads; I would have seen someone following me.

I got to the office, parked right by the door, and went in. On my way out, I thought about putting my sunglasses on but decided against it given I was just popping across the street to Whole Foods. It hurt too much to try and maneuver my bag to the other shoulder to dig for the sunglasses. Pregnancy was not kind to my forty-three-year-old body!

When I walked outside and got in my car, I noticed a man standing about two cars away on the sidewalk. I started the car and drove across the street. I went into Whole Foods and shopped slowly. It was evening by the time I was done—no need for those sunglasses while I pushed the filled cart slowly to the car. I saw that same guy who had been standing outside the doctor's office walking toward me. I opened the trunk of the car and began putting the bags there.

He continued walked quickly toward me. "Rielle, I am from the *National Enquirer*. Are you pregnant with John Edwards's baby?"

To my right, a photographer appeared out of nowhere and began snapping pictures, circling all around me.

"Are you six months pregnant with John Edwards's baby?"

"Please leave me alone. I don't know what you're talking about." I kept loading my groceries. I just kept repeating the same thing over and over to every question he asked: "Please leave me alone. I don't know what you're talking about. Please leave me alone."

"Are you Rielle Hunter?"

"I don't know what you are talking about. Please leave me alone."

He kept firing questions while the photographer snapped photos. It was an ambush.

I remember someone coming up to me, a fellow shopper, and asking if I were all right and asking if I needed any help. Team *National Enquirer* buggered off, and this shopper said to me, "What were they doing? I have never seen anything like that." I said, "Yes, thank you. I'm all right," and got in my car. I called Andrew.

As I drove away, I saw the so-called reporter in his car and the photographer in another car, a blue SUV.

I told Andrew that the *National Enquirer* had just photographed me in the parking lot of Whole Foods. He laughed as though he thought I was kidding. "I'm not kidding. This isn't a joke. I was just photographed by the *National Enquirer*."

"You're serious?"

"Yes!"

I related as much as I could. "Shit," Andrew said. "Okay, let me find him. Are they following you?"

"No, they're not. I saw their cars. They are not."

"Okay, I'll call you back."

Johnny was on the campaign bus preparing for an event when John Davis told him that Andrew was on the line. Johnny told me he said, "I'll call him later," and John replied, "It's urgent."

Johnny went to the back of the bus and got on the phone. "What's up?"

"We have a problem, boss. They photographed her," Andrew said.

"Who?"

"The *National Enquirer*. They photographed her in a parking lot. It's really weird, boss. She acts like nothing happened."

When Johnny told me about this exchange later, we both wondered why Andrew said that. If you know me, and Johnny does, it's an odd thing for Andrew to say, so it stuck in Johnny's head when Andrew said it. Of course, now we understand that Andrew had an entirely different agenda. Was he trying to deflect from himself?

Was he insinuating that I had tipped off the *National Enquirer*? Believe me, I have been accused of that countless times. In fact, in 2009 I signed a statement under oath saying that I had never directly or indirectly contacted the *National Enquirer* or any other tabloid, or received money from them, directly or indirectly. Shockingly enough, I am actually not a big fan of the *National Enquirer*. Aside from stalking me via satellite, completely invading my privacy, printing the worst possible pictures of me, and continually making up stories, the publication's staff has continually and relentlessly attempted to contact me and anyone who knows me. The *Enquirer's* audacity never ceases to amaze me. In fact, recently the *Enquirer* contacted one of my lawyers to offer me yet another interview for compensation. The only compensation I would accept from the *Enquirer* would be if it agreed to shut down forever!

Andrew called back with Johnny on the line. I related to him everything about the incident. He said that he had to go do an event but that he would call back.

I drove back to my house and, instead of turning into the driveway, drove by it. Sure enough, within minutes I saw the blue SUV inside the gated community, headed toward my rental house. I started following him. He knew I was following so he sped up and lost me. I drove to Andrew's rental house, put my car in the garage, and went inside. I called my lawyer, Rob Gordon, and told him, "So I was just photographed by the *National Enquirer*. And there's a bit of a problem. In the photos, it will look like I'm seven months pregnant."

"But you're not," Rob said.

"I am."

"You're pregnant?"

"Yes, I am."

"But John Edwards isn't the father."

"He is."

It may have appeared as if I was running around blabbing that John Edwards was the father of my baby. Simply not true—I hadn't even told my lawyer!

Johnny called from the back of the bus. He was livid. He was screaming at me, one of the two times he had ever screamed at me during our entire relationship. Andrew was sitting next to me (we were in his home office), and he said, "Just tell him I'll say the baby is mine."

I looked at Andrew as if to say, "Don't be ridiculous." I didn't repeat what Andrew had said to Johnny. I simply discarded it.

It was very dark outside by the time Johnny and I hung up. Andrew drove me back to my rental house in their white van. We went from their garage to my garage, and once inside, I pulled all the curtains in my house.

By the time Andrew had gotten back to their house, Cheri had noticed the *National Enquirer* guys peering in her window. She called 9-1-1. Apparently, the *Enquirer* had rented a room for golfing, inside the Governors Club which gave the *Enquirer* staff access to the gated community and entitled them to be there. I don't know what exactly happened with the *Enquirer* over at Andrew's house, but I was told there was screaming and yelling between them and the Youngs, and the cops came. The *Enquirer* was booted out of the gated community.

Johnny and I spoke on the phone off and on that entire night. He did not sleep a wink. He wanted out of the race but his conflict was that he didn't want to be forced out by a tabloid. I totally understood not wanting to be bullied.

The next morning, without any sleep, Johnny had his run time and workout and then did the *Des Moines Register* debate. I was surprised that he did a very good job.

Elizabeth joined Johnny on the bus with the kids later that afternoon. They went to some sledding event; Johnny spent his time doing phone calls about this little tabloid problem that he was still hiding from Elizabeth. She had no idea.

Johnny told me that, during this time, Andrew and he spoke on the phone and Andrew suggested to him, "Why don't I just say I am the dad? Nobody will care about two staffers having an affair."

"Andrew, that's crazy."

"Yeah, I'll have problems getting her on board anyway."

Unfortunately, the suggestion alone planted the seed. And I'll bet having Elizabeth right there with Johnny helped that little seed grow into a full harvest within a few hours, changing his thinking from, "That's crazy," to, "Uh, maybe that will work."

I believe Johnny was looking for a life raft to keep himself float-ing, without her finding out, while he waited for a natural exit from the race, not to be forced out by a tabloid. I don't believe his saying yes to Andrew's idea was ever intended to keep his bid for the White House alive.

Andrew mentioned his idea to me and I rejected it. *Again.* "Do you realize how stupid that is? No one is going to believe it."

I got a call from Johnny when I was standing in the kitchen of my rental house. It was dark but I don't know if it was dark outside or just inside because the curtains were still drawn to keep the *National Enquirer* people away. Johnny said, "Andrew says you are the only one who is not on board with this idea."

"*What?* Cheri is on board?"

This was the first time that this crazy idea started to seem real to me. I never thought it was going to fly because what woman would ever say yes to her husband publicly claiming paternity for a child that wasn't his? It never occurred to me that there are people in this world who want to be rich above and beyond *everything* else. I later learned from the Youngs that Andrew sold Cheri the idea by saying that if they did this, they would be financially set for life. Knowing Johnny like I do, I thought, but did not share with the Youngs, that this was very strange thinking, mixed with very big assumptions on their part. Of course, I didn't know at the time what was going on with Bunny's money.

I also thought that no matter what these crazy men thought, Cheri would be my out. And now I had none. They all wanted to do this.

I reacted the way most seven-months-pregnant women would: I began to cry. And I cried, and I cried, and then I cried some more.

I did not want any part of this. It went against all my belief sys-tems. I said over and over, "No one is going to believe this! It's stu-pid! It doesn't make any sense."

I remember sitting in my bathroom crying when Rob called. I picked up and said hello through my tears, and he asked what was wrong. I couldn't believe he was asking me that and lost it. I screamed, "What's *wrong*? What's *wrong*?"

He immediately said, "Let me rephrase: any new developments?"

Somewhere in between phone calls, tears, and the pregnancy pain I was in, I let go. I gave up. I surrendered. I didn't want to fight

anymore. I didn't want to cry. I made a decision to let go of everything I believed—just let it all go. And what came to me when I did
that, when I let it all go was no matter how stupid I thought this was,
I would do whatever Johnny wanted me to do. I did not want him to
blame whatever was going to happen on our daughter. I didn't want
Johnny to hold over our daughter's head that his being pushed out
of the race or my saying no to this stupid decision was in any way
her fault. And more importantly, I didn't want her to blame herself
if he did. After all, she has enough going against her already. Okay,
I would go along but I wasn't actually going to say that Andrew was
the father. I was going to say what I believed: it was nobody's business, and my decision to bring my daughter into the world, my pregnancy, doesn't have to do with John Edwards. Another nondenial,
but it was what I believed.

Of all the things that happened in my relationship with Johnny,
the thing I regret the most is going along with this stupid idea and
allowing this lie to go public. After this happened, whenever a choice
came up again that I thought was not the right way to go, or I felt
that Johnny's interests were in conflict with what was best for Quinn,
which happened more than a few times because Elizabeth was steer-
ing his boat, I held my ground. I would not waver: my daughter
always won. She still does.

The next step was for Johnny to tell Elizabeth this fantastic news—
Andrew and Rielle had just further ruined their lives. This was to be
followed by Andrew talking to Elizabeth. As I remember, Johnny had
just finished doing *Today*. He and Andrew talked and he told Andrew,
"The next time we talk, Elizabeth will be here."

Johnny told Elizabeth that I had been photographed and that
Andrew was the father of the baby. I suspect that because of her
trust issues with Johnny, Elizabeth wanted to talk to Andrew directly.
And here is what's so crazy about that: Andrew never flat-out told
Elizabeth that he was the father! He alluded to it, saying that he
and Cheri were having problems and they were working things out.
Elizabeth asked him when it happened, and Andrew told me he said,
"The first time it happened was at the Dave Matthews concert."

And that was it. Elizabeth just accepted it. It was what she wanted
to believe. She thought I was a whore and Andrew was a piece of dirt,

so it fit the storyline in her head perfectly. And now she felt really justified for blaming and heaving more of her anger on Andrew and me. We had, after all, nearly ruined her perfect public life.

Of course, Johnny was still trying to get the story killed. The *National Enquirer* wanted Johnny to sign an affidavit verifying paternity. Johnny tells me that he vividly remembers the look on his press guy Mark Kornblau's face. Mark was saying, "Okay, so we need to sign this affidavit and it's done."

And Johnny said, "Yeah, I am not going to do that. I am not going to say that under oath."

The justification, of course, was—signing an affidavit for a *tabloid*? Fuck them.

Johnny said he will never forget the look on Mark's face. It was the moment when Mark knew the truth.

So now the statements. Andrew's new lawyer helped write his, and they sent it to the *National Enquirer*. I had mine written up without the last add-on line after lots of pressure from the campaign.

"They won't believe it unless it comes from you."

"Oh, so now I have to say it? *No one is going to believe this.* What does it matter? I am *not* saying Andrew is the father of my child. I will say it's nobody's fucking business."

And then there came the moment: "*Whatever you want.* I am tired, I hurt, and I want to have my baby in peace. Please—all of you—leave me alone."

Here is my statement issued per my instruction *only* to the *National Enquirer*:

"The fact that I am expecting a child is my personal and private business. This has no relationship to nor does it involve John Edwards in any way. Andrew Young is the father of my unborn child."

Of course, my statement doesn't even make any sense. It's no one's business, but here, let me tell you who the father is anyway?

I still can't believe anyone bought it but they did. The mainstream media did not pursue it. I was very surprised and very happy about it.

And the fact that I lied? I let it go. I was making a baby, and her emotional and physical well-being was of the utmost importance. She was my priority, and, honestly, it wasn't that hard to let it go. My reasoning was, "Hey, I lied to the *National Enquirer*. I lied to liars. Do you really think they expect people to be honest with them?"

Here's a newsflash: The *National Enquirer* is filled with lies, including my own.

SIXTEEN

Band on the Run

"Never go on trips with anyone you do not love."

—Ernest Hemingway

AFTER ALL THE STATEMENTS had gone to the *Enquirer*, and Johnny did not sign any affidavit, Andrew got it in his head that we needed to get away, specifically to Bunny's private island. That was all he was talking about. Clearly he wanted to be on an all-expenses-paid vacation via private plane, but at seven months pregnant, I did not want to be flying, traveling, or away from my doctor. Not to mention I had no desire to be in a bathing suit! So once again, I was not happy about a new development. I didn't want to leave my couch, much less North Carolina.

I told Johnny over the phone, "Andrew wants to go away when the story comes out."

"I think that's a good idea," he replied.

Fabulous.

Andrew took care of all the logistics. I was told to pack clothes for warm weather and that I would not need my passport. I had no idea where we were going or how we were getting there. I was just told that we were leaving at five in the morning on Tuesday. The story was slated to come out on Wednesday.

I packed for a week, figuring it would be one, maybe two at the longest. I left everything in my house as it was. I felt like running away was stupid. So what if the press surrounded my house? They would get bored and leave in a few days. I would be just fine camping on my couch with the shades closed.

However, I had already decided that I was going to do what Johnny wanted, and if he thought it was a good idea for me to leave when the story broke, so be it. It wouldn't be for long. He was going to be out of the race soon. The other thing about me is that once I decide something, I am no victim or complainer, though I do make lots of jokes about the situation. I am on board one hundred percent.

Normally it's a path that I choose, and I take full responsibility for it. Whatever happens, I fully accept the consequences.

But this was a whole different ball of wax.

I have never been down a road that I knew, before walking down it, was the wrong way to go. So I felt right off the bat that the chances were high that things were not going to end well, especially given the idea sprang from the Youngs' greed.

Andrew and Cheri picked me up at around 5 A.M. They were alone because their children were staying with Cheri's parents in St. Louis.

It was chilly outside. I was wearing jeans and the black cashmere sweater that Johnny had brought me when I was going to the mountains at Blowing Rock. The sweater was so big and bulky that I barely looked pregnant.

We met Tim Toben near his house and Tim drove us to the FBO at the airport, where we got on a plane that Fred had chartered for us. I do not know what Fred thought at this time given I hadn't spoken to him. I really don't think he actually knew that I was carrying Johnny's child—not yet. I believe he was just helping us get away from the media because Andrew asked him to.

Once on the plane, I discovered we were going to the Westin Diplomat in Hollywood, Florida. Of course, I had been there before, more than once with Johnny. It would never have been my choice to stay in a huge hotel with minimal privacy.

When we arrived at the hotel, I sat on a couch in the lobby while Andrew and Cheri checked in. I have heard a lot about me being a demanding diva about hotels and suites and such. I will just say the

Let the nightmare begin! Leaving North Carolina with the Youngs in the wee hours of the morning, December 2007.

size of the room never matters to me, but how a room feels does. Andrew and Cheri picked the room and got an ocean-view corner suite; I got the adjoining standard room. I suspect it would be used as the nanny's room if there were kids in the suite. This would be the case throughout all of our travels: they always got the huge, expensive suite and I got a standard room. At the Four Seasons Resort in Santa Barbara, they had a suite that cost about three thousand dollars a night. I was in the standard room next door to their suite, which cost around seven hundred dollars a night. Don't get me wrong—the Four Seasons is the Four Seasons, suite or no suite. I'm just saying, they got the suites, not me.

When I got to my room, I was feeling really sad and couldn't pinpoint the sadness. It wasn't related to this stupid drama; it was something else that I couldn't quite fathom. I called my ex-husband, Kip. I wanted to tell him I was pregnant before he saw it in the *National Enquirer*. He picked up and said, "It's so weird that you're calling—I was just going to call you. Humphrey died."

After we reminisced about Humphrey, my little Jack Russell terrier that I had when we were married, I told him my news. "Just wanted you to know, I am with child, a little girl, and is it okay, do you mind if she uses your name?"

He replied, "I would be honored to have your child have my name, for as long as she wants it. And the father?"

I was silent.

Kip said, "I take it you don't want to talk about the father and I believe it is none of my business."

"Thanks. I appreciate that. I love you."

"Love you too."

When the *Enquirer* cover appeared on the Drudge Report, it said, "LOVE CHILD" with a picture of me, in pain, walking out of the doctor's office without sunglasses. Lo and behold, the mainstream media bought it and left me alone. I was surprised to discover that some people are dumber than I thought.

Naturally, Jonathan Darman chimed in with an email:

> Not sure if you're still checking your e-mail, but I wanted you to know that I'm thinking of you. Hope everything's OK and that, apart from all this madness, you've been happy. You don't have to respond to this, understand why you wouldn't, but it felt weird not to be in touch and let you know that you're on my mind. A lot has happened in the past few months—I've been on leave in Washington, taking care of my father who has been in the ICU, gravely ill with acute leukemia. Lots to talk about…someday. Just know that you're my mind and would love to talk, whenever and if ever you can. XO J

Johnny called to tell me that some woman, a big fan of Elizabeth's, a woman named Melinda who wrote for *Slate*, told Johnny that she was hearing everywhere that I was talking to everyone and that he should really shut me up. This really upset me, and I started crying. "Let's see—I have gone against everything I am about and believe in, I have lied, I am in hiding, and now you are accusing me of talking to people? *I have not talked to anyone.*" It was very annoying, to say the least.

We hung up and Johnny called back to tell me that, during the whole conversation that we had just had, he had forgotten to turn his microphone off.

His camera guy assured him that he hadn't listened in.

Fabulous.

Meanwhile, Cheri, shopper of the century, went on a spree and began filling the suite with supplies: food, a coffee maker, whatever, even a little tiny Christmas tree. She kept very busy, as did Andrew with his many massages.

No matter how much I would have loved to, I couldn't get into the vacation mode. This was no vacation for me.

Meanwhile, Elizabeth had amped up her campaign of bad-mouthing Andrew, and it was getting back to him. He started to lose it: "I have done all this, and she just keeps bad-mouthing me." Emotions were running high in that corner ocean suite. I was privy to the first of many fights that Andrew and Cheri would have.

Nick Baldick called Andrew. Andrew had stopped working for the campaign in October or November; apparently the campaign was running out of money and staff had to be cut. Nick was Andrew's new boss at Nick's 527. (A 527 is a tax-exempt group that raises money in order to advocate issues.) Andrew's only job appeared to involve getting money for the 527 from Bunny.

Andrew told me Nick called and said, "Dude, way to take a bullet. Can you get me more money?"

Andrew was clearly offended by this. After all, he was still taking the bullet. He was very emotional, he was being bad-mouthed by Elizabeth, his wife wasn't being nice to him, he was very, very busy getting massages, and now he had to *work*?

Andrew didn't want his vacation to end, and I believe he convinced Fred, that it wasn't yet safe to go back to North Carolina because the *National Enquirer* was probably not going to let this go. (Gee, I wonder why?) So it was decided between them that we should go to Aspen and stay at Fred and Lisa's house for Christmas.

My warmest clothes were what I left North Carolina wearing. I had packed as I was told to—for warm weather. As for cold weather gear, all I had was Johnny's cashmere sweater and one pair of jeans. So Cheri and I went to the mall. I bought an extra-large goose down Juicy Couture coat on sale for two hundred dollars and a pair of UGG slippers. That was my entire pregnancy winter wardrobe.

We left Florida by private jet and stopped in St. Louis to pick up the Youngs' three small kids, and their babysitter, car seats, toys, and suitcases. The plane was *packed*. Then we all flew to Aspen. Whatever glamour traveling by private plane afforded, it evaporated immediately with the addition of three small children. We were now a traveling circus. Andrew and Cheri were having fun: they had their kids back; the kids were happy too. They were all looking forward to their skiing lessons and all the winter wonderland activities that Aspen has to offer to nonpregnant people. The insanity of it all never escaped me. The traveling was more uncomfortable, especially now with three small, very loud children who weren't mine. For the most part, though, I was still happy.

But wow—Aspen was *cold*.

I remember Cheri bitching *a lot* about how Fred and Lisa's person, who was supposed to help, was of no help. And their babysitter was of no help. The reason Cheri and I would never be close pals is that she is really not a happy person nor adapts easily to change. Such behavior makes an uncomfortable environment to be in, to say the least. Thankfully Fred and Lisa's house was huge, and Cheri stayed very busy out of the house with ski lessons, indoor sports arena activities, and other winter kid stuff.

I spoke to Lisa while we were there and it lifted my spirits greatly. She asked me if I had a name for my daughter yet. I said I liked Frances, but her dad wasn't sold on it, so I wasn't sure yet. I never offered up who that dad was. But when I spoke to Lisa, I immediately got the feeling that it was all going to be okay.

Lisa also found me a doctor in Aspen to visit for a checkup. I went and really liked the doctor but was uncomfortable about having my baby in Aspen. I still didn't know where I was going to give birth, but it was now certain that it wouldn't be in North Carolina because the *Enquirer* had already staked out my doctor's office there. I thought often about leaving the country but I really wanted her to be born in America.

We had to leave Aspen because Fred and Lisa had promised the house to someone else for New Year's and they couldn't get out of that commitment.

Andrew chose San Diego. Why, I have no idea. We flew privately to San Diego, minus the babysitter this time.

I had a junior suite at the Loews Coronado Bay, where I immediately fell asleep upon hitting my room. The Youngs had big problems with their room and with the hotel service. I don't know what was going on with them. They were very unhappy but fortunately were in a building far away from me. They ended up in an extra-large, two-bedroom suite on the water, but to Cheri it smelled like pee or something. She was complaining all about it. And then—OMG—the unthinkable happened: Andrew forgot her birthday! She did not let that go. He was punished on and off for that for as long as I was with them.

We spent New Year's Eve in San Diego having room service in the Youngs' pee-smelling suite overlooking the water, watching the ball drop in Times Square on TV.

Meanwhile, Johnny was campaigning like a madman, 24/7. He would call Andrew's cell or Andrew would connect me to him somehow. I just remember Johnny being in that totally different reality—the campaign bubble—surrounded by people who wanted to hear what he was saying, and relying on subjective people for his information. He was also very sweet to me on the phone. I could feel how much he loved me and missed me.

We went on a private plane back to Aspen—more cold and more altitude—which I wasn't thrilled about. But hey, whatever. The Iowa caucuses were around the corner, and then it would all be over.

At around 5:30 in the morning, I was awakened by Cheri screaming. I got out of bed, and Cheri was in the entryway of their bedroom going at it with Elizabeth on the phone. Elizabeth tracked Johnny's phone calls and had seen a call to Cheri's cell. Elizabeth's tracking had started in December 2006. This is something that never changed, even well into 2010, long after they were separated, until Johnny got a phone under his own name where she couldn't track his whereabouts or his calls.

I watched the Iowa caucuses in Fred's den. I couldn't believe Johnny came in second, but more importantly, I couldn't believe he was staying in. I had a bit of a reaction to this because I expected that he would be getting out after Iowa. He was planning on getting out and thought he would come in third. Now, he couldn't exactly make a graceful exit when everyone around him wanted him to continue. Whatever.

I retired to my bedroom. I had more pressing matters to think about, like where I was going to give birth, an issue that became more important each day because I could no longer fly after thirty-six weeks of pregnancy.

I picked Santa Barbara. First of all, that place is heaven on earth. Second, and more importantly, my dear, dear friend of fifteen years, Bob, who is the sweetest soul and a great source of comfort for me, lived there. I wanted him to be with me when I gave birth, no matter where that birth took place, so why not just go to him?

I refused to budge on this. Maybe this was diva behavior, but I was tired of all the traveling, living out of a suitcase, and the cold weather and the altitude. I was at the end of my rope and about to give birth.

Our odd journey across the country ended up putting me in the most divine city for my daughter to come into the world.

I have more admiration for people, especially celebrities, when I learn that they chose to live in Santa Barbara. When Oprah Winfrey, who lives in Santa Barbara, was at my house in Charlotte, we briefly chatted about it. I said to her, "There is nothing wrong with Santa Barbara." And in total agreement, she replied, "There is *nothing wrong* with Santa Barbara."

And to be able to be born there? Yes, my daughter is indeed one lucky little girl.

SEVENTEEN

The End of Just Me

"The moment a child is born, the mother is also born. She never existed before. The woman existed, but the mother, never. A mother is something absolutely new."

—BHAGWAN SHREE RAJNEESH

FTER THE NEW YEAR, I sent Jonathan Darman a brief email that said, "Thanks for your e-mail. Sorry to hear about your dad, but happy you get to spend time with him. We will talk again one day. Until then, lots of love."

He responded, "Good, I hope that day is soon. You know where to find me. Love, J."

While we were staying at the Four Seasons Santa Barbara, Andrew was house-hunting with a Realtor, and he was telling people that I was his sister Jaya. We all went and looked at a few houses. None of them was right for our living situation, which was comical: pregnant mistress in hiding, three small kids, and a never-been-in-therapy, often-fighting married couple. And then just when we thought we would never find anything suitable, a big beige house in a gated community in Montecito, California, became available.

The house also came with a hefty price tag: twenty thousand dollars a month. But it worked because there was enough space for us to have our own ends of the house. As much as I loved the Youngs (and I really did at that point), I needed privacy for my new baby and me. I am a private person and need my own space. We did have some common areas: the kitchen, the TV area off the kitchen, and the laundry. But I would be also able to close my door to my section and shut them out (or so I thought). They had the other end of the house, with the master bedroom, an extra bedroom for the kids, and an office for their busy work of building their five-thou-sand-square-foot, two-million-dollar dream home back in North Carolina. Of course, I never stopped to think at that point how they could build such a house on a political staffer's salary. Neither of them came from any money. In fact, it was very clear that they didn't. So how much money could they have possibly made from the sale of their other house? It's clear now, but at the time I just never thought about it.

Even as rich as he was, Fred gave Andrew a lot of push back on the hefty rent. I mean, come on, twenty thousand dollars a month is twenty thousand dollars a month. So Andrew basically spelled it out very clearly, stopping just short of directly telling Fred that Johnny was my baby's father. Apparently this is when Fred went to Johnny directly and asked him for the first time if he was in fact my baby's father.

And Johnny said no.

Johnny lied to his friend.

Johnny called me screaming. The second and only other time he has ever screamed at me. "What is Andrew doing? Fred said Andrew all but said directly that I was the father of your baby!"

"Stop screaming at me! I didn't talk to Fred nor do I have any in-terest in your anger."

We hung up.

This happened somewhere between January 7th and 11th. It was at the Four Seasons Resort in Santa Barbara, right before we moved into the big beige house. I believe Fred had no idea what the truth was when he offered to help us get out of North Carolina. Nor do I believe he was doing it to follow Johnny's instructions. I believe Fred was telling the truth when he publicly said that in August 2008. I also believe Fred did not think that his financial help was a campaign violation. The Fred I knew would have never knowingly violated a campaign finance law! I believe Fred helped because that's what Fred did: he helped people. In fact, Fred continued helping me way after Johnny's political career was long over.

Also around that time, I found a doctor I trusted. I was still in a great deal of pain. I wasn't moving much, just to the tub and back, and spent a minimum of five hours a day soaking.

My doctor had a great sense of humor. Naturally, because I was now living under an alias, I had no medical records, so he had to redo all my blood work. He asked me in a very jovial manner, "Who are you running from—the dad?"

"Nope," I replied, smiling, without offering an answer.

He handed me a copy of all my blood work, and said, "Well, here, you might need this in case you run away from me before your baby comes out."

The other great thing about being back in California (the land of the free, wacky, and celebrity) is that when you fill out your medical forms, there is a line for your legal name and then next to it a line for your aka. Of course, I wasn't about to write Rielle Hunter. As much as I liked my doctor, it seemed unwise to trust anyone with my real name right now. I listed only Jaya James.

Once we moved out of the hotel and into the big beige house, I went shopping for baby stuff. I went to a store called Chicken Little and got everything I needed. There was a lady there who was also pregnant with a girl. She was so great—she just flew through the whole store: "You need this, you need this, you need this"—one-stop shopping. You name it, I got it: changing table, stroller, car seat, Baby Björn, baby clothes, Diaper Genie. One day and five thousand dollars later, I was ready to have a baby.

Andrew and Cheri went car shopping and bought a Lexus SUV for Cheri. I don't know Lexus models very well, but whatever it was, it was pricey—a far cry from Cheri's minivan that she drove back in North Carolina. They also began shopping for everything under the sun that they felt they needed to make their lives extra happy. Andrew bought a top-of-the-line treadmill, full weight-lifting gym for the garage, a new large HDTV for their bedroom (the ones already in the house were just not good enough), plus toys, basketball nets,

In the big beige house, February 2008. I had ventured way beyond uncomfortable—tipping the scales at a whopping 166lbs!

motorized cars, and a huge trampoline with a net for the back yard. And clothes! Those kids had more clothes than I had ever seen. They also hired a home school teacher for the kids.

January 23rd, 2008: I read in the indictment four years later that, on this day, Andrew received another check from Bunny for two hundred thousand dollars. This is crazy to me because the Youngs were still telling me that they needed to be reimbursed for all the money they had spent on me so far, which they claimed came from the sale of their house in Raleigh. *Their* money, not Bunny's. And they went on to hold this "*their* money" thing over my head a lot of the time. Cheri would scream at me, "This is *our car*! We bought it!" (She was speaking of my used BMW.) And silly, stupid me, I believed them. So in reality, they had now almost seven hundred thousand dollars from Bunny. The checks went to Cheri and were deposited under her maiden name. Andrew was no longer putting any money into my account; that had stopped December 4th, 2007. In total, he had deposited thirty-eight thousand dollars into my account over a period of seven months. To me thirty-eight thousand dollars is a far cry from seven hundred thousand dollars.

And as crazy as that sounds, it got even crazier.

Andrew was also employed by Nick Baldick at the 527. Andrew probably got a hefty commission on his Bunny money that he got for Nick. He also told me that when he started working for Nick, he got a raise and was making more money than he did working for the senator. Although, given the facts (and fiction) that later came out of Andrew's mouth about money, I have no idea what was actually true about his employment with the 527.

On January 25th, I got an email from a woman named Susanna that said:

> Jon asked me to contact you. Dick Darman passed away this morning after a difficult struggle with leukemia. Jon, Emmet, and Willie all had an opportunity to say goodbye. Please keep the Darmans in your thoughts and prayers. I will be in touch as soon as arrangements are made.

Another note came two days later:

A memorial service will be held for Dick Darman at St. John's Episcopal Church in McLean, VA, on Saturday, February 9th, at 2 p.m. St. John's is located at 6715 Georgetown Pike, McLean, VA 22101. All are welcome and encouraged to attend. Any correspondence for Jon or his family can be sent to [address]. Jon is so lucky to have such thoughtful friends. Hope to see you on the 9th.

I felt for my friend Darman. I know what it feels like to lose your father to cancer. I sent flowers to the address with a note saying, "My thoughts and prayers are with you."

Johnny called me very early the next morning to tell me that he was going to announce that he was dropping out of the presidential race. His decision happened very quickly—it was like he woke up that morning and he was just done. He didn't know when he was going to be able to call me again. Overall, he just sounded frazzled. He said, "I just decided I am out of this." He was in full scrambling mode. "I haven't told all the people that I need to. I need to go."

I was unhappy about him neither having any way to call me nor not telling me of a way to contact him before we hung up. I was about to give birth to his child, and now he "had to go?"

"Okay."

"Bye."

I did not hear or see his "family-by-his-side," out-of-the-race goodbye speech because I was at a doctor's appointment. I was standing on the sidewalk outside the doctor's office after the appointment when a friend rang me to tell me about his speech. She had seen it. Then I got some more calls, one from Rob Gordon, as Cheri drove me back to our big beige house in her new Lexus.

I did not hear from Johnny, which upset me. I felt abandoned. Nine months pregnant with his child, and he drops off the face of the earth?

Of course, he did call eventually. He was finally able to go to the beach house and call me from the beach landline. I think we didn't speak for about a week, but it felt longer to me. He told me he was going to buy a disposable phone, one that he could just keep putting money on, with no permanent records involved.

Once Johnny had the disposable phone, he would just call me directly whenever he wanted and whenever he could. Andrew was no longer needed as telephone operator. Uh-oh—I had a feeling that someone was going to feel rejected. I suspected that not being able to talk to his great love was going to be a big problem for Andrew.

My due date, February 15th, came and went, and my daughter was not remotely interested in joining me in the world yet. Missing my due date was emotional. For nine months I had expected and hoped to have a baby by a certain date yet there I was, still pregnant! On top of that, I was so, so uncomfortable.

After continual checkups, in which my doctor made sure everything was okay, he told me that he was going to let me go until February 26th, when he was on call. Those last two weeks felt like an eternity! Normally I would have seen all the doctors in their practice and then whoever was on call would deliver my baby. But because I was a transfer, I saw only my doctor and I really wanted him to deliver my baby. He clearly had a lot of experience, something I could tell when he walked into a room. Out of all the doctors I saw, I felt blessed that he was the one to bring my girl into the world.

He told me I would go into the hospital on February 26th to begin the process of induction. When February 26th arrived, my friend Bob picked me up. We took pictures with the Youngs and their kids. It was my last night as a pregnant woman. I wanted photos of me weighing 166 pounds. I was fifty pounds pregnant! I had privately been photographing and documenting my belly as it grew and changed over the months. It really was an amazing, wonderful journey becoming a mom. It really was nothing short of a miracle. When I learned later that these pictures had been uploaded onto the Youngs' computers without my consent or knowledge, and that they'd been making copies upon copies, showing them to God knows who, the violation I felt was beyond words.

As I bid them goodbye, I told the Youngs I would call them and let them know what was going on. I arrived at the hospital, checked in, began induction, and began about three hours of *"Oh my God, this hurts!"* I began to walk the halls until I couldn't move anymore because the pain was excruciating. They gave me something for the pain but it didn't help one bit. My body was acting like it was in full

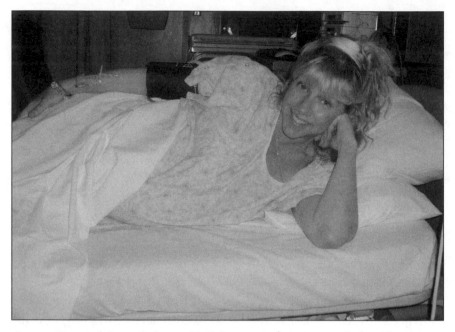

Cottage Hospital Santa Barbara, CA, February 26th, 2008. Just before the un-
bearable pain began.

labor, yet I was only one centimeter dilated. They gave me an epi-
dural but it didn't work quite right, and Quinn's heart started doing
weird things. They broke my water to stick a monitor on her head,
and I then went through the most terrifying couple of hours of my
life, listening to her heart beat erratically, lying paralyzed as half my
body was still feeling the contractions, looking into Bob's eyes. He
kept saying, "She's fine, she's going to be just fine."

My doctor finally got to the hospital and told me he had been calling to check on me and waited on purpose. What was happening was
not that uncommon. He said we could let it go a little longer, or I
could opt for a C-section now.

"Get her out now."

"Okay. Let's get ready."

Bob started putting on the scrubs they gave him (in order to meet me
in the operating room) as they began wheeling me out of the room. I
asked Bob to call the Youngs and tell them I was going in for C-section.
I signed the consent papers as they wheeled me down the hall.

Cottage Hospital Santa Barbara, CA, Feburary 26ᵗʰ, 2008. In labor—walking the halls.

The second we got into the operating room, Quinn's heartbeat returned to normal. They said, "Wow, look at that! Her heart is beating completely normally—she's fine."

My doctor opened me up and went in to get my girl. He said that she had the umbilical cord wrapped around her three times. I heard her cry, which brought tears to my eyes. They brought her over to my face and I was absolutely blown away by her beauty. I was not expecting her to be so beautiful, so pure, and so flawless. She took my breath away.

Quinn's first day. My dear friend, Bob, took this picture—it's my favorite.

My first words to her: "You are so beautiful. I love you." And then I kissed her cheek.

Welcome to the world.

And then I silently thanked God.

My sweet girl, Frances Quinn Hunter, came into the world on February 27th, 2008, at 9 A.M. on the dot.

What was so surprising to me—something that I had no way of knowing before that moment arrived—was that as much as I loved her father (more than I had ever loved any man), I hadn't even begun to touch love until Quinn came.

EIGHTEEN

Changing Diapers, Changing Everything

"If you are going through hell, keep going."

—WINSTON CHURCHILL

WAS IN RECOVERY for a long time before I was returned to my hospital room. A nurse handed me a phone from the recovery room wall. It was Johnny. I filled him in on my last twelve hours. We talked until a nurse said, "We have your daughter, and she is hungry." I asked the nurse for just a few seconds and told Johnny that I needed to go. I remember that vividly because it would be the very first time—with millions to follow—that, when given the choice, Quinn won when it came to who got my attention.

I handed the nurse the phone and she hung it up as another nurse brought my daughter to me. Without any problem at all, Quinn immediately latched on to my breast and that was it—she was home. Breast-feeding is weird. It's a feeling, a connectedness that is incomparable to anything I have ever experienced. It is incredibly loving, fulfilling, and draining—all at the same time.

I was in the hospital for a few days and did not sleep for a long time after the surgery. I was filled with adrenaline. The Youngs had my room overflowing with flowers and sent me a sweet card (which I still have) that read: "Jaya, congratulations on this precious soul that you have brought into the world. Quinn is such a beautiful angel and so lucky to have you as a mommy! Much love from all of us! We feel blessed to be a part of your and Quinn's life. We love you! Andrew, Cheri, Brody, Gracie, & Cooper."

Cheri stayed with me in my room the first night, sleeping on the little chair that pulled out to become a sleeper. She was great. I saw a side of her that I'd never seen before and have never seen since—protective and vulnerable at the same time. Her feet were freezing, so I told her she could borrow a pair of my socks, which she did. She had these big pink fuzzy knee-highs on. She complained to the nurses about how loud they were at their station outside my room and they eventually moved me to another room.

My recovery lasted a brutal seven weeks. It hurt so badly to move, let alone attempt to walk. And it became apparent immediately that Quinn never wanted to be away from me. They took her to the nursery to give me a chance to sleep, which lasted about ten minutes. They brought her back, wailing, and she calmed down as soon as she was next to me.

From there on out, that is how we rolled. She was glued to me unless she didn't want to be. Her choice. I am from the school of thought that insecurity is a deep-seated feeling that can set in as a baby if you didn't experience the security you needed the moment you needed it. During the first two years of Quinn's life, she was never away from me for more than two hours. She went everywhere with me. That's just what she wanted and needed. And believe me, from the get-go, she let me know what she needed.

The second or third night in the hospital, Bob stayed with me as I spoke to Johnny throughout the night. I got no sleep because I needed to nurse Quinn every hour. They told me she had to gain weight or they were going to start her on formula. And it worked. My milk fully came in and she gained the weight she needed and then some.

I left the hospital in a wheelchair. The Youngs took it upon themselves to videotape this moment and later either give it or sell it to

ABC to help them sell their book. They also used photographs of me leaving the hospital for their book. I have no memory of being videotaped or photographed. I was so discombobulated and in pain, feeling very vulnerable as I carried my sweet little girl—her first time outside into the world. I can't begin to convey how invaded and horrible it makes me feel to have that moment used on TV without my permission. There just aren't words to describe the awfulness of it.

When we got back to the big beige house, something different came over me. The part of me that sensed—that knew—something was not right with the Youngs came to the forefront of my awareness, probably connected to my need to protect Quinn.

I believe Cheri viewed herself as a stellar baby nurse and sincerely thought that she would be helpful to me once I was home with Quinn. At least that was the sales pitch they gave Fred and me for why we all needed to be together. I believe it was the *National Enquirer* or Fred—or both—who raised questions about the validity of a family that goes traveling around with a pregnant home wrecker.

Anyway, the argument from the Youngs was always that I needed them because I needed to have Andrew helping with logistics and Cheri to help with the baby. Yeah, well, they needed me as their meal ticket.

I actually needed help, but it wasn't the help that Cheri wanted to give, and she was *not happy* about that. Cheri had no interest in helping me get food or coffee or doing baby laundry, or any kind of help that would really assist me. She wanted only to have her hands on Quinn. And the more anger Cheri indirectly expressed, the more I distanced my daughter from her and all the Youngs.

Early one evening, they came to me and said, "Bye, we are leaving, driving up the coast for a few days. See you later." They were all packed, kids already in the car.

"*What?* What do you mean you're going away for a few days? I don't even have a car! What if there is an emergency? Could you please wait until I get someone to come here and stay with me, in case there is an emergency?"

They were *pissed!* How *dare* I ruin their plains? They were working so hard to keep their marriage together, and I was ruining it for them.

I called Bob, who dropped everything and arranged to come and stay with me. And then, in typical passive-aggressive fashion, Andrew and Cheri said forget it, they weren't going, and it was all my fault. If you want the definition of a complete nightmare, try a single mom recovering from a C-section, breast-feeding a newborn baby, no help in sight, in hiding, and living with the Youngs.

Johnny was headed to LA to be on *The Tonight Show with Jay Leno*. He would also be meeting Quinn for the first time—on my birthday. Naturally, I was excited about my two loves meeting for the first time.

Bob, Quinn, and I stayed at the Beverly Hilton. We had two adjoining rooms. Johnny was at the Hyatt Regency Century Plaza in Century City. Bob went to fetch Johnny and, much later, drove him back to his hotel.

Johnny was so sweet with our daughter. I took pictures of him holding Quinn for the first time. She looked right at him with a look of love that she still gives him. I have never seen her look at anyone the way she looks at her dad.

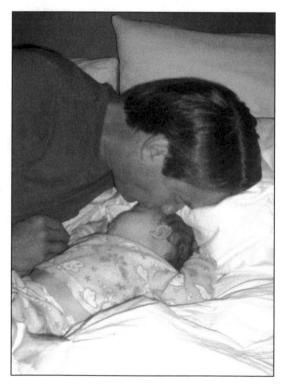

We hung out for a while, and then Bob took Quinn into the other room while Johnny and I had dinner alone.

The next day, my birthday, Johnny joined us right before our room service dinner was delivered. He told me that he needed to answer his cell if it rang, because Elizabeth was in a screaming-at-everyone

The Beverly Hilton, June 2008. No matter what was going on publicly, Quinn has always known her father loves her.

meltdown mode because Johnny was in LA and there was a young girl who used to work for the campaign who lived in LA. Elizabeth had her fired because she was pretty. Johnny couldn't remember her name, which made Elizabeth even crazier. She thought he was lying, and not being able to remember her name was his cover. But he really couldn't remember her name.

By this point I knew that Elizabeth was not remotely interested in the truth. She was always so far from reality and never asked the right questions, so she constantly fought the wrong battles. Sure enough, his cell rang and he picked up.

But it wasn't Elizabeth; it was our future president Barack Obama. What I gleaned from the conversation was that the future president was "phone banking" him. This was one of many calls that Johnny received under the umbrella of Obama looking for Johnny's endorsement. After all the small talk (basketball mostly), Johnny said something like, "Today is no different from the last time we talked. I haven't decided." He hung up and apologized for picking up. He didn't know it was going to be Obama.

Johnny never wanted to be Obama's vice president. However, he operates by watching how the world unfolds, and even though he didn't want that job, he did want to see if it was actually a job he was supposed to have. Unlike a lot of politicians, he was in this for service, and service to him actually means serving the world where you are needed. And more often than not, that job isn't the job your ego wants. Even though VP would have been an incredibley stupid and reckless path to embark on at that time, I actually don't think it was so delusional of him to wonder which way his life was headed. After all, there have been plenty of politicians who kept a love child or their double lives under wraps for years.

After I watched Johnny on *The Tonight Show*, I took pictures of father and daughter sleeping side by side for Quinn's baby book.

Johnny's feelings about me had changed a bit since I became the mother of his child. His appreciation for me grew. His respect for my strength and fortitude, for all I had been through alone, deepened his love for me. I could feel all of it the second he walked in the room, and it bowled me over as he was holding Quinn.

The Beverly Hilton, June 20th, 2008. Johnny and Quinn have always had a lot to say to each other.

Quinn and I drove back to Santa Barbara and into a shitstorm. Cheri's sister and her kids were visiting, and Cheri and her sister ganged up on Andrew, telling him what an awful human being he was for putting poor Cheri through all of this stress. Andrew's birthday was March 23rd, and Cheri purposely did not acknowledge it to punish him. After all, he'd forgotten her birthday back in December when they were in San Diego. They were also really freaked out about money and not getting reimbursed for the money they had spent on me.

Andrew was having his car shipped out from North Carolina and asked me if I wanted to ship out mine as well. (The BMW was mine if they were in a good mood and theirs if they were in a bad mood.) I asked how much it would be, and he said under a thousand dollars. That seemed like a good deal to me, and boy, did I need some freedom from the screaming and yelling that was coming from their end of the house. I felt badly for Andrew. We were such good friends, and it was difficult for me to listen as Cheri was so mean to him. He would go outside by himself at night, sit by the outdoor fireplace, listen to music, and drink. It was easy to see why he had fallen in love with Johnny. He had the same abusive wife stuff in his own life.

Andrew and Cheri were pissed about how much money I had spent to go see Johnny at the Beverly Hilton. How dare I spend money like that? They had gone from being supposedly flush with cash to being insanely frantic about money. And Johnny wasn't remotely interested in talking to Andrew. Andrew used what little time they did spend speaking to complain about how hard his life was. Cheri blamed me and she rode Andrew hard about how awful I was. To attempt to take the heat off himself, he joined the bandwagon and blamed me as well.

Cheri used to say to me, "I feel like you are judging me for my decision to do this." And believe me, I tried hard not to, but she was right: I could never get past what a stupid decision it was to agree to this whole situation and then play the victim.

So imagine how I felt, having lived through this insanity, when I discovered in January 2010 that Andrew and Cheri had actually received nearly a million dollars from Bunny and claimed that they had used that money solely to pay my expenses! In reality, the money that they spent on me was closer to seventy thousand dollars than seven hundred thousand dollars.

Mimi came out to LA for the weekend. She picked up my car that had been shipped to LA and drove it to Santa Barbara. Mimi was trying to help make some peace in our household. She played with the kids, cooked dinner, and tried talking to the Youngs without me. Then she came into my room and said, "Yeah, I don't know what you do with that. They are unconscious victims, unable to take responsibility or see their part in this."

I replied, "You do the only thing you can. You wish them well and walk away."

During her visit, Mimi took my camera and downloaded my pictures onto my computer. Cheri was in the kitchen and came in to my part of the house. I made the big mistake of showing her a couple of pictures of Johnny and Quinn, which, along with my very personal pregnancy photos that I didn't show her were uploaded to their computer without my knowledge or consent.

I was talking to Johnny regularly, telling him how "off" and "crazy" the Youngs were, and that I really need to get away from them. Andrew would tell me, "Please tell the senator to call me." I said okay and I would relay the message. When Johnny wouldn't call, Andrew and Cheri blamed me. In their eyes, I wasn't asking Johnny to call Andrew; his not calling had nothing to do with Johnny not wanting to talk to Andrew. Johnny and I became one and the same person in their eyes. Cheri was big on telling Andrew, "I told you so; John Edwards is an evil man. I've been telling you this forever. And now look what you've done to our family over and over again."

The month of April was a living hell in the big beige house. I stayed away from the Youngs in my side of the house with the door closed as much as possible, shielding my sweet girl from their miseries. If that weren't bad enough, I got frozen shoulder during this time, which is not uncommon after surgery but it made lifting a baby carrier—which you need to do to get out of the house—very difficult.

The Youngs' children were very busy with their home schooling, and Andrew was spending a lot of time getting dental work, which I gathered was cosmetic (it looked like veneers). When all of that wasn't happening, he and Cheri continued spending time in their office working on plans for their North Carolina home.

I also thought the Youngs were complaining to the only person who would listen to them: Fred. He offered to help with the situation. Andrew told me that Fred had offered to reimburse them for every expense they had incurred for themselves and for me. In true victim mode, I'm sure that Andrew was telling Fred that they were in this difficult financial situation because of Johnny and me, so Fred did what he did best. He offered to help.

Fred told Andrew to create a spreadsheet listing everything they had spent. Andrew and Cheri did this for days. Andrew was very concerned about writing everything down and the accuracy of it all, which I now understand, because he had already had a great deal of money from Bunny that Johnny, Fred, and I did not know about. He told me that he couldn't exactly list things like massages. (Andrew loved his massages.) He was going to lie about a bunch of stuff.

At this point, I had the sense that they lied about most everything related to money and would claim to Fred that it was all my spending. In reality, Cheri would go to Target, spend six hundred dollars, add in a few pairs of socks and shorts for me, and claim that the six hundred dollars was my expense.

I remember telling Johnny while I was on a walk with Quinn, "Something is way off with them and money. Their whole focus is on money. It feels like they are constantly obsessing, fighting, and scheming."

Johnny started thinking about what Elizabeth—among many others—had told him about Andrew over the years, connecting the dots. "Wow," he thought, "maybe he is a thief after all."

They were so anxious about any money I was spending that even if I went to the grocery store, they were unhappy. They had gotten me a credit card under Andrew's account, and that is what I would use to pay for my groceries or anything else. Every time I spent "their" money, no matter how meager the amount, they would *not be happy*, even though I knew that Fred was reimbursing them for everything I was spending.

I felt like I was living in a war zone.

When Andrew and Cheri finished that lengthy expense sheet (a sheet that, naturally, I never saw), I asked Andrew for the total amount. When he said "$325,000," my jaw dropped. What?

I immediately asked what happened to the two twenty-five-thousand-dollar checks that he had told me Bunny had given him.

"Oh, I never deposited those, given what happened with the *National Enquirer*."

My head was reeling. Oh my God, I knew my expenses: used BMW, a house full of mostly Pottery Barn furniture, thirty-thousand-dollar C-section, baby gear, a years rent for the house I had lived in for two months in North Carolina, and the thirty-eight thousand dollars he gave me over seven months in 2007. Add it *all* up and it's not even close to $325,000. In fact the grand total for all my expenses was between $150,000 and 180,000 (with Cheri's love for Target, there is no way for me to decipher which ones were actually my expenses or were ones she just claimed were mine).

Andrew told me that after all the expenses were paid he was going to split the remaining cash three ways between himself, Cheri, and me. I was to use that money to live off and after that, he told me that I would be responsible for my own expenses.

They wrote me a check for $9,850.

I deposited the money into my account and it posted on May 8th, 2008.

So just to be clear, at the beginning of May 2008, Fred reimbursed the Youngs for every single cent I spent—and then some!

I told Johnny how much money Andrew said that Fred had given them and also told him I believed that Andrew and Cheri ripped off Fred, charging him way more than what was spent. Johnny later told me that Fred believed the same thing. I believe that Fred knew the Youngs were charging him more than they had spent, and that he hoped that after this one-time payoff, the Youngs would just sort of disappear. I don't believe he ever confronted Andrew about overcharging him. We could all feel that something was really off with Andrew but we had no idea to what extent. We had no idea that he had received over seven hundred thousand dollars from Bunny. One could actually even say zero dollars of Bunny Mellon's money was ever spent on me, because it turned out that the Youngs had actually sold their house in

Raleigh for a large profit, and they did have plenty of their own money to cover all of my expenses until Fred reimbursed them for everything.

Countless press reports year after year said Bunny's money paid for my expenses, yet not one report stated that Andrew double-dipped and Fred actually paid for everything. I have stood in the kitchen of my little rental house and screamed in frustration (more than once), "Where is my million dollars? You are going to send Johnny to jail for money that I didn't even *get*? That he supposedly solicited for me?"

Speaking of screaming, one day, around the time that Fred gave the Youngs the $325,000, Cheri got so mad she was screaming at me at the top of her lungs: "*You are not who you think you are!*" She physically came after me. I shut my door in her face. Shortly thereafter, there was more talk about why they shouldn't give me their BMW. (Cheri always maintained it was their money that was spent on me.) I said, "Listen you guys, you do whatever you need to, I don't care. Take 'your' car that Fred just paid you for. I don't care. I am done here. As soon as I find a place to live, I am leaving."

And that was it for me. No more Youngs. Though we were still sharing a living space, there was essentially no personal interaction between us after Cheri's outburst.

Strangely, as though nothing had ever happened between us, on Mother's Day they knocked on my door to give me balloons and a card for Quinn. They asked me if I wanted to come to brunch with them.

I thanked them and declined.

And then came the endorsement that sealed their hatred of me forever. Johnny had called me and said Hillary was kicking Obama's butt in West Virginia. Johnny and I had an interesting discussion about why that was.

I suggested, "Maybe they just like her better, maybe it doesn't have anything to do with race. Or maybe it does. I don't know."

"I am thinking about endorsing Obama. What do you think?"

This was May 13th. Obama had been calling Johnny since he dropped out on January 30th. I replied, "I don't care."

He said, "You could talk me out of it if you wanted to."

I did an internal scan to see if I had any feelings at all about his endorsing Obama. Nothing came up. No thoughts. No feelings. I replied, "I have no opinion or feeling about this at all. It just doesn't matter. Do whatever you want."

So he said to me, "I don't know what I'm going to do yet but I will call you before I endorse him, if I do."

I said, "Okay."

The next day I was in a store on State Street in Santa Barbara, wheeling Quinn in her stroller. She was just about to fall asleep, so I was doing laps in the store to keep her moving as she transitioned into naptime. My cell rang. It was Mimi. "I just heard on NPR that your boy is going to endorse Obama."

"Really? Cool. I haven't heard." As I was talking to her, Andrew called. I said, "Hold on," and switched over.

Without even saying hello, Andrew asked, "Is he endorsing Obama?"

"I don't know. Last I heard was he might. Nothing definite."

Andrew didn't believe me. He was all up in arms. "They are saying he is going to. He is flying to Michigan and he's endorsing him."

I replied, "Well, that's news to me. I haven't heard." I wondered how many times I would have to say, "I don't know, I haven't heard." I just didn't remotely care about any of this. I had checked out of the world of politics and into the world of motherhood.

We hung up, and then I cruised around State Street a little longer until I, too, was tired. Quinn and I headed back to the big beige house.

I walked into my section of the house and turned on the TV. There was a big rally on CNN (I think), all waiting for Johnny. It was a long wait. The cameras were on the empty podium. Everyone was waiting. I thought, wow, that was fast. It looks like he is actually going to endorse Obama.

My phone rang. It was Johnny. "What are you doing?" I asked. "I just turned the TV on and everyone is waiting for you."

"I told you I would call you before I endorsed Obama, so I am calling."

I laughed. "I didn't realize it was going to be so soon."

"Yeah, neither did I. I'll fill you in later. Right now I gotta go endorse Obama."

"Okay, have fun. I'll be watching." I hung up, smiling at how funny my timing always seems to be. Not knowing a thing, I had just walked in and turned on the TV and didn't miss any of it.

Andrew and Cheri were on the warpath. They couldn't believe I didn't tell them that he was going to endorse Obama. No matter how many times I told them I didn't know, they continued to call me a liar. They were now beginning to act as if there was some great conspiracy against them. And as I said, they had turned Johnny and me into one person, the ringleader of this big bad conspiracy against them. The paranoia was absolutely unreal.

Soon after that, thank God, all the Youngs went away. They claimed they were going back to North Carolina for more work on their new house, but I had seen brochures on the counter for the Las Ventanas al Paraiso in San José del Cabo, Mexico, which is where I suspected they were actually headed after they dropped their kids off somewhere.

Fred and Lisa flew out to see me and meet Quinn for breakfast on May 21st, 2008. Lisa came with yet another box of clothes for Quinn. We had a lovely breakfast at the Four Seasons Resort in Santa Barbara. I took pictures of Lisa holding Quinn. I felt a little uneasy for them because Fred didn't look well and I had seen that look before on my father's face. His energy and complexion looked similar to Fred's about six months before he passed away.

At some point over lunch Fred said to me, "I want to help you. What do you need?" I said, "I need a place to live." He asked, "Where do you want to live?" I thought about it for a second and replied, "I would love to stay in Santa Barbara; it is pretty wonderful here. And I also would need some money to live on." He said, "Done. Start looking for a place to live and let me know when you find one."

"Okay, thank you for your help!" So Quinn and I started looking for places to live; we looked at everything under the sun. I had no idea what my budget was, nor could I find anything that would work for us: furnished, private, and clean. Or affordable—Santa Barbara is very expensive.

Lisa called me one day and said, "Fred wants to give you fifteen thousand dollars a month."

I thanked her and promptly told Johnny what Fred had offered, and he was floored by his generosity.

Now knowing my budget, I continued looking for a new place to live, with and without the Realtor. One day when Quinn and I were out house hunting, without my consent or knowledge, Andrew and Cheri videotaped themselves going through my living space and some of my belongings, including my checkbook. In our settlement agreement, this videotape is officially called the "Santa Barbara Walkthrough Video." I would actually call it something else and before the civil case I had against them settled, I was willing to bet that a jury would, too.

Thank God, I finally found (on my own, through some ad online) a fully furnished gated house that would work perfectly for six thousand dollars a month. So on June 4th, 2008, I packed up all of Quinn's and my stuff and, with Bob's help, loaded my car and said goodbye to Andrew. Cheri wasn't there. As I drove away from the big beige house, I thanked God that I was free from those crazy people. And I admit it: I hoped that I would never see them again. And even though I thought that I knew the Youngs, I still had no idea just how deeply disturbed they really were, or how far they would go for vengeance.

NINETEEN

The End of
My Mistress Stint

*"Celebrity and secrets don't go together. The bastards
will get you in the end."*

—GEORGE MICHAEL

LIFE WITH QUINN in the new rental house was heaven.
Although, compared to life in the big beige house, everything
felt like heaven. For Quinn it was eat, play, and sleep all the
time. I remember Iris the housekeeper saying to me one day,
"This is the luckiest kid I have ever seen. She gets all of you
all the time."

One of the things on my to-do list was to have all my stuff packed
up from the rental house in North Carolina. The big, bulky furniture
(that Fred now owned and gave to me) was to be put in storage; my
clothes, personal belongings, camera, hatbox, and father's ashes were
to be shipped to me.

Fred told me he would take care of this. Lisa asked if I would email
her a detailed list of what was where, which I did. The hatbox was
on top of my armoire, my camera in the camera bag in the front hall

closet, and my father's ashes on the mantle. Of course, I had no idea at that time that I was drawing a clear map for Andrew and Cheri to go rifling through my house or through my belongings in North Carolina, helping themselves to whatever they wanted. Or that they would take another "walkthrough" video. In this video, Cheri is going through all the contents of my hatbox, which contained all of my very personal mementos. As she is taping an item, you can hear Andrew say to her, "We're taking that, you don't need to tape it.

Cheri replies, "I know, but I want to tape it anyway."

At one point in June, Fred told me that Andrew told him that he had my father's ashes with him in Santa Barbara. I replied, "What?" That's what Andrew had told him. He had my father's ashes and was going to bring them to me. He was going to call me. I never heard from him. Later in September, Mimi found my father's ashes in the closet of my rental house in North Carolina when she went to pack up all my belongings. She also found my hatbox there. I did not leave my hatbox, which was filled with many personal mementos (including the videotape I thought I had destroyed), or my father's ashes in the closet. They had been moved.

Johnny was going to be in LA for some meetings, so I thought, why don't we just do what we did before? He stayed at the Hyatt Regency Century Plaza, we stayed at the Beverly Hilton, and Bob picked him up and dropped him back at his hotel later. We stayed for three days and two nights, June 19th to 21st. I took a bunch of pictures. One night Johnny ran into a woman he knew in the parking lot of the Hilton. I would later read that she talked to the press about that.

On June 21st, Johnny ran over to the Hilton to see us before we left in the morning. I took some pictures of him and Quinn—he had on a sweaty running T-shirt. One of the many photos I took that day was doctored and appeared in the National Enquirer as a "spy photo," claiming it was taken a month later. It was taken on June 21st and it was stolen from me. I don't know whether the National Enquirer stole it or if it bought the photo from someone who stole it. It was stolen either from my camera before I deleted the image, or from my computer. I would guess from my computer, or someone took a picture of it as it was on my computer, hence the doctoring of the photo. The bottom line is that I took the picture, I own it, and someone stole the image.

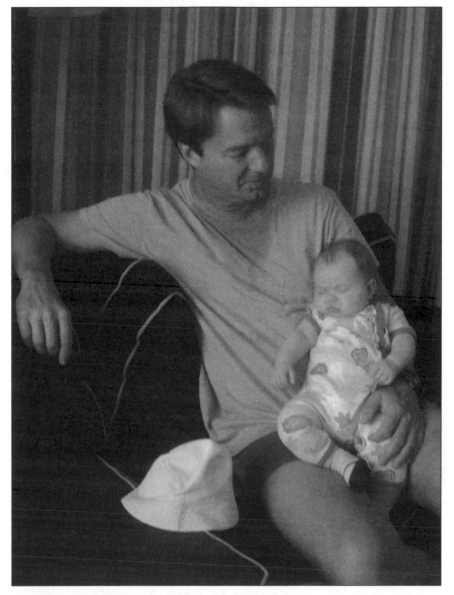

The Beverly Hilton, June 2008. I took five photos that morning; the picture taken ten minutes before this one was stolen from me and appeared in the *National Enquirer* as a "spy photo."

At the end of June, I flew my younger sister Melissa and her two daughters out for a visit. She is the only sister with whom I have a relationship. For her birthday, I took everyone to the Four Seasons for lunch, and for her birthday present I gave her my Cartier watch. It was a man's Panther watch that I had bought right after my father died in 1990. I gifted it to my sister because it was something of mine she always loved.

It was an emotional and sweet birthday lunch. Melissa took a picture of Quinn and me that ended up (without my knowledge or consent) on the cover of the *National Enquirer*. My sister claims that she did not sell it to the *Enquirer*, even though she owns the photograph. She claims she must have accidentally emailed it to my other sister, the one who has gone on TV bashing me more than once, who must have given it to the publication.

Melissa would also be one of the people (given that she was staying with me) who had access to my computer and my camera. I hate to think that there is even a possibility that my own sister would do such things, but when these things happen to you and your property, you can't help but become a little paranoid. I don't believe it was her, but my mind did go everywhere, including to my loved ones.

To this day, I have no idea how the *Enquirer* got those photos. I do know that I did not have anything to do with it. And one of them, the "spy photo," is stolen property—my stolen property.

Why don't I just sue the *Enquirer*?

Believe me, I have had many serious conversations with lawyers about this very topic and, who knows, maybe I will one day sue them. Right now my plate is full with other lawsuits. Rob Gordon, one of my early lawyers, joked to me one day long ago that when all this is done, I could open my own law firm. No kidding: criminal law, family law, First Amendment—what an education I have received.

Funnily enough, on my sister's birthday, while we were dining at the Four Seasons Resort, I got an email from my old pal Jonathan Darman, which read:

> Hello my old friend, I don't think this email address works for you anymore. But I've been thinking about you a lot lately. And knowing you,

you probably know that I've been thinking about you so I figured I'd send a message out there and it would find its way to you somehow. Hope the past few months have been good for you. I'd love to hear where you are and what you're doing. It has been a thousand years, I mean that seriously, for me, since last we spoke and I'm sure it feels that it has been for you as well. I would love to be back in touch. At the very least, know that I'm thinking of you and sending you much, much love. Warmest, J

I didn't respond but wished I could have. I missed Darman.

In mid-July, Johnny scheduled a meeting in order to be in LA for one night only—July 21st, 2008. Bob and I arrived at the Beverly Hilton in the afternoon, and Bob went inside to check in. It was packed. Apparently there had been some media conference held there that day but was ending. I was a bit freaked because it was so crowded, but Bob assured me that the desk had told him that it was over and all these people were clearing out, which turned out to be the case. I went to the room without passing one person, which was easy to do from the parking garage by taking the stairs and avoiding the lobby. That was the route Johnny would take later that evening as well.

I do not believe that the *Enquirer* had been tipped off and was waiting for us. I had been there since three or four in the afternoon. I believe that, as usual, someone spotted Johnny as he was coming in and alerted the *Enquirer*, which was there waiting for him when he left later that night—or, I should say, early in the morning. The *Enquirer* claimed it was tipped off and had photos of us together. I know the publication didn't have photos of us together unless there was one taken with surveillance cameras inside the room because we never left the room. And I don't buy that the *Enquirer* was tipped off early on because, if that had been the case, *wouldn't a photographer have been waiting when we arrived?*

I remember people saying, "What? They don't even have a cell phone camera? Where are the photos?" Of course, the *Enquirer's* big smoking gun was the "spy photo" that was stolen from me—a shot taken a month earlier. Not to mention the security guy told Johnny that he heard the reporter screaming into his phone, "Where's my photographer?!"

The Beverly Hilton, the night the *National Enquirer* confronted Johnny on his way out, July 21st, 2008. Quinn's T-shirt says *ME for President*.

In any case, we had a great visit. Johnny was so sweet and happy to see me. He really wanted to stay the whole night, which I thought was a bad idea and think had something to do with the fact that I had never slept a night without Quinn and I didn't want to. Later, we had fallen asleep for a while, and when I woke up, I wanted my girl back. I told him he should probably go. Bob brought Quinn back to our room. And Bob left us so we could say goodbye. He planned on meeting Johnny at the car. Johnny kissed Quinn goodbye, kissed me goodbye, and left. I had no way of knowing that when he left that it would be the last time I saw the man that was filled with optimism, the man I had fallen in love with.

About thirty minutes after the door had closed, I realized that Bob had not brought Quinn's favorite little binky back with her. I called Bob and said, "Do you have Quinn's binky?"

He said, "I'll bring it to you when I get back."

"When you get back? Aren't you already back?"

"No, I'm still waiting for John."

"*What?* He left here, like, thirty minutes ago." I hung up and called his cell.

He answered, "I guess you figured out what happened."

"No, I have no idea. Where are you?"

"I am with security." He told me what had happened. The English *National Enquirer* reporter was sitting on a bench by the bathrooms waiting for him and asked him if he was at the hotel visiting Rielle Hunter and if he was the father of her baby. Johnny walked right by him up the stairs and was met by a guy doing weird things with a video camera—not behaving like a normal videographer, but making erratic motions with a small camera, which made Johnny turn around and go back down the stairs and into the bathroom. The reporter attempted to come into the bathroom as he screamed questions, but Johnny held the door closed until a man said, "This is hotel security." At that point, Johnny opened the door, and the security guy escorted Johnny out of the bathroom (the reporter was no longer standing there), through the gym, and up to the top floor of the hotel.

That's where he was when I called him. Security was going to get him back to his hotel. He was trying to figure out whether he should have security get me out too. I said, "No, I don't want them to help me out."

The security man got him back to his hotel, and Johnny tipped him a few hundred bucks. Clearly that wasn't enough money to keep him from talking, or maybe the security guy was a Republican, given his interview on Fox News was the first to air on the mainstream media, creating a feeding frenzy.

Johnny remembers the *National Enquirer* claimed to have filed a criminal complaint against the security guard, but the cops claimed it was an incident report and no charges were filed. The *Enquirer* also claimed it had pictures and/or video of Johnny and I leaving the room together and said it had video of me entering the room to see Johnny. *Nope.* Impossible, because neither event happened.

Johnny got back to his hotel, and we talked on the phone for at least an hour. Bob called saying that he had found a way out for me, that I should just get dressed and leave my suitcase, walk down the hall to the stairs, and take the stairs all the way down past the boiler, past another door, and then out to the street, where he would be waiting for me. I was not thrilled with this idea because I had not slept a wink. Bob thought that the longer I waited, the more surrounded the hotel would be. My room phone began ringing. The *Enquirer* still had no idea which room I was in, or the reporter would have been out in the hallway. But I took my ringing phone to mean that it was just a matter of time before they had someone on every floor.

So I did what Bob suggested. I got dressed, packed everything in my red suitcase, took my purse, and put Quinn in the Baby Björn on my chest with a towel over her head. I took the route Bob suggested and passed two maids on my floor beginning their morning cleaning routine, but no guests—and no reporters.

Bob was waiting by his car. There was a guy on the street with his back to us, wearing a backpack. I got into the backseat, lying on my back with Quinn on my chest, a towel over both of us. Bob got in and we took off. A car was soon pursuing us. Bob whizzed through traffic, paparazzi in pursuit. This was the first time I'd ever been chased by paparazzi in my life, but, of course, the first thing that popped into my head was a joke. I looked down at Quinn lying on my chest, and said to her, "Who the heck are you, Princess Di? You leave one life and start the next one the same way you left the last?"

Johnny called from LAX. "Did you get out?"

"Yes, we're being chased right now. Bob is trying to lose them. Let me go, I can't talk right now. I'm lying in the backseat with Quinn on my chest, both of us covered by a towel. This is dangerous. Call me when you land."

Bob, race car driver extraordinaire, lost them in Bel Air. He pulled into someone's driveway behind the hedges. Bob thought we should split up because they obviously knew his car. Given we were in LA and close to my old neighborhood, I called one of my dear friends who lived close to where we were. She was able to come right away. We put Quinn's car seat in her backseat and Quinn and I got into the car. She drove me over to another friend's house right down the street from my old house in Benedict Canyon. Quinn and I hung out there until my friend was able to drive us back to Santa Barbara.

While I was in her daughter's bedroom changing Quinn's diaper, Rob my lawyer called to tell me the *Enquirer* had just called him and told him it was running a story about catching Johnny with me at the Beverly Hilton. "Yeah," I moaned slowly.

Rob asked, "Why didn't you call me?"

"Sorry, I'm not even home yet. It just happened. Sorry."

Minutes later, Fred and Lisa called. "Oh my God, what can we do? How can we help you? Just tell us and we will help you. What do you need?"

I asked, "How do you know already?"

"It's online."

They read it to me over the phone. I was horrified.

My friend drove Quinn and me back home to Santa Barbara. There were no reporters outside my house—yet. They hadn't figured out where we were living, but I knew it was just a matter of time.

Johnny told me he and Andrew had spoken, and that Andrew offered up more lies and cover-ups. "Why don't you just say that I was there?" he'd asked. I stopped listening. I was not interested in any more Andrew Young lies.

And I flat out told Johnny that if he had anything more to do with Andrew, he was the biggest idiot in the entire world. But that still didn't stop him. Regardless of how "off" I believed Andrew was, Johnny still loved Andrew and was still considering going through with Andrew's brilliant idea of creating a new job for Andrew, starting some sort of poverty foundation. It seemed to me (once again) that Johnny was afraid of hurting anyone who he thought was loyal to him or whom he thought loved him. And to me, (once again) that pattern was ANNOYING.

I believe Johnny finally settled on some crazy story to tell Elizabeth about how I begged to meet with him. There was no hanky-panky because Bob was there the whole time, but I pressured him to meet me because I needed help. Andrew was not paying child support and I needed money. (He hit all of Elizabeth's preexisting ridiculous story lines—me the gold-digging whore, Andrew the shitty person.) So good naïve guy that he is, Johnny went along with it because he was afraid that if he didn't, I might go public with our affair.

The mainstream media frenzy began. ABC figured out where I lived and began parking outside of my house, running video cameras constantly. I became a prisoner in my house. Johnny was thinking it would be great for me to leave the country. I actually agreed with him. I wanted no part of his lies or the media.

Fred came up with the idea of St. Croix. I had never been so I was on board. Unlike my North Carolina house, I packed up the California house as if I were leaving for good. I didn't know whether, in fact, I would be returning. During these few days of packing, my computer crashed. No way was I getting it fixed. My house was surrounded by media that hadn't yet made themselves known. They were lurking, pretending to be people who parked on the road to look at the view, but I could spot them pretty easily.

Elizabeth was relentless about Johnny doing an interview to tell the truth, as long as it was the truth she wanted him to say! After the interview, when she learned the whole truth, she did everything in her power to keep him or anyone else from talking. More on that later.

I believed that Johnny doing an interview about our relationship was perhaps the worst idea of the decade, right behind Andrew's idea of claiming paternity for Quinn. But the pressure was on, not only from Elizabeth but also the media. Apparently, ABC kept claiming that it had a friend of mine who was talking to the network and will-ing to go on camera.

I kept saying to Johnny, "There is no friend of mine talking to ABC and willing to go on camera. I know who my friends are."

I figured it was probably Pigeon O'Brien again. I called Jay and asked him if he could find out who this ABC chatting "friend" was. He said he was going to ask his friend, Chris Cuomo.

Apparently Elizabeth was pushing for this interview relentlessly, and Johnny was out-of-his-mind crazy. Every time I talked to him he was someone different on the phone, ranging from expressing these very raw emotions of, "I love you and Quinn so much," to act-ing completely detached from me. Clearly it was not the best time to invite a camera crew into his home.

I wonder if the media had just worked themselves up into a pack of projected anger because they were just so pissed at themselves for letting the story go in December. Everyone now claims to have never bought the Andrew Young story. If that's true, why didn't they blow it up back when Johnny was actually a candidate? Why were they so hell-bent on ruining him now, when it didn't actually matter? It seemed like a total power move to me.

George Stephanopoulos apparently told Jennifer Palmieri (Eliza-beth's press person/friend) that if Edwards had actually conceived a child while Elizabeth had cancer, he was a monster. So Johnny got it in his head that people would accept an affair but not that he was Quinn's dad. His mind took hold of what Stephanopoulos said and wouldn't let it go.

My vote was to say nothing, but if he did, tell the whole truth.

The day before I was set to leave for St. Croix, Fred reminded me that I needed my passport, which was in the hatbox in my North Carolina home. He said he would take care of it, meaning he was going to have someone go into my house, into my hatbox, get the passport, and FedEx it to me. My passport was right on top in the hatbox. I felt fine about having someone retrieve the passport from the hatbox because I believed that private tape of us had been de-stroyed. We also needed a certified birth certificate for Quinn. Great. I have to leave the house. I put on a hat and got Quinn in the car. By the time I got on the freeway, I was being tailed by paparazzi.

They were dangerous—cutting people off and driving like maniacs. I got off the freeway—they followed. They weren't even trying to hide. I called 9-1-1 and the dispatcher directed me back onto the freeway and to the nearest highway patrol station. The 9-1-1 dispatcher stayed on the phone with me the entire drive. When I got off the freeway, there was an officer waiting for me. She told me to turn right, which I did. The van tailing me followed and made a right turn from a left lane. The cop pulled the van over, and I drove away and directly into the highway patrol station behind the building.

After the van's driver was ticketed, a highway patrolman escorted me to the county office to pick up Quinn's birth certificate. He waited and escorted us home. When I got home, he said, "You live in my jurisdiction. My name is Dana. Here's my card. I'll write my cell down. Call if you need anything. You see anyone who shouldn't be here, whatever, I'm happy to do a drive-by whenever you need."

"Thank you so much." I was very grateful for the protection, especially given I had a small child. Most paparazzi get into this weird adrenaline frenzy when they are in pursuit, which can make them oblivious to safety, to say the least.

Very early in the morning of August 6th, two days before Johnny was set to do the biggest-mistake interview of his life, Fred arranged for a car to drive Quinn and me to an FBO south of Santa Barbara. I talked to Johnny on the phone most of the way. The driver got on and off the freeway at least once to make sure we were not being followed. That's the other thing you learn about the stalking media: their day doesn't usually begin before 8 A.M.

We got on a plane and took off. Quinn's first ride in an airplane was on a private little plane for just the two of us. We stopped for fuel in a Southern state—I believe it was Alabama—and the FedEx package containing my passport was waiting for me.

It was dark when we arrived in St. Croix. A man named Ricky greeted us at the FBO. He worked for a lawyer friend of Fred's. Ricky was a St. Croix native and fabulous. He called Quinn "Little Mama." I don't know what I would have done without his assistance during our time in St. Croix. He was floored by the way I looked. He couldn't believe I was the same woman in the pictures. Yeah, not the greatest photos of me, but on the plus side nobody recognizes me, so it's kind

August 2008, right before wheels up—headed to St. Croix.

of genius. Ricky handed me an envelope; in it was the latest *National Enquirer* story with its smoking gun "spy photo." When I saw it, my heart sank. I recognized the photo immediately, even though it had obviously been doctored. I knew that someone must have stolen it from me but I had no idea who or how.

Do you have any idea what it feels like to get to a mental place where you no longer trust *anyone*? You no longer have the ability to talk to anyone about anything, especially not over the phone. We (Johnny, Fred, and I) also wondered if the *Enquirer* was listening to our phone calls and had some sort of tapping device on our cell phones. We could not figure out how the *Enquirer* was getting information that no one outside of us knew. Mimi was suspicious that her house was bugged. Mimi and I had long before stopped talking on the phone about anything that would be considered newsworthy about my personal life.

Ricky took us to our new hotel, The Buccaneer, and after a long search, we finally found the reservation. Fred had put it under another alias as I had requested, but I was exhausted and it had slipped my mind.

The next morning I woke up feeling very isolated and sad. Our room was dark, which didn't help my sadness. It was the bottom floor, out of the sun's path and surrounded by trees. Ricky thought we should move rooms. He went out and searched for a brighter room.

He found a room that overlooked the pool and the bay. It was much brighter, and despite the fact that the mattress on the king-sized bed was at least seventy years old (Quinn and I sank into the middle of it), it had a large bath, and at least if I couldn't go outside for fear of someone recognizing me, I could at least watch other people enjoying themselves poolside.

Traveling with a small child, with no crib and no help at all, is difficult in ways that, if you've never had a kid, you would never think about, like where am I going to put her when I go to the bathroom? The car seat winds up being a savior. But your car seat can't take her for a five-minute walk and it can't take her into the other room for a two-minute break. I was the only caregiver. My attention to her, my unwavering vigilance in protecting her safety, is never turned off. And after she finally snuggled down and fell asleep, instead of relaxing and a little down time, I was met with the most publicly and emotionally devastating night of my life.

TWENTY

She Is Not My Child

"The limit of every pain is an even greater pain."

—EMILE M. CIORAN

THERE WAS NOTHING IN LIFE that could have prepared me for Johnny's interview. And as devastating as it felt, life did go on after that. Through my tears and the blunt-force pain I felt rippling through my entire being, I looked down at my sweet girl, who was safe and sleeping peacefully right next to me.

The entire interview was excruciating to watch. Obviously this was a man who needed serious mental help. Rob Gordon would call after every commercial break and stay on the phone with me, which really helped with my initial shock. The disbelief, pain, and awfulness of it was so multilayered. Johnny denied his love for me, denied his relationship with me (which was ongoing), and made me and my friend Bob, whom I loved so much, seem like blackmailers on national TV, without any regard as to how it would impact Bob or his family. And worst of all, he continued on his path of lies concerning Elizabeth—how great and strong and wonderful she is, how strong his marriage and his love for Elizabeth are, and how much the Lord and Elizabeth have forgiven him. Irritating and painful, yes, but all of that paled in comparison to hearing him say, "It is not possible that she is my child."

Nothing—nothing—prepared me for that.

I watched the man that I loved more than any other man in the world deny our child, the greatest love of my life, his own flesh and blood and, like most people, wondered how could he do that?

I believe one, he had a twenty-year habit of fixing things by lying about women. Two, he was temporarily insane.

Here's the thing: no one who is *not* off his rocker would do that, especially if he believed he could get away with it. Clearly he was not going to get away with it and he just wanted to stop the pain.

And as much as I hurt—and boy, I wish that experience on no one!—I also knew he did not need my judgment or anyone else's. He needed help. Think about it: sane, healthy people do not deny their children, especially on national TV, simply because they are afraid of their abusive spouse's reaction. Only a mentally off person would do that.

When Johnny was indicted, I read an opinion piece by Ruth Marcus in the *Washington Post*, in which her first line read, "John Edwards is pond scum." All I could think was, "Pond scum? Did he go on national TV and deny the paternity of *your* child?" I mean, the judgment is unbelievable. A lot of people believe his cheating on Elizabeth and fathering a child while she had cancer was his worst action. Knowing the truth of their decades-long–no intimacy/abusive relationship and being the mother of the daughter he denied, I would beg to differ. Listening to him deny our child broke my heart and obviously confirmed to me that he was in dire need of help.

I had spoken to him earlier in the day, before the interview aired, as he was scrambling to write some sort of statement. He thought that ABC had screwed them and that some of the content had been leaked, thus starting a media firestorm (talk about ratings for ABC!). However, he told me that he believed the interview had gone well.

He honestly thought it had gone well.

This was not a well man.

After I watched the interview, I told him, "Wow. That hurt."

He said, "Sorry, but it didn't mean anything."

It's very weird to be so disconnected from your public image, which doesn't remotely match the reality of your life, the way my

public image doesn't as I am writing this. When it's so far off, it's understandable how he could get to a place where he gives the public
what they want: that public guy, *John Edwards*, which is not, nor has
it ever been, the Johnny Reid Edwards I know.

Back then I didn't understand that the way I do now. I didn't sleep
at all that night. And the barrage of, "Who is Rielle Hunter?" was just
beginning. What appeared on screen with that terrifying image from
the *National Enquirer*, coupled with what John Edwards himself said
in that interview, could make anyone reasonably assume that I was
a gold-digging, blackmailing whore, with whom he did not father a
child, and whom he did not love. "A serious mistake in judgment"
was all I amounted to.

I honestly had no idea how our relationship could ever recover
from that.

The next day, unfortunately, Ricky brought me a computer, upon
which I would receive yet another blow—a much lesser one, but
wow, it still hurt. Jonathan Darman wrote a piece called, "What
Rielle Hunter Told Me." Besides the invasion of privacy, the real pain
was the last paragraph:

> That October, the *National Enquirer* wrote a story claiming that Rielle
> and Edwards were having an affair. Rielle called me to ask, should she
> put out a statement denying it? I asked her if she would give a statement
> to *Newsweek*, which seemed to make her mad. She said she was talk-
> ing to me as a friend, not a journalist. Though she said that our conver-
> sations had been "between you and me," we had never actually gone off
> the record. Our conversation ended abruptly. I never got to ask her the
> most important question: whether she had had an affair with Edwards.
> I tried to contact her several times in the months that followed, but she
> didn't return my calls. It occurred to me she was saddened that she had
> come to think of me as a friend, but I saw her as a story. In December,
> the *Enquirer* ran an article claiming she was pregnant with Edwards's
> child. (Edwards denies he is the father, and has offered to take a pater-
> nity test to prove it. Prior to the child's birth, an Edwards aide, Andrew
> Young, told the *Enquirer* he was the father of Rielle's child. An Edwards
> adviser, speaking on Edwards's behalf, declined to comment for this
> story. Rielle did not respond to e-mails I sent her last week seeking

comment.) In early January, I was surprised to receive an e-mail from her saying she was thinking about me and hoping I was OK. I haven't heard from her since. But I believe she really did hope I was OK. When my father died later that month, she sent me flowers.

My friend, who just a few weeks before in July had sent me an email saying he missed me and sent me his love, was now claiming (even after I sent him an email saying everything was off the record in October 2007) that we really never went off the record and how sad and stupid I was for viewing Darman as a friend.

Yes, he was painfully correct on that. How sad, because if what he said is true, that would mean that either he lied to me, and pretended to be my friend, and this his warmth, his feelings, his invitation to his father's funeral was all in order to get a story. Or he lied to his readership, hiding and covering his real feelings in order to get a story and advance his career.

Sad indeed.

My real friends and my sister Melissa were flipping out over the way Johnny threw Quinn and me under the bus and about what the media was saying about me. Pigeon O'Brien, the woman who tipped off the *National Enquirer*, was now making the media rounds working her on new public career as my close friend of twenty years. I can still hear Angela Janklow, my dear friend from New York City that I've known since we were sixteen years old, screaming, "Who is this Pigeon person claiming to be your friend?" I was the (trash) talk of every dinner party my friends attended and every grocery line they stood in. They were all upset and very concerned about my well-being. Outside of Mimi, the media were having trouble locating any of my real friends, mostly because they did not know who they were. I asked my friends not to speak to the media and told them that I was hurt but did not want to engage the media publicly.

First and foremost, I am a mother, so my biggest concern was and is for Quinn, her temporarily insane father, and their relationship. Crazy or not, he was still her dad, and I wanted to make sure that she always had the opportunity to have a good relationship with him.

St. Croix, the place where I watched the interview, was not at all where I wanted to be. I didn't feel good there. And naturally, the

National Enquirer found out that I was there, and reporters were lurking everywhere, so that kept us inside most of the day. Prisoners in our hotel room, I reached my end. How many times can one read and reread *A Fly Went By*? I was done. I did not want to run from the media anymore. I thought if I stopped running, there would be no more chase. I called Fred and told him that I was done with running. I really just wanted to go back to Santa Barbara, the place that felt like heaven on earth. Fred had already paid for the house through December 4th.

Thanks to being officially revealed by John Edwards, and then thrown under the bus, my life was now going to be different. I understood that Johnny's actions were going to drive the *National Enquirer* and the media to hunt us even more vigorously in order to prove that he was Quinn's father. I was just going to have to adjust.

Keeping Quinn safe was my foremost concern. I wanted to hire security. Fred thought that was a great idea, and I thought that with that addition, we would be fine. I would just buy more big floppy hats for Quinn and big sunglasses for me. If our picture was taken, so be it. I was done with the charade.

Johnny was still in terrible condition and had gone to stay with his friend John Moylan in South Carolina. Johnny called me from John Moylan's a few times. Then Johnny and John Moylan went to see Bunny. He called me, I believe, from her house to ask if I knew anything about checks Andrew had received from Bunny. I told him Andrew told me he received two for twenty-five thousand dollars each and told me they were never deposited. Johnny said, "That's not what I'm talking about."

I had no idea what he was talking about, nor did he tell me. I assumed he did not want to tell me over the phone because he thought our phone calls were being traced or recorded. And then the feds started investigating, so we never actually talked about it, which is what the lawyers advised us to do. No one ever told me what had happened. Needless to say, I was floored when I learned in 2010 that Andrew had received around $725,000. Even with that information, I never fully believed it or realized the extent of the Youngs' deceit until I saw the actual checks and amounts in the indictment. Only then did I finally put it all together. Andrew and Cheri played us all.

Johnny later told me that Alex Forger, Bunny Mellon's lawyer, discovered the checks written to Bryan Huffman, a decorator, and he signed them over to Cheri Feister (Cheri's maiden name) and Cheri had endorsed the checks. Alex told Fred about them, and Fred told Johnny.

Johnny had no idea what Fred was talking about. Apparently Fred was furious upon making this discovery, even though I think he always sensed that Andrew had been taking advantage of him.

Leaving St. Croix, Quinn and I flew privately to Miami and then boarded a commercial flight to LAX. A car met us at the airport, and on our way back to Santa Barbara I called Fred, telling him we had made it and thanking him for how wonderful he was to Quinn and me. Fred was an amazing man. I know a lot of people who don't have half the heart that Fred did. Fred always managed to see the bright side. He was filled with optimism and always wanted to do the right thing. Fred's passing was a big loss to our world.

We got back to Santa Barbara. It was a beautiful drive, and I was happy to return. As soon as we got inside, I called the highway patrolman on his cell.

"Hi Dana, it's Rielle Hunter. I was wondering if you, by any chance, would like a job? Also, if you aren't too busy right now, is there any way you could do a drive-by? I have three strange cars parked outside my gate."

TWENTY-ONE

Goodbye, Santa Barbara

"Conflict cannot survive without your participation."

—WAYNE DYER

LISA BLUE CALLED ME very early in the morning. She seemed very uncomfortable and awkward. After speaking to her for a little while, I was finally able to get out of her that Johnny told her to call me and end our relationship.

"What? Are you serious?"

She was serious.

"Lisa, tell him to call me directly."

"He can't, because of Elizabeth."

"What, are we in high school? Johnny told you to tell me that he is breaking up with me? Lisa, I love you. Tell him to call me directly."

She called me back and patched Johnny through to me on a three-way call. Then she put her phone down and went in the other room so he could talk to me directly.

He told me he had finally told Elizabeth everything, including that he was Quinn's father and promised her that he wouldn't ever speak to me again.

I listened to him for a few minutes. He was just talking and talking and sounded completely off his rocker. I believed it was true that he had finally actually told Elizabeth everything, which is what triggered more of this craziness. He was saying things to me like, "I have never loved you. I was not in love with you. I have loved one woman." He was talking as if he were giving an interview, not like we were having a conversation. He was that weird, disconnected, false-persona guy, the same guy he was during his interview with Bob Woodruff, talking all over the place. The big problem for me was that he actually believed what he was saying as he was saying it.

"Okay," I said. "Listen to me. You have to trust me. Have I ever told you something that wasn't true?"

"No."

"Okay, listen carefully. You are not yourself right now. You have been traumatized and you have gone temporarily insane. I cannot let you go into the world. I cannot leave you in the hands of Elizabeth and her abuse until you have returned to your normal self. If then you want to end our relationship, I will be fine with that, but right now, I am not allowing this to end. You cannot cut off your connection with me. Do you understand what I am saying?"

"I'm not sure I agree with you."

"You don't have to agree with me but you cannot stop talking to me right now. Your daughter needs you."

Quinn's favorite vibrating, musical seat, which enabled me to cook or take a shower.

That got him. He wasn't going anywhere.

To this day he has no memory of that phone call. I, on the other hand, revisited that call in my head many times over, wondering why I didn't just let him go. The only rational explanation I can come up with is that I didn't want to cut him out of my life at that point because I didn't want to cut him out of Quinn's life.

He called again the next day, sounding much better, but still not anywhere near himself. He informed me that Elizabeth wanted me to sign a confidentiality agreement that I would never, ever tell anyone the truth about our relationship, except Quinn. I could tell my daughter who her father is.

I balked immediately. "No, I will not sign that."

"I need you to. She is going crazy. She screams at me all the time."

"So let me get this straight," I said. "In order for Elizabeth to save face, she wants my daughter to grow up living a lie? That is never going to happen."

"She's going crazy. She is afraid you are going to tell the world the truth."

"I have no desire to talk to anyone but I am not signing a confidentiality agreement. I went against what I believe is right once. That will never happen again."

"I am stuck between both of you. And she is screaming at me constantly."

It was that simple: he wanted me to give Elizabeth her way so she would stop screaming at him. She could scream all she wanted; it wouldn't change my mind.

He sighed. "You're both impossible. She is never going to change."

"So be it. I am not signing anything."

It still amazes me the extent to which people do not understand that most of the mental and emotional pain that we experience is caused by not getting our way. We want something other than what happened or is happening. Once, Johnny and I were having a conversation, and he said, "But it's more complicated than that." I said, "No, your mind makes it complicated. It's actually quite simple. The world isn't going the way you want it to, and that is what's causing the pain."

Also, at this point, Andrew wasn't getting what he wanted—*more money*— and he was driving Fred crazy. Fred really wanted Johnny to talk to Andrew and get him off his back.

Johnny finally agreed to meet with Andrew. In that meeting, Johnny asked Andrew, "What are those checks you got from Bunny?" And Andrew lied to him, saying he didn't know what Johnny was talking about.

Now it seems to me if Johnny had actually told Andrew to solicit money from Bunny, all Andrew would have had to say was, "What do you mean what are those checks? That's the money you told me to get for Rielle."

Apparently Andrew also told Johnny during this meeting, after Johnny told him there was not going to be a foundation funded by Bunny, that Cheri found a sex tape and described the tape in a vulgar, inaccurate way. Andrew was blackmailing Johnny.

Johnny had finally had enough of Andrew. From all accounts, it appeared that Andrew had stolen money from Bunny and had taken complete advantage of Fred. I was telling Johnny that Andrew was bad news and to stay away from him, the very same thing that Elizabeth had been screaming for years, and now Andrew was blackmailing Johnny with a sex tape. He also claimed to have voicemails and emails he was going to share with the world.

From Johnny's point of view, Andrew couldn't hurt him because he had already told Elizabeth that he was Quinn's father. He had faced his biggest fear and was still alive. He was done with Andrew. Praise the Lord.

Johnny called me after this meeting to tell me what Andrew had said about having a tape. I didn't believe Andrew and thought he was bluffing. I told Johnny that I had destroyed the tape in December 2006 and didn't believe Andrew was telling the truth about that, especially given the way he described the tape.

Elizabeth, being so brilliant at manipulating the media (and right out of the James Carville school of how to win—get your story out first), was on the cover of *People*. She didn't speak to them on the record but directed her brother and best friend Hargrave to speak. The piece was all about how she was coping with her anguish and determination to keep her family together, and how she had made the agonizing decision to forgive John for the sake of her family. I read that and couldn't help but wonder what she meant when she said forgiveness, because it certainly wasn't anything that I recognized as

The Santa Barbara Zoo, 2008.

being forgiving. Was it somewhere in between her vile rants, using her kids as pawns, and attempting to hold Johnny hostage in his own home, all while she attempted to get me to sign off on allowing my daughter to grow up under a lie? I wouldn't call any of that forgiveness. As usual, my irritation was triggered from the spin being so far away from the reality. My irritation was not caused by Elizabeth spinning reality but by my own thoughts about her spinning reality. Shockingly enough, the world was happening the way I think it shouldn't be. As usual, I let it go quickly.

At the very end of August, a surprising and glorious thing happened. It was late morning, Quinn was snoozing away during her first nap of the day, and I was watching TV next to her when John McCain named Sarah Palin as his vice presidential running mate. Right then and there, I smiled wide because I knew in that moment my sweet girl and I had just become yesterday's news. Sure enough, the mainstream media, the tabloids, and the bloggers all packed up and moved on to the great state of Alaska to focus on (stalk, uncover information, trash) their new media darling, Sarah Palin.

Quinn's first Thanksgiving, Santa Barbara, CA, 2008.

September was peaceful and uneventful. Bliss in Santa Barbara. Johnny and I spoke on the phone every day. He was still not well, not himself, and very detached, but he had started seeing a therapist. Nothing had changed in his marriage. From Elizabeth's perspective, Johnny had ruined her life. Privately, she blamed him much more than she blamed me. I also heard she blamed the old mistresses and still harassed them from time to time but directed most of her abuse and punishment at Johnny. And the poor guy, they don't have any locks on the bedroom doors, so no matter where he was in that house, or in the barn, she would find him at all hours of the night to scream bloody murder at him for hours on end. Sometimes she would even hit him.

She also began to write her book *Resilience*. It's sort of a sad joke that she would be writing a book about how resilient she was and how she overcame her tragedies, including infidelity, at this point in her life. In her defense, given the success of *Saving Graces,* she was already set to write another book. Still, she could have also told the truth.

Fred called me at the end of September. He was on his way to the Mayo Clinic. We talked about moving my stuff out of the house in North Carolina. Mimi was doing it all, and was going to send him all the invoices and so forth. We also talked about the used BMW that I was driving around, which now belonged to him. I let him know that the registration was expiring soon and would need to be renewed but I didn't have the title. When I asked Fred what he wanted to do about that, he said, "I'll send you the title. You keep the car. I have enough cars. I have cars in Aspen, Texas, and one in North Carolina. I don't need another car. You can have it." I was completely floored by his generosity. I couldn't thank him enough.

Fred also expressed to me his frustrations about Johnny. Like me, Fred really wanted him to step up to the plate and to stop placating Elizabeth. I did not know then that it was the last time I would ever speak to Fred.

Fred passed away on October 30th, 2008. He had wanted Johnny to speak at his funeral, but Lisa Blue understandably vetoed it. Johnny went and didn't speak. For obvious reasons she didn't want me anywhere near the service. Fred's highly publicized gifts to me colored all the great deeds of his lifetime. To this day, that saddens me whenever I think of it.

I spoke to lawyer Abbe Lowell on the phone a few times after Fred passed away because he was helping Lisa at that time. Rob Gordon had signed off on me speaking to Abbe directly. By this time I was timid about talking to anyone new, but Rob said, "You will see when you talk to him, he's a great guy." Rob was right about that. Rob also signed off as my lawyer and continued on as my friend. Abbe told me that the feds were now investigating, so I was now going to need a criminal lawyer *and* a family lawyer.

My lease was up at the beginning of December, so Quinn and I moved back to New Jersey. I was so excited to be back in New Jersey because I missed Mimi and the boys so much. The press reports were hilarious, making up all kinds of nonsensical speculation about why we would be landing back in New Jersey. The truth? I missed my best friend and I felt too isolated in Santa Barbara. As a single mom, my adult interaction was all too rare. Living with loved ones was very enticing to me, to say nothing of having emotional support.

I also had no idea what my finances were going to be like. I had enough money from Fred to last for a while, but then what? I didn't know.

TWENTY-TWO

Jersey Girls

"Patience, n. A minor form of despair, disguised as a virtue."

—Ambrose Bierce

N THE BEGINNING of December 2008 Johnny went to Haiti with the director and producer Paul Haggis and called me as soon as he arrived. Quinn and I had just arrived in New Jersey. Johnny was sounding almost like his old self. He said, "I have to tell you something very important."

I braced myself for whatever was going to come out of his mouth.

"I love you. I really love you."

I almost laughed. This was his important news from Haiti?

"I know that."

"No. I really love you."

He was saying it as if he had just figured it out. Apparently, being away from Elizabeth got him back in touch with his feelings.

"I know that, even though you forgot it."

He called me every night from Haiti. It was nice to have him back, even though it was brief. As soon as he returned to Chapel Hill, Elizabeth's abuse resumed, and he went back into his self-preservation mode. I felt that no matter how awful the abuse was, he was never going to leave her now that she was dying. What would be the

Central Park, New York City, December 2008. Quinn and I had a fun ladies' lunch with my friend Glory Crampton at Serafina. After lunch we took a stroll through the park.

point? He was going to suck it up and endure all her hostility. After all, didn't he deserve it? Most of the world seemed to think so, and deep down, I believe that he thought so, too. I prayed that Quinn would still have a father left when Elizabeth got through with him. I continued talking to him, hoping our conversations would help minimize the damage to his psyche.

The *National Enquirer* showed up at Mimi's door within days of our arrival back in New Jersey. Mimi called upstairs, "It's started."

I thought she was talking about the cable guy, who was scheduled to arrive at 8 A.M. to hook up the cable in our room in the attic. Quinn and I came downstairs and Mimi was waving a letter from the *Enquirer*, a pitch letter offering compensation for an interview. What a joke. As usual, I did not respond, so as usual the story trashed me, saying I was down and destitute in New Jersey.

Quinn's first Christmas was in South Orange, New Jersey. We went into Manhattan a few times to see the Rockefeller Center tree, have lunch with Glory Crampton, and have lunch with Rob Gordon. Christmas in New York always feels so magical. Quinn *loved* New York City. She would begin singing as soon as we went through the tunnel and didn't stop until she fell asleep on the way home.

We adjusted to life in New Jersey quickly. I found Vanita, who is a great babysitter. We enjoyed Music Together and My Gym, where we met other Jersey moms and tots and began doing a ton of mommy-and-me things.

Quinn's first Christmas. She loved Winona and was obsessed with walking her. Winona's leash would hang on the front door and Quinn would crawl over to the door, grab the leash, and follow Winona around the house attempting to put it on her.

Understandably, Elizabeth was hell-bent on making my life as miserable as possible while she rewrote history and finished her book. She rejected the fact that Quinn was Johnny's daughter simply because he believed and said he was. Even though he never denied paternity to his lawyers, they were really pushing for a DNA test because that's what lawyers do. After months of going back and forth, Johnny finally said to his lawyers that he was offended by it. There was no denial of paternity. He wanted to stop fighting them and just move forward.

And we tried, but Elizabeth stopped us at every point.

I read in the tabloids that I demanded a paternity test, eighteen thousand dollars a month in child support, and ten million dollars. Perhaps stupidly, I never demanded anything.

But I did get pissed off many, many times in 2009. Could I have made Elizabeth's life *really* miserable? Yes, I could have. I could have gone public, nailing her to the wall, and believe me, I fantasized about it more than once. But I felt that if I stepped over Johnny and took control, it would emasculate him, which would have been a very bad thing for Quinn. So no matter how much anger I experienced, I chose to wait for Johnny to work out whatever he needed to with Elizabeth.

I remember when he called me to tell me that Elizabeth had Oprah coming to their house. Johnny and I were both baffled as to why Elizabeth would do that. I had no idea how she was going to deflect Oprah when she asked the only question that anyone cared about: is John Edwards Quinn's father?

Johnny said, "I have no idea what Elizabeth is doing."

Apparently Elizabeth was very nice to Johnny the day Oprah was at the Ponderosa.

However, she resumed her screaming at Johnny the day after she taped *Oprah*, saying it was all his fault that she lied on *Oprah* for him. He told me he said, "You lied for *me*? How about you lied for you! I didn't tell you to do *Oprah*. I didn't tell you to write a book."

Of course, everyone wanted to know what she was going to say. And when *Oprah* aired, it resulted in all sorts of cars and vans parked outside Mimi's house. The media called her cell phone constantly and even tried to friend her on Facebook, all in pursuit of me. Mimi really wanted me to end the charade and speak the truth. She was getting very frustrated at Johnny and Elizabeth's bullshit because it had now invaded her house, and believed that my waiting, instead of fighting or speaking up, was just making it worse for all of us.

Elizabeth was constantly afraid that I was going to go public. In Johnny's typical passive-aggressive way, he dealt with Elizabeth by leaving the country during her media stint. He called me every day from wherever he was. All the while, Elizabeth talked about how noble he was and how he was such a perfect husband, except for that one-time thing.

For me, it was odd to watch her talk about how much I wanted attention and that she was not going to give me what I wanted, by naming me, which I heard was her one condition for all the people who interviewed her, thereby creating even more of an air of mystery around me than if she'd actually said my name.

As I said, I did get pissed off a few times, like the time I was standing in the kitchen making coffee. I had just put Quinn in her high chair when I looked up and saw a camera pointed at us from outside on the front sidewalk.

And while Elizabeth paraded around on TV as the poor victim wife who had overcome her husband's one-time-only shortcoming, giving a tour of the twenty-thousand-square-foot house that Johnny paid for, Johnny's youngest daughter was living in an attic in New Jersey because Elizabeth was preventing Quinn from having access to her father's health insurance or sustained child support, and preventing Johnny from publicly claiming paternity. She was in a constant tirade, using her cancer and Emma and Jack as weapons in the war against a father trying to take care of his daughter. Elizabeth made sure that Emma and Jack knew that *that woman*, Rielle Hunter, was responsible for all the misery in their family. All the pain she was experiencing was because of Rielle Hunter. She drilled that into their heads.

My heart broke for those kids. How sad for them to grow up in a household like that.

Whatever Elizabeth's feelings were about me, the law states that Quinn deserves the same as what her siblings are receiving from their father. And yet, thanks to Elizabeth, that wasn't even close to happening. What was going on for Quinn every month was a fight for the small amount of money that was being sent. One month we had no money; my lawyer gave us a thousand dollars out of his own pocket so we could eat.

So yes, at times I experienced some anger. But did I want to litigate and fight Elizabeth? No. I wanted my daughter to have her father and have him intact. If I were fighting Elizabeth, it would only increase the abuse directed at him. I would then be helping to destroy him.

Around that time, the *National Enquirer* reported that I was going to be interviewed by Barbara Walters or Diane Sawyer. Elizabeth went ballistic that I was going to do any interview and ranted at

Johnny for many long nights that I was going to ruin their family and their children by going public. For the life of me, I couldn't understand her thinking. Her actions were teaching her kids that to lie and deny is better than telling the truth, if the truth turns out to be a truth you don't want.

Johnny had always and consistently told me the same thing: if I wanted to speak to the media, I should, whenever I wanted. He said, "Whatever you choose to do, it will not hurt my relationship with Quinn."

I was not going to speak to the media but I believe I did surprise him once, only because I had no way of telling him beforehand. He was in a depression from his regular all-night lashings he was getting from Elizabeth and didn't call me for a few days. During that time I got an invitation that I saw no reason to turn down: I was invited to Barbara Walters's home.

Barbara and her team had been trying for a long time set up a meeting between the two of us, but I just wasn't interested and didn't want to waste her time or mine. But when they threw in Barbara at her home? Now *that* sounded pretty interesting. Where did Barbara Walters live? What did her apartment look like? What would she be like at home? Yes, my interest was piqued.

So Mimi, Quinn, and I went to Barbara's for a casual lunch. And the meeting never got out! I was so floored that it never leaked. Barbara kept her word, and everything ended up being just like she said it would be: off the record. In my life, that was a first.

Her home was exactly as I imagined—a grand old New York apartment overlooking Central Park. It was a fantastic experience and one I don't regret. What surprised me was how much Barbara appeared to want my interview. She was really angling hard for me to talk to her. I mean, come on, she is Barbara Walters; why would she want my interview so badly? It just didn't make sense to me. She even threw in that she and my oldest and very good friend Angela Janklow had known each other forever, and not only was Angela's father her agent, but Angela's parents were her very close friends.

Barbara was clearly positioning herself to help change the incorrect media portrayal and she just might have had the chance had the network's news program *20/20* not rolled out the red carpet for the

Youngs, enabling them to spew their BS on national TV. Of course, Barbara screaming at me on the phone, trying to bully me into doing her interview also didn't do her any favors.

Early one June morning, the feds came knocking on our door. Mimi let them in, and I promptly told them I couldn't talk to them. I called my lawyer and put him on the phone with them. Vanita, my beloved babysitter, took Quinn out for a walk during this visit. While they were out, a photographer with a long-lens camera snapped a shot of Quinn over Vanita's shoulder. The photo was published all over the place; Vanita was heartbroken. So what are the paparazzi and the feds doing at the same place at the same time? After the feds left, we got in the car, and I discovered that I was being followed. The feds denied having anything to do with it. I asked them about it when I went to testify and walked into a media firestorm. Gee, I wonder how the media all knew I was going to be there? The feds insisted that I testify before the grand jury at the beginning of August. It was crucial; they couldn't wait. (The investigation went on to last another two years.) But it was a problem for me because the grand jury meets only twice a month, and I couldn't get childcare in August. I could get it in September or October, but none of Quinn's babysitters were available in August. The feds gave me no choice, however; they needed me in August.

Johnny and I had both agreed that Quinn and I should move to North Carolina. He had been looking for houses for us over the phone while he was at the beach. I would find one online, and he would drive by or see if he could get inside to check it out. We had decided that Quinn and I should come look at some places the week after I testified.

He called me the Saturday before I testified. He was concerned that they were going to exploit Quinn by having me do the "perp walk" in front of the cameras. I told him I had floppy hats for her, and that that was not my biggest concern. I was mostly concerned that I was still breast-feeding and she had never been away from me for more than two hours and when she had been away, it was with people she knew. So my only choices were to leave her for nine hours in a strange place with someone she didn't know or bring her with me, where she could be with my lawyer, who she knew, and the woman who was going to watch Quinn. I could see her during my breaks and at lunch, but that would mean being in front of cameras.

The feds told me they would take me in the back entrance of the courthouse, away from all the cameras. Yeah, right. We pulled up and there were cameras surrounding the front *and* the back. I got out of the car and pulled Quinn out of her car seat. There were cameras behind us, with photographers screaming, "Ms. Hunter! Ms. Hunter!" As we walked, Quinn liked to look directly at the cameras, the way she just had with Vanita in June when the paparazzi got a clear shot of her. She was curious about all the screaming people. I turned Quinn's head and told her to look at the guys in front. Of course, there were cameras at every angle. I was later raked over the coals in the media for bringing my daughter with me and accused of purposely turning her head toward "the" camera, as if there were only one. A news station took two clips of the exact same video footage with me turning Quinn's head and spliced it together, (I assume to make our walk longer than it actually was to use as B-roll) but some reporters, including from *The New York Times*, were unable to decipher that it was the same clip spliced together and claimed that I turned Quinn's head toward "the" camera not once but twice. Underlying message: what a terrible mother.

After I testified, Jim Conney, one of Johnny's lawyers, thought it would be best if Johnny didn't talk to me indefinitely. Given we have a child together, not to mention the insanity that we were attempting to deal with, I thought that advice was terrible.

A week later Quinn and I flew to North Carolina, just as Johnny and I had already discussed. We looked at a bunch of houses in Wilmington, only to learn from my lawyers that Elizabeth and Johnny had decided that Wilmington wouldn't work. We learned this, of course, after we'd been traveling for three days and had decided on a house.

My lawyer told me that Elizabeth needed to pick where we lived. So she began house hunting.

And I'm sorry, but how crazy is it that Elizabeth had gone out house hunting for a child that she wouldn't allow her husband to furnish with health insurance or publicly acknowledge as his own child? What kind of logic in her head allowed her to do that?

Quinn in the U-Haul, helping me pack it up. She loves to help me with any and all chores.

By this point Mimi had reached the end of her rope with Team Edwards and the media circus; she was pretty adamant about wanting us out of her house. I had given her a departure date and when that day came, I had packed up our stuff and put it in a U-Haul, but we still didn't have a place to go because Team Edwards had not yet signed off on a house nor given us the money to move. I was going to go and stay at my lawyer's beach house in New Jersey. And then, in the very final hours, Team Edwards sent a link to a rental house in Southport, North Carolina.

My lawyer suggested that we stay in the rental house for two months and look around North Carolina to figure out where we wanted to live. He said, "You should check out Charlotte. I hear great things about Charlotte." Not a bad idea.

The beginning of October 2009 found me pulling a U-Haul for the first time ever, with Christine (my babysitter who flew from Santa Barbara to help me move) and Quinn in the backseat, all headed south, out of New Jersey into the great state of North Carolina.

TWENTY-THREE

Father of the Year

"Hell hath no fury like a hustler with a literary agent."

—FRANK SINATRA

FTER A GRUELING month-long nightmare looking at every house available in Southport, North Carolina, with a Realtor who was working for the "Team," we finally headed to Charlotte. The second that we drove into Charlotte, I was happy. It was autumn. Trees were everywhere and stunning. Charlotte has trees like no other city I have ever seen, and I love trees. Charlotte is a fantastic place to raise a child and call home.

The first house we looked at was perfect for us. Quinn loved it. She didn't want to leave. It was on a private street, making it difficult for paparazzi to get to us. It had a screened porch (good to keep the mosquitoes at bay), a garage (good for privacy), and a back yard (heaven for Quinn). It's not easy to find all those qualities in Charlotte housing.

But there was a problem. Elizabeth wasn't the one to find it so she would not allow Johnny even to go look at it. Elizabeth had to be the one who controlled all the money for the house and she was the only one who was allowed to find the house.

211

I was really losing patience with this control freak insanity. Johnny and Elizabeth and the Southport Realtor then got together with Amy Lothrop, a Charlotte Realtor, and searched Charlotte. They put in two offers on houses that didn't go through and then purchased a house on Providence Road that was very nice, even though it was on a very busy street, which made it bad for the media but made it more affordable. I was very excited about moving to Charlotte and ending the house search. I must have inspected at least a hundred houses.

I packed up the U-Haul *again.* About two hours into our drive from Southport, pulling the U-Haul to the new house, it occurred to the "Team" that Quinn and I should not be allowed to move in without signing a child support agreement, so they quickly pulled something together. Obviously, they had all the power, and this was a shitty thing to do at the last minute while we were in transit. The agreement was so ridiculous that my lawyer said, "There is no way I am allowing my client to sign that." And I agreed with my lawyer. One of their demands was to charge me rent on the house they had just bought for Quinn. The rent was to be taken out of the child support, which would have left us with basically no money. The "Team" said, "Fine. She and her daughter can't move into the house."

So there I was at the Marriott in Charlotte, U-Haul attached to my car, toddler attached to my hip, and no place to live. Through my tears, I asked the Team Edwards Realtor if he could stay for a day and help us find a place to live, given our terrible circumstances, made even worse because we had just spotted a weird van in the parking lot. Clearly, the *National Enquirer* was stalking the hotel. (And, in fact, they published pictures of Quinn and I in the parking lot the following week.) Thank God that, aside from all the agendas he had to work around, the Realtor actually had a heart. He stayed and helped us find a rental house.

I didn't put my full name on the lease, and our landlord had no idea who we were. She didn't even know my name and the Realtor wouldn't tell her, citing privacy reasons. Of course, she found out soon thereafter because it was all over the news and the house was surrounded with media people. My neighbors quickly learned the media game and were very protective. It is amazing to me how many people do not like the media. I got texts or phone calls the second an odd car was spotted near my house.

After the lease was signed, I drove with Quinn for three hours to Apex, North Carolina, to meet the movers the following morning at the storage unit. (In September, Mimi had put all of my stuff from the rental house in Chapel Hill into storage.) That night, after three stops, we finally found a hotel near the storage unit. I fed and bathed Quinn and put her to bed. I got a text message from Johnny—I hadn't spoken a word to him since I testified in August. The text read, "How's Quinn?"

I was so angry that I almost threw my phone across the room. I thought of many replies, including, "Sleeping peacefully until you woke her up with your stupid text," and, "Your daughter is great only because she has a mother who lives and breathes for her," and "Your daughter is great no thanks to you, *motherfucker!*" Instead, I didn't respond. I know better than to take an action in reaction. It gets you nowhere but the same place you've been before, and that was not a place I was interested in returning to. I wasn't even sure how he got my new cell phone number. It turns out the Southport Realtor had given it to him.

And because the Realtor had given my number to Johnny, Elizabeth made the Realtor into the reason that she and Johnny were not going to make it as a couple and were going to divorce. I am not kidding. She really blamed a Realtor, a twenty-three-year-old kid she had known for a few months. It was *all* his fault. She *screamed* at him!

Once we settled into the rental, I immediately did what all mothers would do: I found Quinn a pediatrician, dentist, and "mommy and me" activities.

About a week into our new city, through the lawyers I was told that Johnny had presents that he wanted to give Quinn for Christmas, so a meeting was arranged under a confidentiality agreement. No one ever told me that Elizabeth was going to be there. Had I known that Elizabeth planned to be there, I would have rejected the meeting outright. I didn't want to put my daughter in a position to be used by her crazy schemes. In fact, I didn't find out that she had been at the Christmas present meeting with Quinn until January, when she broke the confidentiality agreement spinning it to the media as Johnny's statement on paternity hit the airwaves. Johnny was in Haiti. When he called, I *screamed* at him. The first time ever. I have never been so angry in my entire life.

Elizabeth was a master at spin. Yes, she got Quinn Christmas presents. But she also would never admit to any behavior that didn't present herself as the moral and wonderful person she believed herself to be, which sadly meant she never admitted to most of her behavior. When Quinn was to go under sedation for dental work at the end of December, Elizabeth called Johnny's parents and *forbade* them from going to the hospital to be with Quinn. They said, "Sorry, Elizabeth, she is our granddaughter. We are going."

Apparently, Johnny couldn't bear to think of not being there for his daughter at the hospital. Elizabeth screamed at him, "If you go to be with her at the hospital, we are *done!*"

He said, "She is my daughter, and I am going."

"I am going to divorce you!"

So after thirty-plus years of marriage, Johnny had had enough of the power struggle and took the first step toward taking control of his own life. He got in his car and drove to Charlotte.

Shortly after midnight on December 29th, there was a knock on my door. All my lights were out. I looked outside and I couldn't see a car. And then came a hammering on the front door. I screamed, "Yes?" My heart was pounding.

And then I heard, "It's me. Open the door."

I opened the door, and there he was, in an overcoat, white T-shirt, dark pants, and black tennis shoes, smiling. "Why aren't you happy to see me?"

Yes, there he was, standing in the foyer, teasing me, as though nothing had ever happened between us.

Quinn almost jumped out of my arms to get to him.

It was so surprising to me that she knew exactly who he was and was so happy to see him, because so far in her life she had only spent about three hours with him, total. She looked at him in exactly the same way she did the first time he held her, the look she gives only to him.

"How's my sweet girl?"

She beamed. She was so excited—actually, she needed to be sleeping. A married mom once said to me, "I can't imagine having an

Quinn's first trick-or-treating outing in Charlotte. Quinn always wants her dad
to sit in the backseat next to her and Johnny always obliges.

infant with no help." I replied that there are actually some real advan-
tages: no arguments, no power struggles about how to do it, and no
frustrations about the type of (opposite) help that comes from a dad.
But then again, having a dad is having a dad, and nothing can take
the place of that important relationship.

And that night there were some badly needed extra hands for
childcare. In order to sedate an infant for surgery there are rules, including no food or liquid after midnight. I finally got Quinn to sleep,
but she was still accustomed to a feeding in the middle of the night
in order to go back to sleep. So when she woke up a few hours later,
she was unhappy and let us know it. We got in my car, Johnny in
front, Quinn and I in the backseat. He turned the heat up high, immediately putting her back to sleep. We drove around Charlotte until
we needed to get ready to go to the hospital at 5 A.M. All the while,
Elizabeth was texting him divorce messages.

We returned to the house, and Johnny lay with Quinn while she slept and I got ready. Then he helped put her in the car. She woke up a little bit and said, "Bye, Daddy," then went right back to sleep. He told me that his parents were meeting me at the hospital and he was going to go back to deal with Elizabeth. I was too exhausted from that night and the past four months, and too nervous for Quinn, to care what he did. I kissed him goodbye and told him I loved him. I got in the car and drove to the hospital.

Grandma Bobbie and Granddaddy were there waiting for us. Grandma Bobbie said to me, "Rielle, I don't know if it helps you or hurts you for us to be here, but we just had to be here. Quinn is our granddaughter and we love her."

Having them with me was a big help. I am so grateful that they were so insistent from the very beginning about being in Quinn's life. I didn't understand at that point the degree to which Elizabeth ostracized them and kept them away from Emma and Jack, or how much it meant to them to be close to Quinn. I still struggle helping Quinn develop her relationship with her grandparents because of the way that I grew up. I am not used to making strong efforts to keep close.

Having a family like Johnny's was a new experience for me. They love unconditionally and they don't speak to the press. Although, Johnny's sister Kathy still regrets that she didn't publicly tell the truth about Elizabeth. Kathy told me that for decades she was frustrated and miserable about her sister-in-law, and no one would address it. The response was always, "She's Johnny's wife." They were not going to deal with it or even talk about it. They prayed for her.

Johnny called on Wednesday night from the beach saying that he and Elizabeth were officially separated. He told me that she had physically attacked him again in a fight (something she later accused him of in an email to a "friend," which made it into the *National Enquirer*, and which she refused to correct publicly). He said that he had finally had enough of her berating him for being such an awful person. He was in bad shape. I felt awful for him.

At midnight on New Year's Eve, he called to wish us a happy new year.

As usual, Elizabeth was tracking his phone to determine his whereabouts and to find out what numbers he was calling. She cited this midnight phone call as the deal breaker for her, even though they were already separated.

When they signed the separation agreement, the actual separation was dated December 30th, which meant that under North Carolina law, they could get divorced one year from that date.

Elizabeth sent me a weird email on the day they separated. It was from one of her hidden email accounts. The name on the account was Joyce Oates. The subject line was simply "Johnny's cell phone number." A month later she sent my lawyer an email, from her office email account, carbon copying me. The subject line on this one read, "A claim against Hunter" and in it she claimed that I was liable under North Carolina law for criminal conversation and alienation of affection. However, she was willing not to pursue claims against me—to settle— if I signed an agreement that was framed around the following parts:

1. "Hunter will not write or talk about John, me, any member of my family, our home, or any conduct of or communication with such persons... except that Hunter may talk to Frances Quinn Hunter about her father."

2. "that in the event that Hunter violates this agreement (and each time she violates this agreement, if she violates it more than once and for each memorialization or copy she fails to tender), she agrees that she will pay the Wade Edwards Foundation the amount of $1,400,000.00 within ten days of notice of violation."

It went on and on, and she signed her name at the bottom. Reading it was so sad to me. My lawyer and I simply ignored it. I told Johnny about it, and he replied, "That's just more of Elizabeth's craziness." I could hear the sadness in his voice.

Once they separated and we were talking again, Johnny and I both moved forward immediately and signed a child support agreement so he could publicly claim paternity. I think because of my intense desire to move forward, to finally be free from all this mess and move on with our lives, I made some big mistakes. I signed a child support agreement that wasn't great at all. It wasn't bad but it wasn't fabulous. I also did a magazine interview that I shouldn't have done or at least should have had PR help with arranging.

People just have no idea what it's really like when the media is after you, camped outside your house, following you around town, popping up in between cars in a parking lot while you're trying to get a baby out of her car seat safely then and she hits her head because a photographer jumped up out of nowhere. I am not asking for sympathy. I am simply saying that there is no parade happening here. We attempt to get from Point A to Point B as safely and privately as we can. Cameras have been following us since I was pregnant. I have had to put big sunglasses or hats on Quinn to cover her face since she was an infant. It's now become something that she's accustomed to. She loves her sunglasses. She has many pairs and doesn't go outside without them.

I now view speaking soon after Johnny had publicly claimed paternity as a mistake. It was too soon (to say the least) and only helped make the media go away a little bit. I just had no idea what kind of

The back deck of Johnny's rental house, 2010. We spent a lot of time there cooking out on the grill and dancing.

legs this story actually had, that it was *not* going to die no matter what I did. Right around the time that Johnny publicly stated, "I am Quinn's father," after he had returned from Haiti, Barbara Walters's producer Katie called to tell me that there was *in fact* a sex tape, and that ABC producers *had seen it.*

"Oh, and by the way, it pains me to ask you this because it is so wrong and I hate my job, *but* I have to ask: Andrew and Cheri also have property that clearly belongs to you, and those ABC producers want your permission to use it."

What floors me about this is that the producers, James Hill and Natalie Shabilat, watched the tape (there aren't words to describe how gross that feels to me) but never publicly disclosed that little fact to anyone. And then to top it off, they went ahead and broadcast one of Andrew and Cheri's many false claims: that I was pregnant on the tape!

I replied to Katie in a louder-than-normal voice, "Whatever photos or tape that the Youngs have that look like mine is stolen property, and I will fucking sue your asses if you use my property."

I hung up and called Johnny, who had just moved into his new rental house, and told him, "Apparently the tape does exist, and I need a lawyer. I need a lawyer fast. Please give me a name."

I called my New Jersey lawyer, Mike Critchley, and he called Wade Barber, the lawyer Johnny suggested, and then I spoke to Wade. And then Wade did something wonderful and brilliant: he brought in my knights in shining armor, two of the greatest lawyers on the planet, and just downright stellar individuals, Alan Duncan and Allison Van Laningham. I truly love them, especially Allison. Besides being downright brilliant, day after day, she selflessly goes the extra mile, never ceasing to amaze me.

Quinn and I left town before the *20/20* interview aired. We went to the mountains to spend the weekend with my dear friend Burr Collier from my horse show days. After watching the fiction-filled interview with the Youngs, followed by a glorious weekend in the mountains, we headed to Johnny's new rental house in Hillsborough, North Carolina.

And there, in his new ultra-green, modern rental house, in the middle of nowhere, Quinn and her dad fell madly in love with each other. They would cook together, catch fireflies, hunt for bugs, do sticker books, and play "Ring Around The Rosie." One great thing about not living with your dad full-time is that when you are with him, you get all of him. When it comes to Quinn, Johnny is completely attentive. Not many little girls get that.

We met Johnny's sister Kathy and her husband, Steve, for the first time in that house. We also celebrated Quinn's second birthday with her grandparents in that house. And when the *GQ* interview hit the newstands on March 15th, 2010, Quinn and I were safely tucked away in that house with Johnny, retreating from the worldwide venom that was directed at me, with the help of stupid pictures, and the souped-up hounding from the media, all wanting my exclusive TV interview.

Eventually I decided to give a TV interview and went with Oprah as my choice. She got my interview for the same reason she gets all the great interviews: because Oprah doesn't operate like everyone else in the news media. She doesn't chase you down. She doesn't bully you. She doesn't attempt to seduce you. The interviews are not fear-based. Your boundaries are respected. She and her team do what they say they will do.

Johnny's rental house, 2010. Quinn loves to help him cook. They spend a lot of time together in the kitchen.

But I have to admit that I was a little concerned when Oprah's producer Jill called one day during the decision-making phase to tell me that Oprah would like to come to my house. I was even more uneasy when Jill told me that Oprah doesn't go to many houses. I thought back over the years I had seen *Oprah* and I realized that was true. People usually go to Oprah—she doesn't go to them. Yes, she had gone to Elizabeth's house, though she didn't go to the Youngs. (Too bad, because it might have explained to us all where the money I allegedly received actually was.) And yet her wanting to come to my house didn't make sense. I couldn't even picture it in my head. Oprah Winfrey, the Queen of TV, at my little rental house? Life just doesn't get more surreal than that. I said yes.

Oprah's people came the day before she did and turned my downstairs into a tiny TV studio. When Oprah arrived the next day, she did not disappoint. Stepping out of a black SUV surrounded by security guards in my tiny driveway, hair and makeup getting touched up as she was being miked, there was no mistaking who the power source was in this operation. The way her staff responded to her arrival, in a flawless, drama-free work mode, was like nothing I'd ever seen before. And as all of this was going on, she yelled out, "Hi Ri!" as if she had known me my whole life.

There were a lot of angry people who did not want Oprah to interview me, to give me any attention whatsoever, to "reward" what they viewed as my bad behavior. I understand that thinking. I even said to Oprah myself, "I sent you a letter back in 2004, when I was all love and light, and you ignored it. I go and have an affair with a presidential candidate, get knocked up, have a child born out of wedlock while his wife has cancer, and *then* you show up at my door. What's up with that?"

She replied, "It's all part of the plan."

The Divine Plan. Yes, Oprah spoke my language.

I thought she did a pretty good job with the interview, given that we had talked a long time, and she only had around forty-two minutes of airtime. There were a lot of things that didn't make it into the interview, and from my perspective, when you want to speak your piece, you want it all in there so that you can feel like, "There, I said it, and I am done."

I believe a lot of people could not understand how I—someone who fell in love with a married man, became a mistress, and hid it from the world—could view myself as a spiritual person devoted to Truth. People have all sorts of ideas as to what makes someone spiritual or how a spiritual person is supposed to behave. For me, pledging an allegiance to a set of rules, concepts, or belief systems does not necessarily make someone a kind, loving, and accepting person. To me, spirituality is a state of consciousness—an inner space of silence, love, peace, and contentment (oftentimes called the Truth). And being devoted to that state of consciousness (or Truth) means you are always honest with yourself, you always tell the truth to yourself about all the concepts, thoughts, and feelings within you that are attempting to keep your mind or your attention away from that inner space of love, silence, peace, and contentment.

There were also questions in the interview that I wished I could have answered more effectively, like, "Do you think you hurt Elizabeth?" I replied that I thought she experienced pain, but you would have to ask her. I didn't know. What I wish I had said was, "Some people believe that outside events or people cause our pain. I believe it's not the events on the outside that cause our emotional or psychological pain, but our thoughts about the events that cause our pain. The pain is already within us; it surfaces when the world doesn't go the way we want it to and given their marriage was a mess long before I got there, and I don't actually know Elizabeth, I don't know for sure what thoughts trigger pain for her."

Of course, that would have probably increased the backlash because it is not the answer most people want to hear!

The written reaction turned out to be mostly venomous. *The New York Times* even compared me to Mahmoud Ahmadinejad, although he is easier to understand, because he comes with a translator. This wasn't that surprising, besides bashing being a great tool to sell papers when you don't have a negative reaction to something or don't have a war raging inside of you, you usually don't take the time to write about it because you don't actually care. So the people who watched the interview and understood where I was coming from, would have said, "Cool," or, "Interesting." And then instead of rehashing it all over the TV or the Internet they would have moved on to their next pressing thought like, "What should I eat for dinner?"

TWENTY-FOUR

The Last Chapter Before the Verdict

"Forgiveness is the fragrance that the violet sheds on the heel that has crushed it."

—MARK TWAIN

ALL FAMILY HOLIDAYS come with their own special challenges, but when you are co-parenting with someone who is also co-parenting with Elizabeth Edwards, it gets especially challenging. I didn't make any plans for Thanksgiving 2010, because it was going to be Quinn's first Thanksgiving with her father and could easily be Elizabeth's last, I wanted to give Johnny ample room to fit in all that he felt he needed to do. Plus Cate's upcoming engagement was in the mix. Johnny's parents are big on Thanksgiving, and Grandma Bobbie was cooking for Quinn's cousin Julie and her entire basketball team from Elon University. Johnny decided he wanted to take Jack and Emma to Grandma Bobbie's, which meant Quinn and I would not be going.

I was unhappy that Johnny would even ask to take Jack and Emma away from Elizabeth on what might be her last Thanksgiving and I

Christmas in Charlotte, 2011

told him so. He said she was fine with it because she wanted to have Thanksgiving with her family at the Ponderosa.

So Quinn and I spent a glorious Thanksgiving Day by ourselves, hanging out, eating, watching movies, and playing games. And we planned on having her grandparents and Johnny come on Saturday for our Thanksgiving dinner, after Cate's engagement celebrations.

The night before our Saturday Thanksgiving, Johnny was summoned to Elizabeth's room to be issued her instructions on what she wanted him to do for Jack and Emma for the weekend. Johnny reminded her that he was not available on Saturday because he was going to see Quinn for her Thanksgiving. Elizabeth then flew into her usual tirade, making it about me and how he chose me over her. And now he was choosing that whore *again* over what he was supposed to be doing for her.

And I know you may find this shocking but I don't actually agree with Elizabeth on this. I don't believe Johnny chose me and I don't believe he chose Elizabeth. I believe he initially chose fear, self-preservation, and what he thought he was supposed to do based on guilt.

But Elizabeth believed he chose me over her, even though this particular event was actually about a dad wanting to be with his daughter for Thanksgiving. And as usual, his only way to deal with Elizabeth when she got like that was to leave the room. He came to Charlotte as planned, and we had a great Thanksgiving together.

Elizabeth got very ill the following Sunday after Thanksgiving and had to go to the emergency room. By the following Wednesday, they told her to get her affairs in order.

As far as I know, that was the last fight they ever had. Once she went into the hospital and the prognosis was shrunk to weeks or days left, Johnny let everything negative that came out of her mouth roll off his back. He moved back into the barn and took care of her.

Having been through the final stages of cancer at my father's bedside, I understood completely what they were going through in her last week. Johnny would check in a few times a day. He was clearly in that otherworldly, death-is-near reality.

As anyone who has been there knows, it is very difficult to go through, sitting beside a dying loved one. A week feels like a lifetime. I am very grateful and happy to report that they did finally find some peace with each other in her final days.

Her passing was strange, an emotional and odd event for everyone on Johnny's side of the family. Everyone had, to varying degrees, been ostracized or attacked by Elizabeth.

His family was truly sad about her passing but they were also very much looking forward to getting Johnny back and being able to spend time with him again.

After Elizabeth passed away, and after I had talked to Johnny, I spoke to Kathy, Johnny's sister. She hadn't spoken to Johnny yet but was afraid to call the house. She wanted to know whether she should just call his cell. This really upset me, to learn that she was afraid to call her own brother's house. I told Johnny about it, and he said, "Years of getting screamed at has had an effect on all of my family. But all of that is going to change now."

Elizabeth's passing was a media event like nothing I have ever seen, especially for the wife of a one-time senator and twice-failed presidential candidate. The tabloids immediately went to work, making up horrendous things about that awful Rielle Hunter and her rush to make wedding plans now that Elizabeth was dead. A stranger actually stopped me in the grocery store less than twenty-four hours after her death and asked me, "So are you just going to wait six months and then get married?"

Many people were triggered to spew their venom at me one more time, reeled in by the story of the brave, graceful Elizabeth, the skank mistress, and the evil husband whom "she cut out of her will," as the CBS Nightly News reported. That is so ridiculous to me—as in, she hated him so much she left him no money? That will show him!

In the months after Elizabeth passed, I regretted not trying to talk to her and come to some sort of truce, for Emma and Jack and Quinn. Because Elizabeth drilled such awful nonsense into the heads of her children about me, it has made it logistically difficult for him to spend as much time with Quinn as we both would like. I'm sure that will change in time, but it's hard now because I feel Quinn ends up getting the short end of the stick too often. She deserves to have her dad in her life much more than she has him. Johnny believes my attempts to talk to Elizabeth would not have changed anything. And at this point, because of how Elizabeth operated, I will take Johnny at his word. He has not been wrong about her once.

In January 2011 I went and met with Jim Cooney, one of Johnny's lawyers. This was the first time I had met him and learned the specifics and magnitude of Andrew and Cheri's behavior. Jim told me how much the checks were for and when they were written—a total of $325,000 by September 26th, 2007 the day before the *National Enquirer* showed up at my door in New Jersey. But because Jim did not show me the checks, I did not see them with my own eyes, and because the investigation was still going on, I felt the feds must have something that I couldn't figure out. They must have something on Johnny, some kind of concrete evidence of an actual crime.

I was actually surprised that the Obama administration's Department of Justice never killed the investigation. Knowing the facts, it still doesn't make any sense to me.

Following Johnny's lawyer's instructions, I wasn't involved, nor did Johnny talk to me about the negotiations of trying to work out a plea bargain. Johnny called around 11 P.M. the night before the indictment. He and his team were hunkered down at the Ponderosa. He told me that he told his lawyers that it just wasn't right, "that you are Quinn's mom and they clearly know how close I am to you." It wasn't right that I didn't know what was going on. "This directly affects you and Quinn. You should know." But his lawyers were adamant about Johnny not telling me because I could be a key witness. Johnny said that his lawyers were going to call me in the morning.

He already knew my position. I had asked days before, "So if you went to jail, what kind of jail would it be? One of those country clubs?"

He said, "Yeah."

"Where?"

"Probably Virginia."

"So Quinn and I will move to Virginia. Virginia is a great state."

I wanted him to fight, regardless of how painful it was going to be for everyone. At this point in his life, I didn't think the best course for him would be to lie, to say he was guilty of something that he wasn't in order to make the nightmare go away. Wasn't that exactly what he did before, lie to make a nightmare go away?

Greg Craig, another one of Johnny's lawyers, never called me in the morning. And right around 10 A.M., the local press started banging on my front door. (Apparently they were still not wise to the fact that I had a publicist and that they were trespassing.) Thank God I had a babysitter that day. She closed the curtains and the shutters. I informed Quinn that it was a camera day, which in our house means no going outside! Quinn was fine with that. It was too hot anyway, and she was happy playing with her babysitter. I then called the cops on the office line as I turned on the TV. Then I called my friend, the pastor at the church next door, and asked him to please come over and tell these local media people to get off my property! That was something I couldn't do, because if they saw me or I uttered a word, they would record it and it would be on the news. Of course, the pastor was accustomed to his neighborly task. He was so sweet and protective of us. He sometimes rang my cell to alert me, "Just wanted

Playtime at Johnny's house is never-ending—from the playhouse, to the trampo-line, to the basketball court, to the pool...etc.

you to be aware, in case you haven't seen them, you have visitors parked outside your house." Anyway, he came over immediately and the first round of press departed. The cops arrived. I told the officer it was going to be a busy media day and asked if he could do some drive-bys. "No problem," he said.

He left, and my cell rang. It was Johnny. I walked upstairs as I picked up. "I take it there was no deal." As I was talking to him, I heard loud aggressive banging on my front door. I looked down from the upstairs window and saw the top of a curly head of hair. "I've got Jim Morrill knocking on my door. Right now. He's pounding away like he owns the place." How scary is it that I can identify Jim Morrill, a political reporter from the *Charlotte Observer* whom I have never met, by spotting the top of his head?

"I've got helicopters circling my house," Johnny said.

"So I take it there is an indictment. At least that's what they're re-porting on the news."

"Yeah, wait till you hear what they wanted. A deal just wasn't going to happen."

"As you know, I'm happy about that."

"It has been moved to the middle district. I have to drive to Winston-Salem."

"Why has it been moved?"

"I don't know yet. I have to get dressed and go."

"Okay," I said. "I love you. And hold your head high."

Had I even thought for a second that he would be having a mug shot taken, I would have said, "And don't forget, no matter what they say to you, the media will get a hold of your mug shot, so don't smile in it, because they don't know yet that you aren't guilty." The same way he should have said to me, given the interview was in *GQ*, "No matter what they say to you, how covered you actually are, make sure you wear pants." Word to the wise: PR people matter.

I hung up and called Allison Van Laningham to tell her that they moved the hearing to the middle district, her neighborhood. My other lawyer beeped in. I told Allison that I needed to take the call; it was Mike Critchley, my criminal lawyer. Mike reminded me not to say a word and to refer all media to him. I said, "No worries there," and told him that I had already told Rosemarie Terenzio, my publicist, to refer all calls to him. I called Allison back. She had the indictment and sent it to me. I read it immediately and couldn't believe it! I was floored, happy, and outraged all at the same time. I really thought, after all this time, that they had to have *something*. I didn't know what they could possibly have but I thought that after two-and-a-half years and millions of taxpayer dollars, they had to have *something*. But it seems like the whole case is hinged on Andrew Young's statements.

Maybe when it's all said and done Andrew could pitch Mastercard for his own commercial: Used BMW for the boss's mistress: $28,000. Rental house for her: $2,700 a month. OB/GYN bills: $2,500. Filling the house with furniture from Pottery Barn: $30,000. Using the boss's mistress as your cover and lying to everyone about the money you solicited using his name but kept for yourself: Priceless.

One evening in July Johnny called and said, "We have to have a hard conversation."

Graduation from her trike! On the indoor playground, 2011.

"Okay," I said, bracing myself. The physical tensing was because of the damage that's happened over the past few years. Before this all happened, my natural reaction would have been to relax, let go on the inside, and breathe—not to tense up. That's what damage does, among other things.

Johnny went on to tell me that the three women he had told me about the first night I had met him were, in fact, not real and that he had made them up.

I thought he was joking. "Oh, come on."

"I'm serious."

"What?" I didn't understand what he was saying.

"I made them up. They aren't real."

My mind was racing. How could that be? He had told me detail upon detail. I remembered the ups and downs of emotion I had felt the night he went to Chicago to break off his relationship there. I had experienced anger like no other. My reality within our relationship had just been ripped out from under me.

Something I said on *Oprah* suddenly flashed in my head. She had asked, "How do you know he isn't lying to you?"

I replied, "He doesn't lie to me. I know him like the back of my hand."

So I asked him straight out, "Why would you do that?"

He went on to tell me that it was a habit triggered by women when they hit on him. Apparently one that started decades ago when his first mistress expressed her plans to leave her husband for him. He didn't want her to think that she was the only one or that he was ever going to leave Elizabeth. He wanted to keep control over the situation, keep her at bay, and his real feelings as well, I imagine.

"So who was real and who wasn't?"

"The three I told you about the first night, the ones after 2004, were fiction. The ones before 2004 are real."

Well, no wonder the media never found ex-mistresses in Chicago, LA, or Florida. They didn't exist.

"So if Chicago wasn't real, who owned the cell phone before the one I bought you?"

"My second ex-mistress."

I thought about all the texts that I had read—they were all from her.

"But why would you—on the first night—tell me about three women like that, right off the bat?"

"I didn't want you to think that you were special."

My mind was still spinning, thinking of all the things I would have done differently had I known this little tidbit of total fucking insanity! Excuse the judgment, but shit! I was mad at myself!

"So here I was, thinking when you ran that you have so many smoking bombs since 2004, but I was the only one?"

"Yes. You are the only one."

"And why did you wait so long to tell me this?"

"I wanted to tell you in 2009, but Cooney told me not to tell you before you testified before the grand jury."

"So you waited until 2011?!"

I continued, "And let me just say, you following Jim Cooney's 'brilliant' advice has done us no favors as far as our relationship is concerned. First, he instructs you not to talk to me for five months after I testified, and now this?"

I started asking details about what was and wasn't real. He immediately went into reaction mode, and I realized that I was interrogating him the way Elizabeth did for years.

So I stopped.

"Yeah, I don't know where this is going to leave us."

He simply said, "You'll adjust."

We hung up. I sat still. Fucking unbelievable. I, too, had betrayed myself. After a couple of minutes of beating myself up with mean thoughts followed by awful feelings, in my head I let go of everything that I knew to be real and true and just sat there. The mind likes to hold on to thoughts, attach and file thoughts to a category called "What I know." This gives us a (false) sense of security and pride. And now my mind had nothing to hang its hat on as far as my relationship with Johnny was concerned.

Johnny didn't do anything out of character. He has a long history of lying about one thing only—women—and I mistakenly thought I was different. I was in love with him and wanted to be special. I wanted to be the only one he didn't lie to. But I had one problem: I was a woman.

Stupid me.

I really don't believe Johnny's lying about women was ever malicious. It's actually very understandable behavior from a passive-aggressive man. One that never learned how to express his feelings and how to stand up for himself. Just like many children who learn how to use lying as a tool to get what they want, he used it as a defense to keep women, intimacy, and real feelings at bay and get what *he* wanted. Interestingly enough, unconscious passive-aggressive men are also frequently partnered with an aggressive witch on wheels, allowing themselves to be the passive good guy, the victim of all the madness directed at them. In reality, the pattern keeps them from taking responsibility for their own feelings and standing up for what they feel.

I misjudged. You don't actually trust other people—you trust your judgment of them. It all takes place inside of you, and when your judgment is wrong, it's you that can't see clearly. The anger and sadness you experience is at yourself for not seeing clearly. But you must forgive yourself because, believe it or not, when you truly forgive yourself, you will be able to see real gifts in what happened. And even though Johnny is who he is, I don't want to label him and lock him into an image that he may no longer fit. Johnny is a very different person today than he was when we met on February 21st, 2006. I actually don't ever want to label anyone, even Andrew or Cheri, because labeling stops understanding. When you label people, you can no longer relate to them or understand them.

In the end, we are all human and we will all betray ourselves from time to time. We all have agendas and, God willing, we will all fall in love.

I fell in love. I followed my heart and I don't regret it. I cannot regret it because I learned a lot; in fact, I grew up. Our relationship and all its consequences helped me to evolve—I am a different person. But more importantly, as any mother knows, I cannot regret our love because it produced the greatest love in my entire life: Frances Quinn.

Johnny does know me well. Just as he said I would, I adjusted.

The government has this argument that Johnny was hiding me in order to influence the election. I don't agree with that at all because Johnny hid me for the last two years and he wasn't running for

My Quinn in the hat—at home in Charlotte.

anything. His defense argues that he was hiding me from Elizabeth, but even after she passed away, he was still hiding me.

I would say that he was hiding me because he was still unable to stand up for his feelings and because his desire to protect his family from emotional pain outweighs his need to be honest about how he truly feels.

Way back when Johnny and Elizabeth separated (it feels like a lifetime ago), he and I automatically, naturally, just went right back together. And to my surprise, I discovered that there were parts of my personality, parts of my good nature, that had shut down and did not seem to be coming back into our relationship. It's like a slice of pure innocence—my youthful, blissful self—went into hiding when Andrew claimed paternity and even more so when Johnny publicly denied our love. Of course, the biggest part of me left "us" when he denied Quinn was his daughter.

I have gone through phases over the course of the past two years. Sometimes I would be happy to be around him, especially seeing him together with Quinn. He is a great dad to her when he is with her. But there were parts of me that did not like him and were not interested in him coming back into the mix. I was protecting myself from more hurt and I was still mad at myself for getting involved with him in the first place, for allowing the hurt to happen.

Around the summer of 2010, I began requesting couples therapy, which I saw as the only way to salvage our once incredible romance. I was met with many "maybe, if I don't get indicted"–type responses. And then I kept thinking, if I could just hold out until the criminal case is over, then we could see where we were and attempt to rebuild. But out of nowhere came, "Oh, by the way, I made up women for basically the first six months of our relationship." I believe *that* severed what few threads I had left holding "us" together.

But I didn't stop just yet, even after that: I gave him a real heart-to-heart talk, which was basically filled with many a "You aren't nice to me," and "I just don't like you anymore" from both of us. And then I threw one final Hail Mary pass: "Will you do couples therapy with me?"

Which was met with his usual passive reply: "I don't know."

Which naturally hit a button in me—the "Can't you take a clear stand on *anything*?" button. He's frustrating because his way of operating is so very different from mine and it's something I don't have a lot of patience for anymore.

So I went ahead and helped him with this one. I said, "*That* answer says it all. I am taking a stand. We are done with the romantic part of our relationship."

And I was. I was absolutely finished.

I woke up the very next day and felt wonderful, in way that I hadn't felt for a very long time. I realized that I had been bogged down, suffering from judgmental overload, with unfulfilled expectations and a few assumptions mixed in. I had been very attached to making our romantic relationship work for so many reasons. He was the father of my child, we were so in love, I had invested so much time and energy into our relationship, and we had been through the wringer. I wanted to prove all the negative media wrong regarding how frivolous our relationship is or was. I just wanted to make it work, darn it! And I finally got to a place where it no longer mattered to me. I finally let it all go.

Quinn surrounded by her "guys." She has named every single one of them, except G-raffe—he was named by her granddaddy Wallace.

True forgiveness is letting it all go.

And when I dropped it all, I felt free, happy, and whole. Many parts of me that had gone into hiding immediately came dancing back. Love was everywhere.

And shockingly enough, once there were no more romantic expectations between us, Johnny was suddenly much nicer to me. Amazing how that works!

Late in the afternoon, we were running an errand with Quinn. When I got out of the car, I looked at Johnny and out of nowhere, I thought, "You're actually quite handsome." I was very attracted to him again for the first time in a long time.

Yep, that's right, my big "taking a stand and ending it" lasted less than twenty-four hours. Oh, but what a difference a day makes. For me it was a new beginning, one I find ironic because it came at the same time as the end of my writing this book.

Johnny said to me later that night as he was kissing me, "You're back. I've missed you."

He was right, and it was so unbelievably simple: by dropping the self-judgment, the disappointment in myself, and my need for it not to end, love came pouring forth again. It felt so unbelievably fantastic to have all those youthful emotional parts back in our relationship again.

Yes, I was finally done with our romantic relationship, but apparently it wasn't done with me. One of the many things that I have learned is that our combined love, the mysterious, unpredictable force that exists between Johnny and me—the very same force that I felt on that first night when I walked into his hotel room at the Regency when I had earlier been afraid to walk across the room—that indescribable whatever it is, it is not to be underestimated.

I really have absolutely no idea what will happen with us. The jury is still out. But I can honestly say that the ending is of no concern to me anymore. The love is here. And as sappy as it may sound, I love living in love.

Epilogue

OHNNY AND I, because of or despite the fact that we fell head over heels in love, have been through so much awfulness, hardship, heartache, and media scrutiny, with the wrath of America directed at us, that I think it would appear to almost anyone that the odds of us making it for the long run are not good.

I am not different from most women in this regard: what I want in a relationship is a full-time romantic relationship filled with laughter that is based on real intimacy, a relationship that causes continual growth, and is emotionally open and honest with off-the-charts sexual chemistry. And even more important to me than my own experience, I want Quinn, the love of my life, to have a full-time dad and a role model that enables her to have a love relationship with real intimacy of her own when she grows up.

I have talked to a lot of women about this, and most women who say they want what I want seem to think that it doesn't exist, that men are men and you will never have all of what you want in one package. And, as a woman, you will always have to fold parts of yourself to accommodate a man or a relationship.

When Oprah came to my house, she asked me one of her standard questions: "What do you know for sure?" It's a great question, but given my perspective, it's a very difficult question to answer honestly. My answer didn't make it into my interview—it was probably too wacky for most people to understand exactly what I meant by it.

I have had some time to think about it and, in 2011, after everything I have lived through—falling in love, working in politics, having an affair with a presidential candidate, getting knocked up by a married man, living on the run, becoming a mother, withstanding the media stalking and bashing, having my private possessions stolen,

the perpetual invasion of my privacy, the court cases, co-parenting from hell, the government's witch hunt, and discovering that I, too, betrayed myself—I actually have an answer to Oprah's question.

Here's what I know for sure: anything is possible, nothing is predictable, and no matter what you think the weather may look like, don't ever, ever leave your house without sunglasses.

Life is weird. And within that, you always have a choice. You can be miserable, criticizing and blaming and crying for the world, *or* you can be happy: drop your judgments, take God by the hand, put on your shades, and just *go with it*.

Erica Jong once said, "Love is everything it's cracked up to be.... It really is worth fighting for, being brave for, risking everything for."

Of course, I would add that if that love is shared with someone who is not your spouse, you might *not* want to step front and center onto the public stage with a run for the presidency.

You can deny it to yourself, you can lie to the world, you can run, you can hide, but no matter what you do, Truth will eventually find you. It's inevitable.

Acknowledgments

MY LIFE is full of love and support from some fantastic people. I want to publicly thank them; I am very grateful for each of them. In one way or another, they have all enriched my life. (And, if you are a member of the media please do not call or bother one person on this list, of course, with the exception of RoseMarie. All calls go to Rose!)

Mimi Hockman: Just a little innocuous "Let's go to the Regency for a drink, I want to relive the love and show you where we sat." CUT TO six years later, your four-year-old God daughter is standing in my closet trying on my shoes. It's all your fault, again! I love you more than you will ever know. Thank you for your never-ending love and support. I am forever sorry for all the media harassment as well as the many subpoenas! You are a beautiful, talented, hilarious woman, a great mom, and the complete definition of a true friend. There is no such thing as too much Mimi. And to Jack and Cole, my sweet God sons: I love you both.

RoseMarie Terenzio: You are a constant source of joy, support, and humor in my life. You became my friend and my publicist in the first five minutes of our initial phone call. This book exists because of you and your "Are you fucking kidding me? You need a book deal yesterday!" I love you. I can't thank you enough.

Steve Troha: My agent and one of my many gifts from Rose. It's been a long road with many laughs. Meow. Thank you, Steve. I am honored to call you my agent, and more importantly, my friend.

Glenn Yeffeth, my publisher: It's been a wonderful experience. Thank you for your patience, flexibility, and courage to publish a book written by such a "crazy mistress." May your courage reward you greatly.

My editor, Erin Kelley: Thank you and congratulations on your new married life!

Leigh Camp, Adrienne Lang, and all the other BenBella folks who worked so hard on this book: Thank you.

Janet Boschker and NorthLight photography: Thank you for the cover photo and the author photo.

Kim Wood: Thank you for always being able to accommodate my hair around my child care or lack thereof.

Tom Steele: Thank you for your edits, your shift key, and your recipes! You are a joy, and not just in the kitchen!

Elizabeth Spainhour from Brooks Pierce: Thank you for your legal eyes on this book.

Hilary Liftin: Thank you for your time on the first proposal. You are a fantastic writer, but, for whatever reasons, I had to write my own book.

Kip Hunter: I love you. Thank you for so many wonderful years, thank you for your name, and thank you for being so completely Kip.

Angela Janklow: How is it possible we both have four-year-olds? And as you know, I will always love you, your loyalty, and all things Willie.

Burr Collier: I love you. You are a constant gift to me and Quinn. And to Burr's gang of friends (especially Helen) that have become mine—thank you for your support.

Glory Crampton: Thank you for decades of friendship; I love you.

All of my California friends, especially my girls Laurie, Maggie, Wendy, Cindy, Amy, Vanessa, Katie, and Annabelle: I love you all.

My Jersey girls: Liza, Chloe, and Eileen—I miss our ladies' lunches!

All of my Charlotte moms, neighbors, and friends, especially Amy Lothrop and Amy Antoniak: Thank you.

Frances, John, Jack, and Francie Hankins: Thank you for being so wonderful.

Dawn, Patrick, and Summer Bannigan: Hours and hours of play with you make the day fly by, and you make Charlotte heaven for us. Thank you. Quinn and I love you!

Ms. Trish, Ms. Ann Marie, and Ms. Willow: Thank you for taking such great care of my sweet girl.

Pastor John Earl: Thank you for your prayers and your constant patrolling.

Christine, Vanita, Hollie, Harriet, and Hayden: Quinn and I love you. Thank you.

Dr. John Vanderheide: Thank you for my bringing my sweet girl into the world.

Dana Smith: Thank you for your stellar protection, and for being such a huge help. And wow, you have such a photogenic arm! Every time I see someone driving recklessly, I still hear your voice in my head saying: Look at this idiot. Thank you for all those laughs.

South Orange Police Department and the Charlotte-Mecklenburg Police Department, Providence Division (especially Sergeant Dave): A big thank you to each and every one of you for keeping us safe. When I see cops on the road, instead of thinking: Oh no, there's a cop! Am I speeding?, I now think: There goes my friend.

Julie Damron: Thank you for your efforts.

Sam Cullman: You are filled with goodness as well as talent.

Lisa DePaulo: Thank you for your integrity.

Jill Barancik: Oprah is very lucky to have you. You are a walking Super Soul Sunday.

Lisa Blue and Fred Baron: A big thank you for always trying to do the right thing. Lisa, I am truly sorry for your loss.

Rob Gordon: I love you. Thank you for the hours upon hours of support especially during "the" interview.

Michael Critchley and Frank Louis: Both of you are grandfathers that care. Thank you.

Wade and Elizabeth Barber: Thank you for your continual work and goodness on my behalf.

Smith Moore and Leatherwood: Thank you for Alan Duncan and Allison Van Laningham.

Alan: Thank you for your stellar work to protect my privacy. I am grateful beyond words.

And Allison: The greatest thing that came from me not burning that tape is meeting you. I love you. Thank you for "Quinn's" beach house and thank you for your friendship and most of all thank you for you.

Kearns Davis at Brooks Pierce: Thank you for your meticulous counsel.

To my spiritual teachers: You are one. I live in love and gratitude because of you. Thank you for your time, support, and blessings.

My "kool" friend: Thank you for decades of friendship and laughs. May you succeed with your life's goal of never being googled.

My dear Bob: A man who really knew his way around a Reuben sandwich. What a joke, and one that would have gotten a lot mileage between us. I miss your laugh and your sense of humor. I am truly sorry for all the pain your family has gone through from this mess; not a day goes by that I don't miss hearing your voice. I love you every day, and miss you always. Thank you for always holding my hand, and, more importantly, thank you for forever holding your God daughter, Quinn, in your heart.

I want to thank my mother and father for bringing me into the world and my father for his sustained love. My father had many faults, but loving and taking care of his four girls was not among them. He would have made an outstanding grandfather. I miss him always.

My sister Melissa, my brother-in-law John, my nieces, Zoey and Allie: I am sorry, truly sorry for the media harassment. I love you all.

Bobbie and Wallace: As far as grandparents go, you are the top of the heap! The unconditional love for Quinn, and your desire to be in her life no matter what was going on melts my heart every time I think of it. Thank you. I love you both. May God continue to shower his blessing on you.

Kathy, Steve, Julie, Bogie, and Stella: Thank you for immediately embracing and loving both Quinn and me. And thank you for all the laughs...and the many more to come!

Jack and Emma Claire: With all of my heart, thank you for accepting your sister Quinn. Emma, you have grown to be so incredibly beautiful inside and out. Quinn and I both adore you, and an extra big thank you for letting her follow you around.

Johnny: Through all the destruction, I (still) admire your fortitude. You came out of it all not only a better person, but more importantly a better father. And, no matter what happens I will always love you, and as you know, I am eternally grateful for your part in co-creating with me the greatest love of all: our daughter. And boy, did we do good on that.

Frances Quinn, this book is for you: You are the definition of a blessing; thank you for being my daughter. No matter what anyone says, or prints, you know the truth, you know who your parents are, and most importantly you know that you are loved. You are my world, you are my heart, I love you with all that that I am.